BECOMING CENTAUR

ANIMALIBUS VOL. 9
OF ANIMALS AND CULTURES

Nigel Rothfels, General Editor

ADVISORY BOARD
Steve Baker (University of Central Lancashire)
Susan McHugh (University of New England)
Garry Marvin (Roehampton University)
Kari Weil (Wesleyan University)

Books in the Animalibus series share a fascination with the status and the role of animals in human life. Crossing the humanities and the social sciences to include work in history, anthropology, social and cultural geography, environmental studies, and literary and art criticism, these books ask what thinking about nonhuman animals can teach us about human cultures, about what it means to be human, and about how that meaning might shift across times and places.

Other titles in the series:

Rachel Poliquin, *The Breathless Zoo: Taxidermy and the Cultures of Longing*

Joan B. Landes, Paula Young Lee, and Paul Youngquist, eds., *Gorgeous Beasts: Animal Bodies in Historical Perspective*

Liv Emma Thorsen, Karen A. Rader, and Adam Dodd, eds., *Animals on Display: The Creaturely in Museums, Zoos, and Natural History*

Ann-Janine Morey, *Picturing Dogs, Seeing Ourselves: Vintage American Photographs*

Mary Sanders Pollock, *Storytelling Apes: Primatology Narratives Past and Future*

Ingrid H. Tague, *Animal Companions: Pets and Social Change in Eighteenth-Century Britain*

Dick Blau and Nigel Rothfels, *Elephant House*

Marcus Baynes-Rock, *Among the Bone Eaters: Encounters with Hyenas in Harar*

BECOMING CENTAUR

*Eighteenth-Century Masculinity
and English Horsemanship*

Monica Mattfeld

THE PENNSYLVANIA STATE UNIVERSITY PRESS
UNIVERSITY PARK, PENNSYLVANIA

Library of Congress
Cataloging-in-Publication Data

Names: Mattfeld, Monica, 1982– , author.
Title: Becoming centaur : eighteenth-century masculinity and English horsemanship / Monica Mattfeld.
Other titles: Animalibus.
Description: University Park, Pennsylvania : The Pennsylvania State University Press, [2017] | Series: Animalibus: of animals and cultures | Includes bibliographical references and index.
Summary: "Explores the history of horse-human relationships over the long eighteenth century, and how these relationships in turn influenced performances of gender. Examines the agential influence of horses in their riders' lives, horses on stage and the early circus, and the politicization of human-animal being"—Provided by publisher.
Identifiers: LCCN 2016043164 | ISBN 9780271075778 (cloth : alk. paper) | ISBN 9780271075785 (pbk. : alk. paper)
Subjects: LCSH: Horsemanship—England—History—18th century. | Horsemen and horsewomen—England—History—18th century. | Human-animal relationships—England—History—18th century. | Masculinity—England—History—18th century.
Classification: LCC SF284.G7 M38 2017 | DDC 798.20942—dc23
LC record available at https://lccn.loc.gov/2016043164

Copyright © 2017
The Pennsylvania State University
All rights reserved
Printed in the United States of America
Published by
The Pennsylvania State University Press,
University Park, PA 16802-1003

The Pennsylvania State University Press is a member of the Association of American University Presses.

It is the policy of The Pennsylvania State University Press to use acid-free paper. Publications on uncoated stock satisfy the minimum requirements of American National Standard for Information Sciences—Permanence of Paper for Printed Library Material, ANSI Z39.48–1992.

To my parents.

Thank you.

CONTENTS

List of Illustrations   ix

Acknowledgments   xi

INTRODUCTION
Of Horses and Men   1

1   WILLIAM CAVENDISH AND HOBBESIAN HORSEMANSHIP   21

2   RIDING HOUSES AND POLITE EQUESTRIANISM   69

3   ASTLEY'S AMPHITHEATRE   121

4   HENRY WILLIAM BUNBURY AND THE MOCK MANUALS OF HORSEMANSHIP   171

Notes   227

Bibliography   251

Index   271

ILLUSTRATIONS

1 Peter Paul Rubens after Leonardo da Vinci, *Battle of Anghiari*, ca. 1603 *37*
2 Abraham van Diepenbeke, plate 4 in William Cavendish, *A General System of Horsemanship* (London: J. Brindley, 1743) *43*
3 Abraham van Diepenbeke, plate 3 in William Cavendish, *A General System of Horsemanship* (London: J. Brindley, 1743) *50*
4 Giambattista della Porta, *De humana physiognomonia libri IIII* (1586), 83 *53*
5 Charles Parrocel, *A Riding Academy*, in William Cavendish, *A General System of Horsemanship* (London: J. Brindley, 1743), 15 *58*
6 Isaac Cruikshank, *Sunday Equestrians or Hyde Park Candidates for Admiration*, 1797 *71*
7 Philip Astley, figures 2, 4–11, in *The Modern Riding-Master, or A Key to the Knowledge of the Horse, and Horsemanship* (Philadelphia: Robert Aitken, 1776), 23–28 *81*
8 William Austen, *The Lucky Mistake, Or the Buck & Blood Flourishing Macaroni L^d—playing a Solo on the Jelly Glassez*, 1773 *82*
9 Sawrey Gilpin, *Set of Eight Horses— The Managed Horse*, 1786 *84*
10 Sawrey Gilpin, *Set of Eight Horses— The Hunter*, 1786 *85*
11 John Vanderbanck, *The Capriole*, in Josephus Sympson, *Twenty Five Actions of the Manage Horse* (London: Printed for and Sold by J. Sympson and Andrew Johnston, 1729), 25 *86*
12 John Vanderbanck, *A Hunter upon full Stretch*, in Josephus Sympson, *Twenty Five Actions of the Manage Horse* (London: Printed for and Sold by J. Sympson and Andrew Johnston, 1729), 26 *86*
13 Joseph Wright, *Mr. and Mrs. Thomas Coltman*, 1770–72 *104*
14 *The Favourite Footman, or Miss well Mounted*, 1778 *107*
15 John Collet, *A Soft Tumble after a Hard Ride*, 1780 *108*
16 John Kay, *Angelo Tremamondo, Riding Master*, 1788 *114*
17 *Ouer The head of the Horse*, in Will Stokes, *The Vaulting-Master: Or the Art of Vaulting, Reduced to a Method, comprized under certaine Rules, Illustrated by Examples*. . . . ([London?]: Printed for Richard Davis, in Oxon, 1652) *130*
18 John Singleton Copley, *The Siege and Relief of Gibraltar, 13 September 1782*, ca. 1783 *145*

19 William Hincks, *Young Astley, the Equestrian Hero*, 1789 *150*
20 *L'Ecole de Mars*, 1808 *162*
21 Philip Astley, handbill, 1782 *166*
22 Samuel Collings, *The Downfall of Taste & Genius, or The World as it goes*, 1784 *169*
23 Henry William Bunbury, *Geoffrey Gambado, Esq.*, in *An Academy for Grown Horsemen. . . .* (London: W. Dickinson, S. Hooper, and Mess. Robinsons, 1787) *185*
24 *A Taylor Riding to Brentford*, n.d. *188*
25 John Collet, *A Taylor riding to Brentford*, 1768 *190*
26 William Hogarth, *John Wilkes, Esq.ʳ*, ca. 1763 *193*
27 Piercy Roberts, *Proof Positive or no Deceiving a Sailor*, 1807 *196*
28 Henry William Bunbury, *How to make the most of a Horse*, in *The Annals of Horsemanship* (London: W. Dickinson, S. Hooper, J. Archer, and R. White, 1791) *204*
29 Henry William Bunbury, *How to make the least of a Horse*, in *The Annals of Horsemanship* (London: W. Dickinson, S. Hooper, J. Archer, and R. White, 1791) *204*
30 Henry William Bunbury, *How to travel upon two Legs in a Frost*, in *The Annals of Horsemanship* (London: W. Dickinson, S. Hooper, J. Archer, and R. White, 1791) *209*
31 Statue over the entrance gate of the Old Admiralty Building, 26 Whitehall, London *210*
32 Thomas Rowlandson, *How to Travel upon Two Legs in a Frost*, in Henry William Bunbury, *An Academy for Grown Horsemen. . . .* (London: Printed for Vernor, Hood, and Sharpe et al., 1808) *212*
33 Henry William Bunbury, *Hyde Park*, 1781 *214*
34 Henry William Bunbury, *A Riding-House*, 1780 *218*
35 Charles Parrocel, *A Riding Academy* (detail), in William Cavendish, *A General System of Horsemanship* (London: J. Brindley, 1743) *222*

ACKNOWLEDGMENTS

My first thank-you must go to Donna Landry for her critical engagement with my work, and for her untiring, enthusiastic, and conscientious support throughout. She has truly taken me under her wing, and has not only shown me new approaches to the study of history and literary studies but has opened my eyes to new cultures and new ways of thinking and of riding; the *Evliya Çelebi* ride was a wonderful, once-in-a-lifetime experience. I am also grateful for the contributions of David Ormrod, whose vast historical knowledge and keen eye for art have been invaluable. Also, the astute suggestions and perceptive input of Rosanna Cox have lent important depth to this book, and have given me a new appreciation of early modern political thought, while Jane Spencer was truly generous with her time, support, and suggestions.

Many other people have been lavish with their time, guidance, and insight. Helen Brooks was kind enough to give me a crash course in the history of eighteenth-century theaters. Elaine Walker, Marius Kwint, and Kirrilly Thompson generously sent me copies of their work, while providing welcome advice and support. Clive Johnson, Hugh Adlington, and Jan Montefiore suggested wonderful equestrian sources, and Jan was exceptional in her always engaging ideas and intelligent conversation. Thank you also to Pete Edwards for some fantastic talks and thoughts, to Richard Nash for introducing me to the wacky world of quantum physics, and to Karen Raber for her excellent ideas and untiring enthusiastic support. I must also thank Jennie Batchelor and Jane Spencer for excellent revision suggestions and an enjoyable PhD viva.

My forays into archival research were greatly helped by understanding staff. The staff at the New York Public Library kindly explained the technicalities of working with rare books, and those at the University of British Columbia were quietly efficient. I would also like to thank the knowledgeable staff at the British Library's Rare Books and Manuscripts reading rooms for their help in tracking down some of my more obscure sources. Similarly, the wonderful archivists at the Victoria and Albert Museum Theatre and Performance Collection were always willing to help, and were obviously passionate about their role in document preservation. A big thank-you must also go to the many people around the world who came to my rescue when sourcing the sometimes very obscure images for this book—you are all wonderful. None of my research in the London archives would have been possible without the generous support of the Federation of Women Graduates Theodora Bosanquet Bursary; the funding was appreciated and, I hope, well spent. Financial support also came from the University of Kent's School of English.

A big thank-you must go to Sarah Horgan, Katherine Korrigan, Courtney Salvey, Jenny JiPlacidi, Gemma Vaughan, Stephanie Decouvelaere, Kim Simpson, Vybarr Cregan-Reid, Amy Lilwall, Robert Maidens, Tom Lawrence, and Petr Barta for their invaluable support, knowledgeable critiques, enthusiastic engagement with my sometimes offbeat ideas, and infectious laughter. You are all fantastic people whom I am entirely privileged to know. I must also thank my family for their unreserved encouragement and support. It is appreciated more than you know.

Finally, the many horses in my life deserve their place among those who have contributed to this book. Noonie, Gambler, and Mayday (along with the many other horses I have been fortunate enough to meet in my travels), family members in another form, are the inspiration for this work. Without their presence, and our days spent talking together, this book would not have been possible. Thank you, everyone.

INTRODUCTION

Of Horses and Men

In 1780 there appeared in the *Gentleman's Magazine* a remarkable piece of writing. It recorded the words from a funerary monument placed in the gardens of John Boyle, fifth Earl of Cork, fifth Earl of Orrery, and second Baron Marston in 1754. While reprinting such information was not unknown, what made this monument unusual was that it marked the final resting place of King Nobby, a horse. By all accounts, Nobby had a good life with Boyle. He "was purchased in a lucky hour" and served as a "faithful servant" for "near 28 years" as a "docile, social, and even a domestic animal." According to the monument:

> [Here] are interred the bones of KING NOBBY; a Horse, who was superlatively beautiful in his kind. He loved his master with an affection far exceeding the love of brutes. He had sense, courage, strength, majesty, spirit, and obedience. He never started, he never tript, he never stumbled. He lived to an uncommon age, and till within two years of his death retained all his natural excellences and vigour. His limbs were sound to his last moments, he having enjoyed the peculiar felicity of scarce ever having been lame or sick during the long course of his life.

He also "performed two journeys into Ireland, without accident and without fatigue. Though he was strong and hardy, his limbs were light and delicate. His mane shone like jet, and flowed gracefully from his crest to his shoulders. His ears were small. He was——Oh! he was all perfection."[1] This interesting and highly anthropomorphized monument points to a multispecies bond that was not terribly uncommon during the eighteenth century. For Boyle, King Nobby was a beloved companion, cherished for his service, obedience, stamina, and strength, while for Nobby, we are led to believe, Boyle was his happily obeyed master.

Boyle was not alone in memorializing a cherished equine companion. As Ingrid Tague argues, while many obituaries or memorials for animals, frequently pets, were intended as satire or comedy, some horse memorials were entirely serious performances of grief and affection for a missed loved one.[2] The 1771 *Annual Register*, for instance, included an epitaph for a horse similar to Boyle's for King Nobby.

> *A Generous foe, a faithful friend—*
> *A victor bold, here met his end.*
> *He conquer'd both in war and peace;*
> *By death subdu'd, his glories cease.*
> *Ask'st thou, who finish'd here his course*
> *With so much honour?—'Twas a* HORSE.[3]

As these memorials indicate, horses were special, unique, and extraordinary animals in the eighteenth century. They were the partners of choice for many men, and it was through their presence that men sought to become, and to be observed as, something other, something powerful, awe-inspiring, even mythical. For men of this period—when the horse was central to agriculture, the economy, and transportation—creating a partnership with a horse was essential to their understanding of the world and their place in it. Horses influenced political discourse, social standing, scientific understanding of rationality, personal identity, and the performance of gender, while frequently transgressing the boundaries between what was considered human and what was understood as animal. Nicholas Morgan of Crolane, for example, argued that "amongst other liuing creatures, the horse is esteemed more noble, & more necessary then others, as well to Kings & other Princes, in the time of warre and peace." For Thomas Bewick, "The various excellencies of this noble animal, the grandeur of his stature, the elegance and proportion of his parts, the beautiful smoothness of his skin, the variety and gracefulness of his motions, and, above all, his utility, entitle him to a precedence in the history of brute creation." And *The Gentleman's Dictionary* defined "horse" as "an Animal so generally known, that to define him, 'tis sufficient to say, he is the noblest and most useful of all Animals, and his Sensible Nature, Obedience, Swiftness and Vigor are at once the Object and Subject of the noblest and most necessary Exercise of the Body."[4]

However, these remarkably similar descriptions of horses from wildly differing time periods raise more questions than they answer about horse-human interactions during the eighteenth century. Why, for example, was the art of horsemanship so necessary for some men but not for others? What was meant by the animal's "utility," and how did it change over the course of the century? How was horse-human interaction understood over the century, and what did the representation of multispecies relationships say about gendered performance? These and other questions about the performance of masculinity and horse-human interaction are the focus of this book. It examines the interconnected world of equestrians in the long eighteenth century, a world related through the horsemanship manuals, memoirs, social satires, images, and ephemera produced by some of the period's most influential horsemen. By exploring the often controversial and complicated considerations of political horse-human communication alongside the gendering of both man and horse, this book seeks to develop new understandings of gender performance and identity, while interrogating changing conceptualizations of "human" and "animal" during the long eighteenth century.

CONFORMATION OF THE FIELDS

Horses were everywhere in seventeenth- and eighteenth-century Europe and interactions with them had a profound impact on the lives of humans, but this very "taken-for-granted centrality of horses to human lives in the past," along with the Otherness of horses in today's motorized Western society, has played a central part in their relative invisibility in the history and literature of the long eighteenth century. We frequently "fail to notice them."[5] As a result, men's preoccupations with their horses and the horses' influence on human lives have rarely been the subject of scholarly investigation. While in recent years there has been a marked increase in scholarly interest in everything equine, much of the work done to date either limits its focus to the pre-1650 early modern period or picks up the story in the nineteenth century.[6] These innovative texts, although they begin the process of including horses and the art of horsemanship in human history, do not focus on the long eighteenth century in Britain. This century remains almost uncharted territory, with the exception of studies of the related practices of sporting art and culture, rather than the central practice of horsemanship itself. Donna Landry's pioneering *Noble Brutes* and Stephen

Deuchar's *Sporting Art in Eighteenth-Century England* are two examples of this tendency; Landry examines the influence of Eastern bloodstock and equestrian traditions on English sporting practices, while Deuchar studies the role of sporting experience in the formation of masculinity. As a result, while scholars of horse-human relationships perpetuate animal studies' current state of "mammalian hegemony," to use Robert Markley's phrase, there is much that we still do not know about the role of horses in human life.[7]

Similarly, scholars know relatively little about masculinity during the seventeenth and eighteenth centuries. Frequently restricted to the description of categories and stock characters, and working under a plethora of approaches, gender studies is only now beginning to entertain masculinities that follow or question hegemonic models and to consider them as a part of larger historical events.[8] According to Karen Harvey, "We still know too little to argue for an ancien régime of masculinity."[9] The emergent status of the study of masculinity has led to a situation where men of the early seventeenth century and those of the late seventeenth and eighteenth centuries appear to be "different species rather than different generations."[10] This separation, as Alexandra Shepard correctly observes, is due more to the methodologies of scholars than to any major shift in identity formation. Study of the early seventeenth century is dominated by an approach that focuses on the patriarchal role of men in the domestic household, an approach that argues that normative masculinity and its many divergent discourses were formulated, enacted, and continuously imperiled through interaction with women—most often wives. Elizabeth Foyster's *Manhood in Early Modern Britain* and Anthony Fletcher's *Gender, Sex, and Subordination in England* embody this approach, and like most texts that approach manhood through the lens of domestic and gendered interaction, both are based on the popular domestic advice literature that was beginning to emerge at the time. In this narrative, the focus is on the gendered power of the patriarchal man over women and how that power interacts with codes of honor. Studies like Foyster's and Fletcher's argue that through the maintenance of control over the household and its residents (of all genders), a man could achieve the patriarchal ideals of hegemonic masculinity and gain honor in the process.[11]

This patriarchal picture stands in rather dramatic contrast to the situation of the later seventeenth and eighteenth centuries, where men's participation in a "public" consisting chiefly of other men has become the primary focus of scholars. As Shepard argues, "Crudely summarized, the long eighteenth century is heralded as the passageway to a reconfigured private domestic order, and to modern gender identities, rooted in notions of binary sexual difference (as opposed to a gender hierarchy which placed men above women on a continuum)." These identities in turn "were increasingly internalized and . . . [were] ultimately connected with a modern sense of self" as part of the longer "civilizing process" identified by Norbert Elias.[12] In these arguments, the socially defined patriarchal head of the household, or his opposite, the cuckold, is replaced in the Restoration period by a veritable proliferation of male identities increasingly defined by interiority of identity rather than "public" displays. While, as Fletcher notes, the way in which pervasive masculinity "involved an internalised identity—an interiority of the mind and emotions—as opposed to a sense of role-playing—is very hard for the historian to judge," the consensus among scholars is that masculinity, as an internalized sense of self, is defined by homosocial interaction rather than by heterosocial relationships that created an externally defined identity.[13] Within this narrative, masculinity prior to 1660 was primarily related to social status, while the "public" man of the Restoration and eighteenth century was of cultural construction.[14] This development can be seen in scholarly arguments on the history of dueling. In the eighteenth century, honor becomes not so much a performance before others, capable of conveying honorable status to the duelists, but an increasingly outmoded display of internal emotion that had little bearing on social status.[15]

While this change in masculine performance was not instantaneous, and while after the Restoration the patriarchal man of honor stepped aside to allow the sexually predatory libertine and the effeminate figure of the fop to take the stage, these characterizations take a back seat to socially or "publicly" defined categories of identity formed in relation to politeness.[16] Politeness had many definitions in the eighteenth century, but in general it can be understood as an artful pursuit of social agreeableness in speech and deportment, sometimes at the expense of truth, for the sake of social and personal improvement.[17] Philip Carter and Michèle Cohen are the most influential authors here, and their work has led the vanguard in the emphasis on politeness as the new and overwhelmingly hegemonic form of masculinity that supplanted most older forms.[18] This aspect of masculinity studies increases the tendency for scholars to point to a sea change in identities somewhere between the seventeenth, eighteenth, and even nineteenth centuries, where there may not be any, or where such change has been overstated. While there is ample evidence that polite culture was indeed a strong molding force in late seventeenth- and early eighteenth-century society, its status as a metanarrative is, as Karen Harvey points out, clearly problematic.[19] Here, it is the post-1660 man of commerce and conversation, most often from the middling sorts, who pushes aside the landed gentleman as the primary figure of investigation, which is a trend that is carried out for the rest of the eighteenth century. As masculinity studies now stands, there is no "comparing like with like" over the course of the seventeenth and eighteenth centuries, a fact that "undermines any attempt to draw a line from the seventeenth-century patriarch to the eighteenth-century polite gentleman."[20]

ANIMAL STUDIES AND PERFORMANCE

Situated within and across the fields of animal studies and masculinity studies, this book aims to begin sketching that line between the diverse forms of seventeenth- and eighteenth-century masculinities by following the lives, publications, and animal-human relationships of horsemen. In doing so, it attempts to unravel the complicated gender performances of men who shared similar interests and forms of gender performance that also incorporate men from the social elite alongside those from the middling sorts. By doing so, the book starts the process of comparing like with like, while including nonhuman animals as an essential component of gendered display. The book focuses primarily on the genre of the horsemanship manual. A form of didactic literature situated, sometimes uncomfortably, between the similar genres of courtesy literature and husbandry manuals, the horsemanship treatises of the seventeenth and eighteenth centuries were written by practicing horsemen interested in personal and public improvement through textual production. Often containing information on correct forms of riding and horse training alongside advice on hunting practice, veterinary care, and ideal masculine behavior, the genre provides unique insight into the lives and practices of horsemen. However, as scholars who work with courtesy literature in their study of gender and identity have consistently illustrated, what is advocated in these and other didactic texts is frequently misleading in relation to personal embodied realities; instead, it provides an idealized view on and representation of morals, social behavior, and identities.[21]

There is a similar danger inherent in the study of horsemanship manuals, with some of the advocated behavior, actions, and languages of display providing only a partial look at equestrian culture of the time. The information contained in the manuals of the seventeenth and eighteenth centuries, for example, does not address the entire horse-working society; the manuals were intended for a socially elite audience, an audience (for the most part) that could afford to purchase, train, and keep horses, and not for men who used horses to work the land or for other labor. Produced by men who frequently knew one another personally or knew their predecessors' work, and who functioned within a close-knit and self-regulating community of fellow horsemen, the manuals are situated within ongoing and enacted discourses of horsemanship practice. As this book illustrates, the authors wrote back to one another while working not only to elevate their own public image and reputations but also to benefit the wider community of horsemen and, by extension in a number of cases, the wider commonwealth of elite citizens.

These authors were also practitioners of the art and instructions they put on paper. Unlike courtesy literature, horsemanship manuals allow for a relatively accurate insight into the lived and embodied experiences of horsemen. While some of the content and anecdotal evidence contained in the manuals often has undergone idealization, much of the practical equestrian instruction, gendered language, and expressions of horse-human relationships were based on the lived experience of the authors.[22] Constructed and published within the close-knit group of fellow horsemen, a group with shared epistemologies, ontologies, and discourses, manuals of horsemanship were intended for direct use within the many riding houses of the eighteenth century. They were frequently written by masters of horsemanship, although there were class variances within this model, who were also consumers of previous manuals on the subject with and against which they discussed their own theories. These masters, in turn, and their reading audience, worked to put the behavioral and practical teachings contained in the manuals into practice. Richard Berenger gives an example of this materiality of the text; for him, "The present Henry [Herbert] earl of Pembroke, (*non corpus fine pectore*) is an illustrious labourer in this vineyard [of horsemanship]: he has honoured the art by composing a treatise upon 'The *Method of breaking* Horses'; and practising what he preaches, instructs the world both by precept and example."[23] Like other horsemen, such as William Cavendish, William Hope, and Sir Sidney Meadows, Herbert practiced what he preached in his 1762 *Method of Breaking Horses and Teaching Soldiers to Ride, Designed for the Use of the Army*. He lived and experienced what was written in the manual, just as manuals of horsemanship today comment in detail not only on external kinesthetic actions but also on (ideal) internal behavior and processes necessary for riding; these constructed elements of embodied subjectivity as a horseman are in turn enacted on the ground and in the saddle, as it were, while interacting with an animal.

This multispecies exploration of gendered performance also questions the unnatural categories of "human" and "animal" (the definitions of which frequently negate the presence of the breed, culture, or individual), not as binary pairs within a teleological ladder of order but as reciprocally informing concepts.[24] As Donna Haraway argues in her paradigmatic *Companion Species Manifesto* (and in its later incarnation, *When Species Meet*), the evolutionary history of all of earth's inhabitants is a story of co-development and opportunism. "Earth's beings are prehensile," she writes, "opportunistic, ready to yoke unlikely partners into something new, something symbiogenetic. Co-constitutive companion species and co-evolution are the rule, not the exception." The history, language, and literature of animal-human interaction is one of recognition of a being both like and unlike ourselves, of the intelligence, subjectivity, objectivity, motivations, and needs of the nonhuman animal, while understanding or seeing the co-dependence and evolution that make up "companion species."[25] For Haraway, there can be no essentialized human over animal, and there can be no human without animal; there are only beings constitutive of both. When this constitutive intersubjectivity is recognized, the traditional parameters of humanism are problematized, and the nonhuman animal—in all of its messy, shared, co-companion situatedness—becomes an acting agent in history.[26] As a result, scholars in animal studies argue that there must be a movement beyond animals as symbols in order to understand how animals are never fully animal and humans are never fully human but amalgamations of both.[27] The inclusion of real, actual animals in the creation and performance of group, individual, human, and nonhuman identity is necessary for Erica Fudge; matter must come to matter, to paraphrase Karen Barad.[28]

Taking up Derridean preoccupations with discursive practices and engaging with Haraway's theories of co-evolution, Barad merges quantum physics and gender studies in an innovative retheorization of performativity. Instead of relying on a Cartesian differentiation between "things" and "representation," or "the inherent distinction between subject and object, knower and known" that dominates much of today's scholarship, Barad argues for a reorientation of focus that radically reworks our current understanding of discourse, performance, causality, and agency. According to Barad, there needs to be *"a causal relationship between specific exclusionary practices embodied as specific material configurations of the world* (i.e., discursive practices/(con)figurations rather than 'words') *and specific material phenomena* (i.e., relations rather than 'things')." In other words, there needs to be a shift away from preexisting "things" and discursive practices, those binaries so frequently at the heart of literary studies that uphold ideas of "nature" and "culture," "human" and "animal," "singular" and "plural," and toward a view of the universe that focuses on the "causal relationship between the apparatuses of bodily production and the phenomena produced." Within this framework, there are no preexisting concepts or things; there are no horses, men, societies, or genders; there are only variously intra-acting material-discursive apparatuses that continually create, alter, and bring into being those ideas or "phenomena." Barad continues, "It is through specific agential intra-actions that the boundaries and properties of the 'components' of phenomena become determinate and that particular embodied concepts become meaningful. . . . Relata do not preexist relations; rather, relata within-phenomena emerge through specific intra-actions." In turn, these phenomena come to matter (both figuratively and literally) in an ongoing process that reconfigures definitions, "boundaries, properties, meanings, and patterns of marks on bodies."[29] In other words, the category and label "man" or "masculinity," for example, represents a continuously becoming state of being because of ongoing and iterative intra-actions with the equally changeable notions of "horse" and "animal." Neither man nor horse preexists the other but performatively comes to create both. As human gender and subjectivity are formulated and negotiated through performance (performance being "the repeated stylization of the body, a set of repeated acts within a highly regulatory frame that congeal over time" and that literally embody our existence in the world),[30] so too are animal gender, subjectivity, and being in the world, according to Lynda Birke, Mette Bryld, and Nina Lykke. However, "non-human otherness" is "a *doing* or *becoming,* produced and reproduced in specific contexts of human/non-human interaction."[31] As Keri Brandt has found for horse-human relationships today, for example, "humans and horses co-create a language system by way of the body to facilitate the creation of shared meaning." This kinesthetic and visually hybrid language "challenges the privileged status of verbal language" while opening the stable door, as it were, to alternative ways of understanding and of being in the world.[32] As this book will demonstrate, through the performance of riding, the rider and horse become something more than either; they make visible the human-animal as hybrid, more-than-singular, transspecies being.

This messy co-becoming is traced through four central models of horsemanship and masculine performance. The first model, the subject of chapter 1, reveals multiple horsemanship communities defined by honor and spectacular horsemanship skill. William Cavendish, first Duke of Newcastle, purposefully displayed himself as partially embodying the animal through skilled, artistic, kinesthetic relationships with his horses in an attempt to become a leading figure in the manège community. He understood himself, and knowledgeable spectators understood him, as inhabiting the body of his horse, and he (and they) understood his horse as embracing his mind to create a hybrid, dual-natured creature: a centaur. This centaur, inherently honorable and performative, opens up fresh perspectives on how the human body and behavior, when interacting with a horse (such as Cavendish's favorite, Le Superbe), were immediately politicized. Cavendish's ability to rein (and therefore reign) rightly was an intrinsic component of centaur status. For Cavendish, to embody the centaur was to embody and perform the political theories of his close friend, Thomas Hobbes, in a way that saw the horse and human become a living example of ideal governance within the body politic. To become a centaur was to perform the ways in which sovereign and subject, through a horse-human covenant, could ensure the continued stability of a nation recovering from the ravages of civil war.

The second model, examined in chapter 2, follows Cavendish's legacy from the country estate into London—increasingly the new home of equestrian practice and changing horsemanship communities. The early eighteenth century saw a separation within horsemanship practice and community belonging that eventually resulted in the creation of two distinct but interconnected schools of horsemanship: the "modern school," interested in mechanistic, noncentauric riding for pleasure, industry, and the performance of polite and commercial virtues, usually performed on Thoroughbred horses—and the "old school," which continued to look at horsemanship as an art form to be learned on "traditionally" built horses for the conspicuous self-display of skill, nobility, and gentlemanly greatness in the Cavendish vein. The riding houses of Mr. Carter, Sidney Meadows, and Domenico Angelo, sites of often vitriolic attacks against men from competing horsemanship communities, saw men of all classes and political allegiances ride together, while criticizing their rivals' ideas and gendered display. Complicating the picture with the new inclusion of women in a traditionally male social space also allows for an examination of horse-woman communication and performed femininities. These urban riding houses revise our conception of London's politico-social spaces, the civilizing role of women therein, and the current understanding of politeness as hegemonic. Politeness, while important for the men of the riding houses in their interactions with women, was certainly not the dominant form of masculinity expected of the communities' members. Instead, men of the new horsemanship communities joined politeness to a discourse of political and personal liberty, a belief in useful commercial endeavor, free and forward riding, and equine independence, to create a notion of masculinity surprisingly martial and republican in form. For men of the more traditional communities, politeness was subordinated to the continuing discourse of refinement, honor, strength, and spectacular personal display of the centaur.

The third model, the subject of chapter 3, traces the career of one of Domenico Angelo's most famous, controversial, and ultimately influential pupils, Philip Astley, and other riders at Astley's Amphitheatre. At this illegitimate theater, Philip and his son, John, joined the comparatively normative practices of all of the horsemanship communities (the modern and old schools of equestrian practice) with performance traditions from the nation's itinerant fairs, and proceeded to (literally) turn them on their heads. With a general focus on the 1788 and 1789 seasons, at a time in which one of the Amphitheatre's most famous horses, the Gibraltar Charger, captured the public's imagination, chapter 3 investigates the theatrical staging of political centaurism at a particularly unstable point in British history. In the Amphitheatre, Philip deviated from previous horse-human performances through the creation of horses who were actors capable of performing identities and genders for themselves and their riders. In an attempt to offset the perceived failure of martial masculinity during the American war, with the help of the Charger, Philip embraced a militaristic chivalry that nostalgically recalled a fictitious glorious past when men were "truly" masculine. John, on the other hand, while dancing on horseback, glorified an identity onstage that was an unstable mixture of the masculine and feminine. With an androgynous emphasis on politeness, refinement, grace, and physical strength, John performed a masculinity and a heroism that were radically different from his father's. However, both the ultramilitarism of Philip and the refined physicality of John were necessary if the Amphitheatre was to succeed in its reformation of the nation's men. With the help of horses, frequently perceived as uncanny for their amazing feats and acting abilities, the horsemanship and manly qualities of the nation's heroes—past and present—were re-performed theatrically in the

Amphitheatre in an attempt to promote gender stability, patriotism, and social stability.

The final model of *Becoming Centaur*, the subject of chapter 4, focuses on one of the Amphitheatre's most vocal critics and the eighteenth century's greatest equestrian satirist, Henry William Bunbury. A social elitist and a purist when it came to his understanding of theater, Bunbury took aim at the illegitimacy of Astley's and the very social and gender changes that had allowed the Amphitheatre and some of the earlier London riding houses to function in the first place. He argued that new equestrian practices, both the horse-human relationships and the masculinities formed by these "modern" horsemanship communities (regardless of how polite, chivalrous, manly, or honorable the riders made themselves and their riding styles out to be), were thoroughly effeminate. Like Cavendish, and, ironically, like Astley before him, Bunbury worked to (re)establish a community of horsemen that looked to older, seventeenth-century traditions of horsemanship and masculinity for the benefit of the nation. Through the elite manège, horsemen would fulfill their civic-humanist duties and become versed in military duty and service to the state. In Bunbury's formulation, to be considered a gentleman, a man had to be elite, independent, a supporter of the king, and against popular Wilkesite liberty. He also, however, had to display appropriate masculine behavior that was expressly anticommerce and traditionally aristocratic, in which sensitivity, social refinement, and politeness in deportment and speech were the norm. For a horseman to be a masculine man who could fulfill his civic duty to the nation, he was also required to "speak" the "languages" of horsemanship with perfection and grace. Men needed to be brave and ready to serve their nation, but they had also to be gentle, sensitive, and expert at interspecies communication. For Bunbury, horsemen were to become socially refined men who embodied both the model of public, properly genteel civic virtue and a sensitivity to social benevolence and fellow feeling, as sentimental masculinity dictated.

These four interlinked models do not provide a comprehensive examination of gender or masculine display over the long eighteenth century, but they do begin the process of thinking through the complexity of experience and representation of horsemanship in the lives of humans in England. By following these men and their changing understandings of "shared trans-species being-in-the-world," this book reveals that for many men, performances of gender were no longer individually determined—or even determined by a human subject.[33] Instead, with a focus "on the *performance* of human-plus-nonhuman—where the constituting discursive practices must be understood to include the material, participating nonhuman"—masculine performance becomes a process of two interconnecting bodies working together (intentionally or not) in a "relationship" to display masculinities that, although seemingly of different species, were at times remarkably similar.[34] Taken together, the horses and horsemen of the seventeenth and eighteenth centuries developed relationships that often mirrored wider changes in normative codes and discourses of gender, class, and human-animal understanding. However, they also developed relationships that were gloriously alternative. It was through the mediating presence of horses that the very humanity (or monstrous inhumanity), masculinity (or its lack), and honorable (or dishonorable) status of horsemen were created and secured. Through horses, men came to know a multispecies identity complete with its own communication systems, modes of sociality, performances, and epistemologies. Horsemen could not be men, successful, or respected, without embodied and communicative interactions with their other half—the horse.

THE ART: A PONY-SIZED HISTORY

All four models of horsemanship and the many understandings of transspecies being discussed in this book can trace their methodologies, and often their ideologies, to a much longer equestrian tradition. As the discussion above suggests, both today and in the seventeenth and eighteenth centuries, horsemen were not confined to one single practice of horsemanship. The term itself encompasses a diversity of epistemologies, approaches, and applications that differ not only over time but frequently between manuals of the same era. The practice of horsemanship in general includes the participation in and understanding of riding (whether in the manège, trick riding, vaulting, ambling, or haute école), along with knowledge and practical abilities in all other aspects of equine care: dressing, farriery, stabling, etc. However, the term *horseman* does not, interestingly enough, encompass the activities of hunting or racing, although both activities frequently were included in the manuals. As for what constituted a horseman in the period, the treatises differ considerably in their definition and will be traced throughout this book. The differences are found between manuals that cover horsemanship alone and those that cover it in conjunction with sporting or racing materials, and they are frequently found between manuals published in the seventeenth century and those published in the eighteenth. In general, however, a horseman was a man who practiced the manège, to some extent, and someone who possessed skill, again to various degrees, in unmounted horsemanship.

The act of educating a horse in the manège is a practice that allows for insight into changing human-animal interactions, definitions, and changing discourses and performances of masculine subjectivities. To work in the manège, or to school a horse, was to practice systematic improvement of both horse and rider, and the manuals incorporate the walk, trot, gallop, stop, and, in the early years of the period under study, tournament activities such as running at the tilt or the *cariere* (running at the ring) in the term. Frequently, ambling and pacing are included in this category as well. John Brindley defined *manège* as "a word that signifies a place, not only set apart for the exercise of riding the great horse, but likewise the exercise itself."[35] For Brindley and others, the manège also included the haute école; however, this usage was not universal, and varying meanings are attached to the term throughout our period. Furthermore, the term haute école itself was not coined until the 1850s, as Elaine Walker has pointed out, but I use it here, along with manège, to aid in the ease of separation between the various horsemanship practices and to allow for further understanding of changes in discourses over our period.[36] As for the haute école (French for *high school*), the term is used here to refer to the manège movements defined as airs above the ground and those categorized as useful to the parade ground. These included the capriole, *terra a terra, balotade,* curvet, *groupade (croupade), passage, piaffeur (piaffe)*, and general leaps and yerks earlier in the seventeenth century.

Both the manège and the haute école, along with their many derivatives, can in turn be traced back to a much longer tradition of horsemanship practice that saw the inclusion of classical riding methodologies alongside increasingly evident Eastern traditions. In general, however, English horsemanship had its origins in the fourth-century B.C.E. writings of Xenophon. His *Hippike,* or *The Art of Horsemanship*, is the earliest surviving Western text on horsemanship, and it created the mold for all subsequent treatises on the subject.[37] His text, itself based on the now lost manual by Simon of Athens, was reprinted, studied, debated, and followed (often to the letter) throughout the eighteenth century, while his ideologies, grounded on "patience and gentleness," and his methodological "observations," which were "true and just," formed the backbone of horsemanship in the early modern and modern periods—as they continue to do to this day.[38] However,

Xenophon's teachings were not known to Western horsemen for nearly two thousand years after their initial publication. In the meantime, texts on husbandry, the history of animals, and agriculture by Greek and Roman authors became the key references for Renaissance and early modern authors of horsemanship manuals. These sources included Aristotle's *Historia animalium* (350 B.C.E.), for breeding and raising horses; Varo's *Res rusticae* (37 B.C.E.), for equine conformation; Virgil's *Georgics* (29 B.C.E.), one of the more popular sources for riding and training horses for parade and warfare; Pliny the Elder's *Historia naturalis* (77 C.E.), which included descriptions of heroic horses and horsemen such as Alexander's Bucephalus and the Scythian cavalry; and Oppian's *Cynegetica* (early third century C.E.), which was the first text to discuss horses in the context of hunting.[39]

The classical tradition in turn fed into European cultures and combined with vernacular customs to create a thriving equestrian and print culture that, as Hilda Nelson points out, saw the publication of equestrian-related texts such as *Les livres des tournois du Roi René* (1460), *The Book of Saint Albans* (1486), and *Le livre de la chasse* (1387–39), prior to Xenophon's reprinting. However, these texts were dominated by vernacular horsemanship traditions, despite the large influence of classical sources, and it was not until Xenophon's manual was republished that this changed.[40] His text was retrieved from Constantinople by Giovanni Aurispa, a Sicilian, in 1423, and may have first been republished in Naples in 1516.[41] Naples was also home to one of the most influential horsemen active during the art's formative years in the early modern period. Federico Grisone erected the first riding academy in 1532, and was one of the first to publish a manual of horsemanship partially based on Xenophon's teachings. His transitional 1550 *Gli ordini di cavalcare* (*The Rules of Horsemanship*) was immediately successful and was quickly translated. His teachings, very much indebted to classical and Ottoman sources while firmly grounded in the more familiar vernacular methods, were taught in turn to some of the most renowned horsemen of his time.[42] His pupil Giovanni Battista Pignatelli was riding master to "the three key French horsemen" (the Chevalier de Saint Antoine, Salomon de La Broue, and Antoine de Pluvinel) who would shift the focus of horsemanship education from the Neapolitan school to France in the late sixteenth and early seventeenth centuries, and who would come to play a significant role in English manège horsemanship under some of the most influential horsemen of the era.[43]

Pluvinel was chief equerry to Louis XIII, master of his own riding academy in Paris, founded in 1594, and the author of two manuals of horsemanship: *Le maneige royal* (1623), republished with the original text as *L'instruction du roy en l'exercice de monter à cheval* in 1625.[44] These treatises, two of the most revolutionary texts of the time (and clear precursors to William Cavendish's manuals of horsemanship), incorporated the more gentle teachings of Xenophon alongside those derived from other classical sources handed down through Grisone.[45] As for de La Broue, he penned the 1593 *Preceptes principaux que les bons cavelerises doivent exactement observer en leur escoles,* which became a standard reference text for many English authors on horsemanship in the early seventeenth century, such as Gervase Markham for his 1607 *Cavelarice.* Saint Antoine, in turn, was transferred to England as part of a coronation gift of horses from Henri IV to James I in 1603. He was to become a central component in the Frenchification of the English manège community, and played an active role in educating a select group of English elite—including Prince Henry, Charles I, and Cavendish.[46]

It was much earlier, however, that the manège first made inroads into England. Before Grisone's manual was translated into English, the practice was already influencing English courtly equestrian culture. Gentlemen traveled to the Italian courts, where they learned the art; they in turn introduced their teachings into England while purposely breeding their own horses to suit their newly acquired horsemanship methodologies and to mirror the horses desired by many European courts. Henry VIII, as Giles Worsley explains, first received horses trained "in the Spanish fashion" by Giovanni Ratto, envoy to their sender, the Marquis of Mantua. Henry quickly became a convert and frequently performed the movements of the manège, including those of the haute école, at court tournaments. This art quickly spread among English courtiers, so that when Nicolo Sagudino viewed a tourney in 1517 he could record that "between the course, the King and the pages, and other cavaliers, performed marvellous feats, mounted on magnificent horses, which they made jump and execute other acts of horsemanship, under the windows where the most serene Queens of England and Dowager of France were, with all the rest of the beauteous and lovely and sumptuously apparelled damsels. . . . The King performed supernatural feats, changing his horses, and making them fly rather than leap, to the delight and ecstasy of everybody."[47] By the end of Henry's reign, such performances and an increasing interest in the art, helped along by the repeated importation of Italian riding masters by the king and the titled aristocracy, led to manège and haute école horsemanship becoming the dominant equestrian practice among the English ruling elite.

Indeed, by the time of Elizabeth I's reign, not only had the manège become an actively promoted component of a young courtier's education, but the art had entered into a veritable golden age exemplified by widespread practice and a marked increase in horsemanship manuals. The first of these manuals, not so much a translation as a rewriting of Grisone's earlier treatise, was Thomas Blundeville's *A New Booke Containing the Arte of Ryding, and Breaking Grete Horses* of around 1560. Others soon followed, drawing on Grisone's and Xenophon's treatises: Thomas Bedingfield's *The Art of Riding by Claudio Corte* (1584) (a translation of Claudio Corte's *Il Cavalerizzo*), John Astley's *The Art of Riding* (1584), Christopher Clifford's *The School of Horsemanship* (1585), and Gervase Markham's *Discourse of Horsemanshippe* (1593) and *How to Chuse, Ride, Trayne, and Diet, Both Hunting-Horses and Running Horses* (1596), the first of many Markham titles to come. These authors and others, much like subsequent generations of horsemen, operated in a "closely knit circle," "exchanging and training each other's horses, while dedicating books to each other."[48]

The erection of riding houses for academies, such as Master Thomas Story's Greenwich school, Sir Humphrey Gilbert's in London, and Sir James Scudamore's in Holme Lacy, Herefordshire, also began during Elizabeth's reign and continued until the Civil Wars. At these schools, horsemen increasingly gathered to learn from the newest imported Italian master in a wholehearted following of the latest fashion in equestrian practice. However, with the reign of James I, the Italian dominance in English horsemanship began to wane. While Italian influences did not disappear, and while young men of elite status both continued to travel to Italy for instruction and sought out the few Italian riding masters working in England, France and French horsemanship gradually came to dominate English and European equestrian circles. In England, for example, Saint Antoine recruited fellow Frenchmen as esquires in the royal mews, while at the same time the growing fame and influence of Pluvinel and de La Broue shifted the heart of the manège to the French court.[49]

During the reigns of James I and Charles I, the Elizabethan golden age of horsemanship showed few signs of diminishing. It was here that some of the most influential texts on the subject were written, among them Michael Baret's *Hipponomie* (1618), Nicholas Morgan of Crolane's *Perfection of Horse-manship* (1609) and *The Horse-mans Honour* (1620), and Thomas de Grey's *Compleat Horseman* (1639). Charles I also continued the practice of the manège and haute école, not only through patronage of the art but, like his predecessors, through personal performance. As a Venetian ambassador to Charles's court recorded, "He [Charles] excels at tilting and indulges in every other kind of horsemanship, and even if he were not prince one would have to confess that he surpassed others."[50] Similarly, while James I by all accounts was not a devoted manège participant, his son Henry and his followers carried on the Pignatelli style of horsemanship—through Saint Antoine's teachings—and formed one of the strongest and most accomplished circles of horsemen of the time.[51]

However, even with the manège's continued popularity, manège horsemanship was never welcomed or adopted in England with open arms, owing to doubts about the art's usefulness for military men and horses and an apparent distrust of foreign methods of riding. In Baret's 1618 *Hipponomie,* for example, the still relatively new art of horsemanship in the manège was struggling to take hold, thanks to the continuing influence of local English custom. As a result, Baret's "earnest desire" was "to haue this now withered and dead Art of *Horsemanship* (being such a famous Art [in Europe]) the more to flourish in this Kingdome, which hath been so long frost-bitten with the congealing rygne of ancient traditions; whereby Custome hath taxed such false impositions upon these noble Creatures, as now they are become most ignoble and base."[52] The threat to the manège continued throughout the seventeenth century, and in 1639 Thomas de Grey, in his *Compleat Horseman and Expert Ferrier,* complained that in addition to a paucity of horses serviceable for the manège, there was a worrying trend of "laying aside of the great Saddle and Cannon, and neglect of the Horse of Menage" in the face of changing equestrian pursuits. For de Grey, the growing interest in sporting riding and racing had made "the most ancient honour of Horseman-ship peculiar to this our Kingdome" "almost vanished and lost."[53] That said, however, there were still champions of the art.

For William Cavendish (1592–1676), first Duke of Newcastle, and many other writers on the subject, horsemanship was a sure method of developing and maintaining physical strength, living a long and healthy life, and, above all, achieving an elite bearing and confidence in addition to skill at arms and warfare. However, the inclusion of sporting pastimes alongside the manège and haute école in the new manuals, and the authors' continual and repeated insistence on the importance of the haute école, suggests a considerable and growing backlash against the use, keeping, and training of horses for such "frivolous" pursuits as the haute école was thought to be. Cavendish wondered what "makes these *Men* speak against it" in his *New Method, and Extraordinary Invention, to Dress Horses, and Work Them According to Nature,* in which he concluded that their opposition was primarily due to their ignorance of the art and their disinclination to "take Paines" to become masters of horsemanship. Those who "think it a Disgrace for a Gentleman to do any thing Well," like riding, were acting on the changing perceptions of the horse as useful in warfare and the protection of the commonwealth, and were arguing that when a gentleman like Cavendish spent vast amounts of his wealth, time, and energy working with horses, he was not producing anything useful to the nation. Likewise, Karen Raber interprets Cavendish's defense of the haute école as a sign of his disconnection from prevailing trends that dictated the uselessness of the practice, even dismissing it as an "obsolete" exercise, and Anthony Dent argues that the haute école was "an elaborate pretense" for any military training.[54] However, for Cavendish, "both Use and Pleasure" could be found in all aspects of the manège, including the haute école. "It is True," he argued, "that if there was nothing Commendable but what is Useful, strictly Examined; we must have nothing but Hollow Trees for our Houses, Figg-leaf-Breeches for our Clothes, Acorns for our Meat, and Water for our Drink; for certainly, most things else are but Superfluities and Curiosities."[55] In his view, not only was the manège of use to the kingdom, but it was also necessary for pleasure, the absence of which reduced man to a state of simple necessity, incivility, and savagery at the expense of the civilized and refining arts. The manège, beautiful horsemanship, was far from a useless pastime, as far as Cavendish was concerned. It remained central to his notion of militaristic and honorable masculinity and continued to define his ideal political animal, as we shall see more fully in the following chapter.

1.

WILLIAM CAVENDISH AND HOBBESIAN HORSEMANSHIP

To turn and wind a fiery Pegasus,
And witch the world with noble horsemanship.
—WILLIAM SHAKESPEARE

"O mine star! how se royal youth carry himself as Alesandare on Becephalus. Now, Sare, advance your pace," [he said,] cracking his whip. "Hold up your august chins—turn in your royal toe."
—MONS. DURELL

In 1667 William Cavendish outlined his approach to the practice of horsemanship in his manual *A New Method, and Extraordinary Invention, to Dress Horses*. "As for Pleasure and State," Cavendish wrote,

> What Prince or Monarch looks more Princely, or more Enthroned, than Upon a Beautiful Horse, with Rich Foot-clothes, or Rich Sadles, and Waving Plumes, making his Entry through Great Cities, to Amaze the People with Pleasure and Delight? Or, What more Glorious or Manly, than, at great Marriages of Princes, to Run at the Ring, or Tilt, or Course at the Field? What can be more Comely or Pleasing, than to see Horses go in all their several Ayres? and to see so Excellent a Creature, with so much Spirit, and

Strength, to be so Obedient to his Rider, as if having no Will but His, they had but one Body, and one Mind, like a Centaur? But above all, What sets Off a King more, than to be on a Beautiful Horse at the Head of his Army?

Thus it is Proved, That there is nothing of more Use than A Horse of Mannage; nor any thing of more State, Manliness, or Pleasure, than Rideing.[1]

Riding was the perfect art, the most profitable science, the method of ensuring a stately bodily grace, and the pastime that was essential for gentlemen to perfect. Horsemanship was an exercise not to be ignored, and it certainly was not a pastime that could withstand imperfect dabbling. Instead, horses and horsemanship needed time, effort, and practice to perfect. But why? Why should a gentleman spend so much time, effort, and money on riding? Why did Cavendish almost beggar himself to purchase new horses while in exile in Antwerp? What was it about horses that could be so beneficial? And what did he mean when he wrote of being like a centaur? These and other questions relating to Cavendish's practice of horsemanship are the focus of this chapter, and while the answers are necessarily somewhat general in scope, they can provide a glimpse into the complicated, technical, competitive, and highly political world of seventeenth-century horsemanship.

Today, most scholars of horses and horsemanship agree that the embodied act of riding was inherently political during the seventeenth and eighteenth centuries.[2] However, the intricacies of this relationship and its performativity still require clarification. This is also the case for Cavendish, that most studied of horsemen, even though Karen Raber has taken up the reins, so to speak, and examined Cavendish's politics in relation to horsemanship. She argues that Cavendish, while he may have appeared to follow Royalist philosophies, harbored deep-seated, and possibly unknown to him, political leanings that diverged from older beliefs in absolute monarchy and fell more in line with the emerging republican philosophies popular in the years after the Civil Wars. For her, Cavendish's horsemanship introduced subjectivities that point more to the "profound, political transformation which eventually reshaped England's government as a representative republic" than to a balanced monarchy or strong class hierarchy.[3] In my examination of Cavendish's political horsemanship, however, I take a different approach. While exploring Cavendish's multilayered discussion of horsemanship, I look to his relationships with his horses alongside his frequent entanglement with Thomas Hobbes's theories of government. For Cavendish, governing a horse was analogous to governing an absolute monarchy or commonwealth organized along the lines of Hobbes's theories. To "bee well setled in [the] Sadle" of horse and state took time and effort, and was entirely a Hobbesian, embodied, transspecies experience.[4] This political embodiment of government in the body of man and animal created a monarchical sovereignty, an experience, I argue, that in turn generated masculine power and honor for the useful display of the horseman's political animality.

WILLIAM CAVENDISH, DUKE OF NEWCASTLE

William Cavendish was "admir'd and honour'd by all good Men," was "for so many years together, the Pattern and Standard of Honor to the Nation," and his "whole Life has been so great an Example of Heroick Virtue" for other horsemen. He possessed "all the advantages of a noble Birth and Education" and had "rendered both, yet more conspicuous" by his "Virtue" and self-improving labor.[5] Educated as a child in the "traditional" masculine pursuits of "Horsemanship, Dancing and Fencing, which accompany a good breeding," Cavendish went on to be an influential man at court, in national politics, and in local affairs.[6] Cavendish was also a forward thinker and an influential patron of the arts and sciences. He established "a courtly academy in the provinces" with his brother Charles at their estate at Welbeck Abbey in the 1630s, and his family became "a vital centre of intellectual and cultural activity" during their interregnum exile on the European continent.[7] Continually ambitious in his political and personal life, Cavendish worked hard to increase his status at court through patronage and unwavering support of the Royalist cause before, during, and after the Civil Wars.[8] As a youth, Cavendish, that "Prince of Horsemen," trained alongside Prince Henry with Monsieur Saint Antoine (who trained with the founding fathers of manège horsemanship, Pignatelli and Pluvinel) and undertook a grand tour in 1610 to improve his courtly skills.[9] In addition, Cavendish "was amorous in Poetry and Musick, to which he indulged the greatest part of his time; and nothing could have tempted him out of those paths of pleasure, which he enjoy'd . . . but Honour and Ambition to serve the King."[10]

And serve the king he did. Cavendish was appointed governor of the future Charles II in 1638 and appointed member of the Privy Council in 1639. As governor, he did not waste any time in expressing his views on matters moral, political, and monarchical in multiple influential letters addressed to the young prince.[11] Cavendish resigned his post as governor in 1641 at the outbreak of the Civil Wars, but he went on to serve as Charles I's captain-general and supreme commander of the Royalist forces in the north. Following his disastrous defeat at Marston Moor and subsequent flight to the continent, Cavendish continued to serve as mentor and adviser to the monarchy through his position within the Privy Council to the exiled government.[12] Also during his exile, Cavendish set to work in penning his many masques, poems, and manuals of horsemanship.

Cavendish's first manual, *La méthode nouvelle et invention extraordinaire de dresser les chevaux,* was sumptuously illustrated, modeled after Pluvinel's 1623 *Maneige royal* and published in 1658 while he was in exile at Antwerp. This printing was small (fifty copies), with the majority of books produced for presentation.[13] Upon his return to England after the restoration of Charles II to the throne in 1660, Cavendish published an English edition of *La méthode nouvelle* that was "neither a Translation of the first [book], nor an absolutely necessary Addition to it." His 1667 *A New Method, and Extraordinary Invention, to Dress Horses* was to "be of use by it self, without the other [book], as the other has been hitherto, and is still, without this [content]; but both together will questionless do best."[14] Although *A New Method* was produced without the plates of the original Antwerp edition, it was still a handsome publication printed on imperial folio and dedicated to the king. In 1737, six decades after Cavendish's death, his granddaughter, the Countess of Oxford, along with the printer John Brindley, reissued the 1658 Antwerp edition in French with the original illustrations from the plates by Abraham van Diepenbeke and Charles Parrocel. After a presumably successful print run, Bindley translated *La méthode nouvelle* and published it in 1743 as *A General System of Horsemanship*.[15]

These texts, similar in content and frequently containing verbatim passages from one another, made the already well known Duke of Newcastle the most influential horseman in England, and one of the most respected on the continent. For example, François Robichon de La Guérinière wrote sometime between 1729 and 1731 that Cavendish "honoured the profession infinitely with the unique study he made of it throughout the course of his entire life; he was considered, moreover, to be the greatest expert of his age in the matter of horses."[16] Like Guérinière, almost all horsemen writing and practicing after Cavendish, well into the nineteenth century, drew on his teachings and ideologies in their own treatises on horsemanship, or indicated their awareness of his importance to the development of horsemanship if they had not managed to obtain a copy of his publications.

Cavendish's manuals were also repeatedly republished in France, Germany, and Spain during the late seventeenth and early eighteenth centuries. William Hope, a student of Cavendish's, even went so far as to reissue entire sections of *A New Method* in his *Compleat Horseman* of 1696, while Claude Bourgelat reworked *A New Method* for his own *Nouveau Newcastle, au nouveau traité de cavalerie* of 1754. Other horsemen explicitly stated their indebtedness to Cavendish's theories, while perpetuating Cavendish's almost mythical status as a great horseman. For example, the Earl of Pembroke simply called Cavendish "great," and the master of horse Richard Berenger thought Cavendish "honoured" the art of horsemanship "with his practice, and greatly enriched it with his knowledge."[17]

Inspired by previous horsemen, such as Federico Grisone, Claudio Corte, and others (with whom Cavendish frequently disagreed on matters equine and equestrian), Cavendish's manuals also proposed a radically new horsemanship methodology. His work explored a method of training that was scientific, rational, measured, and overtly political in its formulation, but his manuals did more than allow him to circulate his ideas. As Karen Raber argues, "Publishing both interjected Cavendish into an ongoing print debate over training methods, and made him a *teacher* of riding skills, rather than simply or only a great rider and trainer in his own right."[18] Cavendish's manuals both engaged with and distanced themselves from existing manuals and discourses of horsemanship written by men of various equestrian backgrounds and classes. In doing so, and in accordance with accepted behavior associated with his rank, Cavendish was not only working to bolster his status as an elite man practicing an elite art; he was also working to establish a form of "cultural capital" that would help confine the practice of horsemanship to those who were by rank and gender worthy of it.[19] Furthermore, these manuals were designed to teach his select group of pupils proper masculine behavior and political ideology, in this case that of Thomas Hobbes.

Hobbes worked closely with the Cavendish family and enjoyed Cavendish's dedicated patronage and close friendship for much of his career. After his graduation from Oxford in 1608, Hobbes was employed as a tutor for Cavendish's cousins, the second and third earls of Devonshire, and instructed them in the classical humanist tradition. While at this post, he became an acquaintance of Cavendish's and his younger brother Charles's, and accompanied Cavendish on his grand tour, after which he began to correspond regularly with the brothers on matters of science and philosophy.[20] Hobbes also seems to have shared many interests with Cavendish, and undertook a collaborative project with him in 1646 for the writing of *The Truth of the Sorde,* a book on mathematics and scientific swordsmanship. When it came to horsemanship, however, Hobbes was not a master of the art. He did ride, though, and was well versed in horsemanship principles as taught by Cavendish, principles he later put to good use when Cavendish commissioned him to purchase Le Superbe (possibly the same Le Superbe who became one of Cavendish's favorite horses) while he was living in Paris.[21] This equestrian connection is especially interesting when we look at the ongoing political discussions and debates between the two men. Hobbes dedicated his *Elements of Law* to Cavendish in 1640 along with his 1646 *Questions Concerning Liberty* (written at Cavendish's suggestion), and it is certain that he frequently discoursed on matters philosophical, scientific, and political with his patron while writing *Leviathan.*[22] Cavendish, in turn, was well versed in Hobbes's theories of government and liberty, and actively participated in ongoing debates on the subjects.

THE CENTAURIC LEVIATHAN

According to Hobbes, there was a distinct process to the creation of a commonwealth that took man from a state of insecurity and incivility to one of prosperity and contented security under a sovereign. To summarize, prior to the development of a political administration, man is essentially by nature in a state of violent and competitive being. Mankind displayed "a generall inclination" for "a perpetuall and restlesse desire of Power after power, that ceaseth onely in Death."[23] Searching for bodily comfort, wealth, honor, and status, mankind was in a state of incivility and war when in his natural state, but paradoxically continually searching for peace as a means of ensuring his security and safety. Only available through the creation of a sovereign body that would regulate man's continual quest for power, this peace was obtained through giving up of some of man's natural freedoms, such as the freedom of independent movement or resistance to a stronger body than oneself. The relinquishing of some of these freedoms or natural rights to a sovereign, or the indication of the will (desire) to relinquish them, was done through a "pact or covenant" that created "subjects" of the natural persons under one ruler. As Hobbes argued,

> the finall Cause, End, or Designe of men, (who naturally love Liberty, and Dominion over others,) in the introduction of that

restraint upon themselves, (in which wee see them live in Commonwealths,) is the foresight of their own preservation, and of a more contented life thereby; that is to say, of getting themselves out from that miserable condition of Warre, which is neccessarily consequent . . . the naturall Passions of men, when there is no visible Power to keep them in awe, and tye them by feare of punishment to the performance of their Covenants.

Covenants created a three-tiered being for Hobbes, where in the first instance covenanting, in effect, served to "reduce" the people's "Wills, by plurality of voices, unto one Will." This resulted in a situation where the "reall Unitie of them all" brought into being and was represented "in one and the same Person," the sovereign. This "*Soveraignty*" was in turn the being upon which the artificial animal Leviathan depended, as without it there would be no life, since the sovereign "is an Artificiall *Soul*, as giving life and motion to the whole body." The resulting "great LEVIATHAN called a COMMON-WEALTH, or STATE, (in latine CIVITAS) which is but an Artificiall Man; though of greature stature and strength than the Naturall," was imagined as an artificial human body, a body composed of a sovereign head and a multitude of persons upon which it rested.[24] Wonderfully hybrid in its creation, Hobbes's ideal commonwealth was at once mechanical (Cartesian), artificial, and alive. His commonwealth was monstrous in its form and consisted of a body and soul brought together through education and skill as art.[25]

Jacques Derrida analyzed Hobbes's formulation of the great Leviathan in his examination of sovereignty and sovereign power. For him, and for many previous philosophers, political man is always a political animal (or *zōon politikon*, to use Aristotle's famous phrase), and as such is a "double and contradictory figuration" of being. Building upon Western epistemological ties to biblical teachings that mandate man's domination over animal life as a natural right, Derrida argues that political man is "*on the one hand* superior, in his very sovereignty, to the beast that he masters, enslaves, dominates, domesticates, or kills, so that his sovereignty consists in raising himself above the animal and appropriating it, having its life at his disposal."[26] This natural right at once placed man in a superior position above animals (along with many humans, such as women, children, slaves, and those of less social power), while also situating the sovereign in a position of the semidivine. In an imitation of God's creation of mankind, political man artificially creates the beast Leviathan through art and law. This ongoing divine domination and creation of animal life within the Leviathan in turn necessitated Derrida's other half of man as political animal. As Derrida argues, there was "*on the other hand* (contradictorily) a figuration of the political man, and especially of the sovereign state *as animality*, or even as bestiality . . . , either a normal bestiality or a monstrous bestiality itself mythological or fabulous."[27] Frequently figured as wolfish by political theorists, for Derrida, political man was at once always superior to animality and animal life and also animal himself. The creation and maintenance of sovereignty by necessity was a violent process only marginally removed from the continuous state of war that the sovereign lifted the people out of through domination and covenants. Furthermore, sovereign power was a fragile thing, and was maintained through absolute actions of men who appeared not much different from the animals their rationality evidently distinguished them from.[28]

In this formulation, then, political man as a potentially ravenous political animal was a contradictory figuration of man as superior to animals on the species hierarchy and of political man as artificially constructed animality close to the divine. However, Hobbes's engagement with Aristotle's *zōon politikon* adds another element to this already complex figuration. While Derrida argues that political animality was bestial in form, and violent toward competing states especially, Hobbes looks to human nature as indicative of man as a political "creature." He argues that Aristotle's formulation was an "Axiom" "certainly False, and an Errour proceeding from our too slight contemplation of Humane Nature." For Hobbes, the concept of *zōon politikon* did not necessarily reference man's fitness for politics but his natural propensity to come together to "delight in each others company" within political bodies. Hobbes argued in *De Cive* that theorists, especially the classical Greek philosophers, thought the formation of a commonwealth or republic was a relatively simple affair. Republics in turn enjoyed "the preservation of Peace, and the Government of Man-kind" through nothing more than a mutual agreement between men in the form of "certaine Covenants and Conditions together, which themselves should then call Lawes." In addition, this theory of civil society was erroneously predicated on an understanding of human nature that saw men's love for their fellow men as a natural occurrence, not as a component of the artificial covenanting process. Instead, political man was not a "Creature born fit for Society" but a creature that sought out the company of others for personal gain: "We doe not therefore by nature seek Society for its own sake, but that we may receive some Honour or

Profit from it." Human nature was not to form commonwealths out of an almost instinctive drive for social interaction or out of any love for our fellow man but was competitive, selfish, and perpetually full of faction, jealousy, and discord. In other words, "All Society therefore is either for Gain, or for Glory; (i.e.) not so much for love of our Fellowes, as for love of our Selves."[29]

Thus, when taken together, these three formulations of political man as animal or animality form a three-sided sovereign that can dominate, domesticate, or kill as a being above the law, and as a being that does so as a social creature interested in personal gain. A remarkably apt image of both Leviathan and Cavendish's centaur, this figuration was representative in form, and could theoretically (for Derrida) include live animals in its formation. However, neither Hobbes nor Derrida, in his deconstruction of Hobbes's theories, explored the role of live animals within the formation of covenants or sovereign states. Hobbes argued that even though animals, such as bees and ants, that appeared to form states did exist, and exhibited all of the elements necessary for the creation of a commonwealth, the creation of a body politic with brute beings was strictly impossible. They were simply not equipped mentally or physically for the task. For Derrida, however, the existence of traditionally political animals necessitated a new approach to theories of power, government, and structure that begins to witness the inclusion of live animals. As a result, he calls for a "restructur[ing of] the whole problematic" of critical examinations of the past; however, Derrida remains oddly silent about live animals in his wolfish tracking of sovereignty as dualistic animality.[30] This chapter begins the process of restructuring our understanding of the beast and the sovereign by taking seriously the constitutive role of animals within the animalized sovereignty of Cavendish and his horses, and it does so while interrogating Hobbes's insistence on the impossibility of animal participation within sovereign states.

Karen Barad takes up Derridean preoccupations with discursive practices in her merging of quantum physics and gender studies in a complex and innovative retheorization of performativity that takes as intrinsic the ongoing influence of matter. Instead of relying on a Cartesian differentiation between "things" and "representation," or "the inherent distinction between subject and object, knower and known," Barad argues for a reorientation of focus that allows the material presence of animals to become essential to our further understanding of Cavendish's animal sovereignty. This reorientation of focus away from Cartesian dominance toward phenomena produced through agential intra-action negates any conceptualization of either party as preexisting the other.[31] As such, there are no horses and there are no riders prior to their ongoing and ever-evolving relationships together; they co-create each other through iterative intra-actions, and through each other performatively generate a physical gendered body. Therefore, when we move beyond figurative animality or bestiality, when a material, live animal is added to the equation of sovereignty, what we see is not only a mythological representation of animality wrapped up in discourses and acts of power in the Derridian sense, but also a lived becoming and a way of being in the world for both man and animal together—a becoming that was but one body and one mind in a commingling of beast and human to create a very real hybrid body of man and animal as more than metaphor or "parallels" to the rider's life, a becoming that was a living, breathing commonwealth, or intra-active, centauric Leviathan.[32]

GOVERNMENT AND HORSEMANSHIP

However, Hobbes would have disagreed with Barad and her theories of animal and human performatively generating each other together. Like many authors of the time, Hobbes shared a philosophy similar to Descartes's and was highly skeptical about the idea that animals could enjoy any form of equality with humans, even though he did afford them a limited, and contradictory, form of rationality and intelligence. Hobbes argued that animals were capable of "Imagining" and hence of "Understanding." They could come to understand commands given either by verbal speech or through some other sign, if given enough time and repetition. This understanding, however, was not a true knowledge of speech enjoyed by humans. Animals could only come to know a limited number of speech signs, such as "a dogge by custome will understand the call, or the rating of his Master; and so will many other Beasts." Man, in contrast, can fully grasp the complexities of meaning inherent within language. Man can understand not only the will of a master, as animals could, but also "his conceptions and thoughts, by the sequell and contexture of the names of things into Affirmations, Negations, and other forms of Speech."[33] Animals could think, or "Deliberate," they could decide their actions upon such deliberation, or have "*Will*," but they could neither speak nor truly understand language in a way that made their will understandable to humans.[34]

Thus, for Hobbes, a covenant required the indication of the will, so "to make Covenant with bruit Beasts, is impossible." This was "because not understanding our speech, they understand not, nor accept of any translation of Right; nor can translate any Right to another: and without mutuall acceptation, there is no Covenant." Man (in this instance in the role of sovereign) was not intelligible to the animal, and because the animal could not think abstractly or speak, he was unintelligible to man. As a result, an animal was incapable of making his desire to covenant clear, to add his own interests to that of his sovereign, of understanding his natural rights to man or of understanding man's conditions of right when presented to him.[35] Being without a covenant was to enter into a situation where "there had been amongst men, neither Common-wealth, nor Society, nor Contract, nor Peace, no more than amongst Lyons, bears, and Wolves."[36]

In contrast, while Cavendish's frequent political musings closely mirror Hobbes's theories of the animal Leviathan, when it came to creating covenants with animals he radically, although unsurprisingly, disagreed.[37] For Cavendish, horses were rational beings capable of understanding and (admittedly limited and dumb) communication with their riders. To formulate his argument on the subject, Cavendish directly engaged with arguably one of the most dominant and persistent theories of animal sentience to come out of not only his circle of scientific philosophers but the seventeenth century: Descartes's "beast machine." Descartes argued that animals were not rational beings. They could not speak, and as a result they were evidently incapable of rational thought or of responding when addressed. "And one should not confuse words with the natural movements which bear witness to the passions and can be imitated by machines as well as by animals," he stated, and "neither should one think, as did certain of the Ancients, that animals speak although we do not understand their language." Indeed, this incapacity for speech, coupled with the apparent inability of animals to perform "certain actions" as well as or better than humans, "proves that they do not have a mind." For Descartes, it logically followed that "it is nature which acts in them according to the disposition of their organs, as one sees that a clock, which is made up of only wheels and springs, can count the hours and measure time more exactly than we can with all our art."[38] There is no rational soul, no thought, and no intelligence within the animal body; instead, animals are mere machines who are interchangeable with automatons that take the appearance of a live being. "Mere nature," rather than rational thought in the form of response, dictates the movement of the animal body in a reaction to external stimuli.

Cavendish, in contrast, explicitly took the side of the "Ancients" whom Descartes so disparaged. Pointing to an epistemology radically different from accepted scientific thought, one intimately connected to the ontologies of horsemanship practice, Cavendish argued that equine rationality was understandable to him because he was a horseman. He observed and communicated with animals on a daily basis and thus had come to recognize that they simply could not possess the level of agency experienced by him, be trained, or perform his instructions without it. "A horse must be wrought upon more by proper and frequent lessons, than by the heels, that he may know, and even think upon what he ought to do," Cavendish explained.

> If he does not think (as the famous philosopher DES CARTES affirms of all beasts) it would be impossible to teach him what he should do. But by the hope of reward, and fear of punishment; when he has been rewarded or punished, he thinks of it, and retains it in his memory (for memory is thought) and forms a judgment by what is past of what is to come (which again is thought;) insomuch that he obeys his rider not only for fear of correction, but also in hopes of being cherish'd. But these are things so well known to a complete horseman, that it is needless to say more on the subject.[39]

Cavendish's horses were fully rational, thinking beings who were more than capable of imagining the future and responding to the past. As such, as Erica Fudge points out, for Cavendish, horses were able to think and had reason as animals, as horses. Horses, even though they were as rational as humans, remained essentially Other in form and being; rationality does not equate with the human, as most earlier philosophers argued.[40]

While instrumental in the history of human-animal relationships, this use of speech as a traditional form of species differentiation was not seemingly applicable to horsemen in the horse-human relationship. This experiential and situated knowledge was directly discussed by John Oswald in 1791 as an important component of his case for animal rights. For him, speech was an entirely unnecessary component to understanding animal intelligence, and "those . . . whose business it is to rear animals, are at no loss to understand their language" because they know their charges. They live and work with animals, and therefore have a unique perspective on their intelligence that was directly in opposition to more institutional philosophical ideas. Indeed, "the huntsman knows by the voice of the hound, whether he is in search of the hare or pursues him, whether he has found him, or has lost the scent. In the same manner the cow-herd can tell when the kine are dry or hungry, or fatigued, whether they are stimulated to venery, or call for their young. . . . Now this would be impossible, unless there were between man and other animals a similarity of intellect, by which they mutually operate upon and move each other."[41] In a similar though more empirical manner, Cavendish insisted on a shared rationality between man and animal expressed through common experience and understandable to him as a horseman. He argued that "altho' horses do not form their reasonings from the ABC, which, as that admirable and most excellent philosopher master HOBBS says, is no language, but the marks and representation of things, he must notwithstanding give me leave to think, that they draw their reasonings from things themselves." Horses did not need language (speech) to make their thoughts and wills known because "the one is as wise as the other. I am reasoning by marks express'd in language, and he is reasoning from the presence or absence of things without these marks."[42] Even though man and horse were mentally different from each other, they were essentially equal when it came to wisdom and rationality. Horses could think, they had will, and they were capable of indicating it through a bodily language; the art of horsemanship was the medium through which their Othered addresses came to be understood.

A complex process generated through years of concentrated effort and practice, horsemanship was founded upon the perfection of intra-active bodily communication. Just as Donna Haraway's companion species are "co-constitutive" today, so horsemen, for Cavendish, were fashioned through the willed kinesthetics of their horses, and their horses were formed through the rational domination of the rider in a reciprocal relationship that, if done correctly, could produce embodied human-animal "symbiogenesis."[43] Ann Game explains this process further. By coming to know the other's "culture," man and horse learn the language of riding, of communication, and over time come to inhabit the other. Horsemanship, for Game, "is the bringing to life of *the* relation between horse and rider, involving a mutual calling up of horse and rider in each other. What horse and rider entrain with is the relation, the rhythm between, the transporting flow, the *riding*."[44] While too egalitarian for Cavendish's hierarchical and absolutist horsemanship methodologies, what Game proposes for understanding her own experiences highlights the coming together, the continual intra-active process of creation, that riding developed for him. In this formulation, the rider learns through practice the art of riding, and the horse learns "true obedience" to his sovereign master's instructions or aids in a mutually communicative process of speech generation. Over time, the horse comes to understand the rider's physical language, and the rider comes to learn the horse's. As such, horsemanship and the subsequent creation of a centaur consisted of more than taking a "gallop from St. Alban's to London, or [making] a horse trample with a snaffle and martingal the old English way." It took years of dedicated effort for ease on horseback to develop, and those "are mistaken vastly, who think themselves great masters, because they have learned to ride a month or two, and have not been thrown."[45] There were "Thousands of things in the Art" of horsemanship necessary for reducing horses by degrees to will the same as a master though covenant.[46]

Horses were not easily brought to obedience, however, making skill in horsemanship especially necessary. As Cavendish argued, "The horse being, after man, the most noble of all animals (for he is as much superior to all other creatures as man is to him, and therefore holds a sort of middle place between man and the rest of creation) he is wise and subtile." As a result, it was because of this middle ground, this superior-beast status, that "man ought carefully to preserve his empire over him, knowing how nearly that wisdom and subtilty approaches his own."[47] Horses could think for themselves, and must therefore be persuaded through communication to covenant.[48] A sovereign horseman, through his excellent horsemanship ability, was to educate them in their rights and the rights of the sovereign by generating "love" in, or becoming "friends" with, his mount. Cavendish's whole goal of horsemanship was "to make the horseman and his horse friends, and bring them to will the same thing," that is, to make the horse "Obedient to his Rider" as sovereign.[49]

A sovereign was to look to art, that peculiar prerogative of the patriarchal divine, and become a sovereign in a material-discursive process of intra-active becoming. This "*Ground* of Dressing all Horses whatsoever" was knowing, after governing himself, how to govern a horse through a combination of rewards (known as cherishing) and punishments. As Cavendish argued, "Hope of *Reward,* and Fear of *Punishment,* Governs this whole World; not only Men, but Horses: And thus they will Chuse the *Reward,* and Shun the *Punnishment.*"[50] The same process of monarchical government espoused by Hobbes, ruling a horse as sovereign took careful judgment and iron control. It was also based on fear.[51] In a theory of horse and human control that was the result of the "Counsel of a Friend" (probably Hobbes), Cavendish argued that cherishing was only to be given in moderation, while "Fear" of possible punishment "doth Much," and "Love" from the rider, or excessive leniency and cherishing, "doth . . . Little." Love was useful to a certain degree, but it was still "Impossible to Dress any Horse, but first he must Know, and Acknowledge me to be his Master, by Obeying me," Cavendish argued. "That is, He must *Fear* me, and out of that *Fear, Love* me, and so *Obey* me. . . . For it is *Fear* that makes every Body *Obey,* both Man and Beast."⁵² Fear created the desire for covenants, ensured the obedience of a horseman's inferiors, either man or animal, and ensured a natural hierarchy of animal and man.

As Elisabeth LeGuin argues, fear, as Cavendish used it, did not suggest being afraid of something or someone. Instead, it was patriarchal in tone and defined as the command "Fear God," or "the physical enactment of respect" toward a father figure.⁵³ Indeed, Cavendish's view of government stipulated that horses and humans "all doe love thee, yett we feare they rodd, / Nott love for feare, butt feare for love, like Godd."⁵⁴ A horseman was to "chastise him [horse or man] like a kind of divinity superior to him," a Derridean sovereign capable of carrying out the artificial, patriarchal, godlike act of creation, of iteratively creating the artificial being called Leviathan or centaur.⁵⁵ As Victoria Kahn argues, in this Hobbesian discourse on fear and love, the "internalization of God's word transformed servile fear into love, the coercion of the sinner into the 'voluntary subject of his creature.'"⁵⁶ For Cavendish, then, a horseman was to be a benevolent but masterful rider who enacted his hard-won governance and became semidivine himself with his horse, like all ideal sovereigns. Therefore, "Sovereignty causes fear, and fear makes the sovereign" or "the best of kings," because it reduces the governed subject to complete obedience.⁵⁷

Obedience was the physical indication of the horse's will to covenant, and once there was obedience, perfection in the art of horsemanship could develop. This was the moment of centaurism and of animalization so prized by early modern horsemen. Philip Sidney, one of the greatest horsemen of the Elizabethan golden age, provided one of the most concise descriptions of centaurism in his sixteenth-century prose work *The Countess of Pembroke's Arcadia*. For Sidney, and for many subsequent horsemen, including Cavendish, a horseman was "as if centaur-like" or as if "he had been one piece with the horse."

> [The horseman] was no more moved than one is with the going of his own legs; and in effect so he did command him as his own limbs; for though he had both spurs and wand they seemed rather

marks of sovereignty than instruments of punishment, his hand and leg with most pleasing grace commanding without threatening, and rather remembering than chastising . . . nor the horse did with any change complain of it; he ever going so just with the horse, either forthright or turning, that it seemed as he borrowed the horse's body, so he lent the horse his mind."[58]

Similarly, Joseph Blagrave, writing in 1669, observed that a rider in a centauric state—that is, being a sovereign or an "expert Rider" on a perfectly schooled horse—would have "small use of a Rod, or any other help, but to keep his true, just, and perfect seat, because his Horse, by the least token of Bridle or Spur, will do all things in such time and measure, as the Beholders will judge the Man and Horse to be but one Body, one Mind, one Will."[59] Over time and with concentrated effort, riding a horse was understood, taught, and experienced as becoming animal, becoming the Other. Horsemen were not awarded the label for their equestrian know-how and ability to follow proper husbandry regimes for their charges, although such ability was important to some degree, but for their ability in the saddle. To ride with the greatest skill was to invite the crossing of species boundaries to literally become a horse-man.

A sketch by Peter Paul Rubens vividly illustrates this becoming of the Other as mutual agential action while making clear the long tradition of such representation and experience in Western society. In his *Battle of Anghiari* (ca. 1603), a copy of the work by Leonardo da Vinci, now missing, the boundaries between animal and human are heavily blurred (fig. 1). The embattled figures in the upper right are depicted with rider facing rider and horse engaging horse in an interesting visualization of equine agency that directly supports the desires of the riders. The horses are shown to be as enraged, as violent, and as committed to the fight as the humans. They do more than reflect the emotional state of their riders as subjectless signboards, and instead seem to feel the emotion of their riders and come to share and express it through intentional action in a moment of being more than pure horse. The first mounted figure on the left embodies this "mixing of the centaur." With the head of the horse conspicuously missing, this centaur, shown *en pasade,* possesses the body of a horse and the head of a human. With his animalness emphasized by the ram's head flourish on his breastplate and the mirrored swirls of the ram's horns and shell ornaments on his helmet and armor, the body of the human rider is contorted and twisted to conceal the equine form of the horse, which is replaced with the

FIGURE 1   Peter Paul Rubens after Leonardo da Vinci, *Battle of Anghiari*, ca. 1603. Photo © RMN-Grand Palais / Art Resource, New York (Michel Urtado).

mastery of the human-animal centaur. Therefore, as Hobbesian political theory developed out of much longer philosophical traditions, so too did the understanding, experience, and display of a horseman as dual-natured. Centaurs were man and animal, obedience and sovereignty, perfection and grace. As all horsemen knew, and as Blagrave alludes to in his reference to spurs, wand, and threatening behavior, centaurs were not always so ideally figured. Instead, they were often temporary states of becoming owing to the rationality and agency exercised by the horse, and they were frequently inherently violent.

SLAVES, SUBJECTS, AND LIBERTY

Cavendish's concept of sovereignty was essentially absolutist. For the most part, he seems to have shared Hobbes's understanding of liberty. Though he defined it slightly differently in each of his publications, Hobbes generally held that a man enjoyed two interlocking forms of liberty.[60] The first was natural liberty, which all creatures experienced prior to the process of covenant. In a 1645 letter written to Cavendish (later published in

Leviathan), Hobbes defined natural liberty negatively, as "the absence of Opposition; (by Opposition, I mean externall Impediments of motion;) and may be applyed no lesse to Irrationall, and Inanimate creatures, than to Rationall. For whatsoever is so tyed, or environed, as it cannot move, but within a certain space, which space is determined by the opposition of some externall body, we say it hath not Liberty to go further."[61] For Hobbes, only when a body's natural movements are restricted by an outside force acting contrary to the subject's will is an agent not free. The process of creating a covenant, in turn, automatically placed some restrictions upon free subjects. By willingly placing himself under the power of a sovereign body, a person gave up many of his natural freedoms in exchange for peace and protection from that very natural state and its concomitant situation of continual war of all against all. Once under the law and control of a sovereign, who was free to act in any way he saw fit, even as a tyrant, the covenanted persons became subject to his power.

Subjectivity came in two forms for Hobbes, in the form of either servants or slaves. A servant was "tyed" and "oblig'd to obey the Commands" of his "Lord" or master, with whom he had created a covenant. Men became slaves, in contrast, through an act of "War." In *The Elements of Law,* Hobbes argued that through warfare the vanquished would automatically have to obey their conquerors in return for their lives, in much the same way that a "Commonwealth by *Institution*" ensured the continued protection of the servant under the sovereign. However, in a "Commonwealth by *Acquisition,*" man "is not suppos'd to have Contracted with his *Lord;* for every one is not trusted with so much of his naturall liberty, as to be able, if he desir'd it, either to flie away, or quit his service, or contrive any mischief to his *Lord.*" The sovereign could not trust the newly conquered to uphold their end of the covenant and obey his orders or laws. Because of this state of distrust, such persons were kept "within Prisons, or bound within Irons, and therefore they were call'd not by the common name of *Servant* onely, but by the peculiar name of *Slave.*" The lack of natural, or physical, liberty, the chaining and imprisonment that restricts bodily movement, created slavery. This state, however, was not permanent. A slave could become a servant in time and, most important, with trust. "The obligation therefore of a *Servant* to his *Lord* ariseth not from a simple grant of his life," Hobbes argued, "but from hence rather." Only when a sovereign could keep a man "not bound, or imprison'd," could a "Compact" or covenant truly take place. Indeed, "where's no trust, there can be no Contract," since a "Compact is defin'd to be the promise of him who is trusted."[62] Hobbes did not provide precise details on how a slave could gain a sovereign's trust in order to move from a state of servitude to one of covenanted sovereignty, although we might gain a glimpse of the subtleties when we move back to Cavendish's horsemanship.

Cavendish argued that the ground of dressing horses (and of governing men) was fear, and that through such fear, love was to proceed. This love was analogous to Hobbes's trust. For Cavendish, where there was love, there was obedience, and where there was obedience, there was true and absolute horsemanship as sovereign. To generate the requisite love in a horse, however, was not a straightforward process, and it was one expressly grounded on a careful balance of reward, punishment, and covenanting through warfare. Only horsemen such as Cavendish, those who had truly mastered the art of horsemanship and who dedicated their labor to the practice, could hope to succeed. In addition, much like creating covenants between people, covenanting with animals took a surprising amount of time, coupled with great skill in government. As Cavendish outlined in his manuals, a rider was to "conquer" his horse "by degrees" through his ability to cherish, punish, and outsmart his mount as the situation and temperament of the individual horse warranted.[63]

Cavendish was most forthcoming on the process of moving a horse from a state of warfare and slavery to one of obedience and servitude when he discussed the process of curing a restive horse. A horse that was restive, like an "obstinate" man ("'tis all one") who refused to obey his sovereign master, displayed more faults than "refusing to advance"; he also was known for "his opposition to the rider, in every thing he possibly can, and with the utmost malice" and "ill-will."[64] A restive horse, in effect, placed himself in direct opposition to the will and laws of his sovereign master as rebellion and refusal to covenant. For Cavendish, "One must therefore gain the horse; for the perfection of a well-managed horse consists in his following the will of his rider, so that the will of both shall seem to be the same." To do so, a rider was to "force" his horse "a little, but not long, because force will make him worse." Tyranny and continual warfare (defined by Cavendish as corrections given by a rider who was unskilled in the timing or strength in which they should be given and who gave in to "force and passion") will not do; "violent methods" like spurring and beating would make the rider "the greater brute of the two."[65] Indeed, if a rider "cannot Punish, & reward, in Juste time," for lack of horsemanship governing skills, then he "cannot Governe, for there Is no more to governe, this world, but by reward & punishmente, & itt muste bee done in the very nicke of time, orr

Else Itt is to no purpose."[66] As Cavendish explained, "when the horseman has spurred the beast so much, that he has made him all over blood and sweat, and put himself into a great heat and out of breath, still so long as he torments the horse, the horse will resist. He will run against a wall, lie down, bite, kick, and commit a thousand such like disorders." Furthermore, "as soon as the rider ceases to beat and spur him, the horse will leave off his tricks: and then the rider thinks himself conqueror, but is mistaken, since he himself gave up the cause by ceasing to beat and spur. The horse therefore finding he has the better, is altogether master of the field." Violent warfare with a horse would only result in a fruitless "duel," like a continued "quarrel" lasting "even to death" between man and beast, a duel that was guaranteed to make the man rely on his passions and tools of violent subjugation. In this situation, ungoverned bestiality and tyranny, not a beast as a sovereign bent on creating and preserving peace, would result.[67]

A true horseman was to look to his superior intellect and governing skills of "*Justice*" and "*Reward*" to bring a horse to trust, love, and join with him in a covenant.[68] To do so, a horseman needed to play upon the horse's rational abilities and the disallowing of warfare seemingly enjoyed by horses in their state of restiveness. The horseman was to create the appearance of a shared will, which, when iteratively performed, would eventually become ingrained as habit. "I mean," Cavendish explained,

> that if in this extremity the horse will not agree with you, you must agree with him in the following manner. You would make your horse advance, and he to defend himself against you runs back: at that instant pull him back with all your strength. And if to oppose you he advances, immediately force him briskly forwards. If you would turn to the right, and he endeavours to turn to the left, pull him round to the left as suddenly as possible. . . . In a word, follow his inclinations in every thing, and change as often as he. When he perceives there can be no opposition, but that you always will the same thing as he, he will be amazed, he will breathe short, snuff up his nose, and won't know what to do next, as it happen'd with the horse that I cured this way.[69]

By following the horse's inclination and creating the appearance of a shared will, the rider is able to place the horse in a state of insecurity and doubt. He is able to shake the obstinate opposition and inherent malice in a rebellious horse, which in turn (and when coupled with the judicious use of cherishing and punishment) allows the rider to proceed with the training program in relative peace.

Cavendish explained this complicated process of understanding, determining, and finally willing in greater detail in *A New Method*. "Certainly there is no Horse but will Strive at the first in the Dressing, to have his own will, rather than to *Obey* your *will*," Cavendish reasoned, "nor doth any Horse love *Subjection,* nor any other Creature." This dislike of subjection or slavery, a universal constant for man and beast, would make a horse resist at first (horses that did not resist were wanting in courage and strength and should be avoided at all costs), "until there is no Remedy" to the situation. Once this state of hopelessness occurred, the horse would come to realize that he must turn to a covenant. He would then "*Obey;* and the Custom of *Obedience* makes them *Ready-Horses*." In other words, "They will Strive all the Wayes possibly they can, to be Free, and not Subjected; but when they see it will not be, then they *Yield,* and not before."[70] There would, of course, be continuous setbacks throughout the training process; the horse would revert to his initial state of warfare against the state of subjection, and if the horse continued to "Maliciously Rebell . . . against What you would have him Do," Cavendish was certainly not averse to violent force. In this situation, the rider was to "leave not *Spurring* of him, and Soundly, until he Obey you." So far, this is the realm of the bestial ungoverned. What made a true sovereign in this undesirable situation, though, was the judicious use of true government in iterative training sessions. "When he Obeys you in the least Kind, Leight off, and send him to the Stable, and the next Morning Try him again; and if he Obey in the least Kind, Cherish him, and make Much of him; and Forgive him many Faults the next Morning, that he may see you have *Mercy* as well as *Justice,* and that you can *Reward,* as well as *Punish*."[71] Thus, through the custom of obedience a horse came to learn, sometimes by carefully measured violent methods, not only to fear, or respect, his rider over time, but also to become happy with his willed covenant and curtailed freedoms within the new horse-man body politic. The horse would then "take pleasure in all that he does: he will even love you, and the exercise you give him."[72] Alternatively, as Cavendish had argued in his earlier manual, he would "be Pleasant, Lively, and in Lust, and take Pleasure in you, and the Mannage."[73] A horse would love his rider, and his rider would trust him as a secure servant to his will; together they would constitute one being with shared interests, objectives, and body.

This ideal of a figurative and embodied sovereign horseman is most clearly illustrated in plate 4 of *A General System of Horsemanship* (fig. 2).

Karen Raber finds this image ambiguous in that it can "be read either as a statement about the significance of his method for reasserting aristocratic class values, or it can be read as a sign that those class values, as Cavendish imagines them, are already being transformed, dislocated, detached from their former place in the 'real' world of political power" on its way to embracing republicanism.[74] Cavendish was concerned with class values and was uncomfortably flirting with some of the emerging republican discourses in his understanding of commonwealths.[75] However, there is another side to this image that supports horsemanship as a highly classed endeavor while unambiguously placing Cavendish's theories within the tradition of absolutist rule. Viewed in the context of his political horsemanship, the image can be read as the pictorialization of Cavendish's monarchical advice, and above all as his personal embodiment and self-propagandized image of a horseman as absolute sovereign.

He is depicted on horseback with the horse "flying" in a capriole as "*Perseus* upon *Pegasus*," and is shown to be a divine being who has managed the submission and humility of his own passions and social inferiors as only elite and properly sovereign horseman were able to do. Above him are clouds on which the pantheon of Greek gods are artfully arranged; they are "brought to ecstasy" because of their viewing of his "delightful wonders" (Et par ses merveilles ravit en extases les Dieux). Because of his exceptional reining, his fear-inducing combination of punishment and love, Cavendish has not only impressed the gods and received honors in return, but has himself crossed over into the realm of the divine. He has become greater than the legendary Bellerophon (the tamer of Pegasus who was thrown when he attempted to fly), and has managed to touch "the seat of the Heavens" (Il monte si haut qu'il touche de sa teste les Cieux) because of his intra-active covenants with brute being.[76] Cavendish himself was "the most absolute and only Master" of horsemanship; he was the master, and all previous authors on the subject, along with current noble horsemen, were his "Pupils." For example, the vice-chancellor and senate members of the University of Cambridge found "both Kings and Princes resorting to your [Cavendish's] Palace, condescending to sit at your Feet," like the horses at Cavendish's feet are shown to be doing, "and intreating you as their Oracle to declare unto them, first where and of what Race to chuse a Horse for the Mannage, and then how to Feed, and Order, and Mount, and to Work, and Raise, and Stay, and Ride in all Voltoes, and Corvetts, Forward, Backward, Side-ways, on both hands, just as the Rider directs." Cavendish, for them, was the only one fit to teach; he was "the

FIGURE 2 Abraham van Diepenbeke, plate 4 in William Cavendish, *A General System of Horsemanship* (London: J. Brindley, 1743). Photo: Yale Center for British Art, Paul Mellon Collection.

only Governour, and Dictator, and Umpire, and such a Master of Horse, as can (when you please) infuse sense, and reason not only into Men, but also into Brutes."[77] Although they are wrapped up in excessive flattery, such comments illustrate that Cavendish had become, through his political horsemanship, a figure worthy and able to support the commonwealth and improve its governors through the spectacle and ceremony of his own centauric greatness, and the application of his divine art.

The image's symbolism further expresses this argument. As Elaine Walker points out, the eleven horses bowing down to Cavendish could represent the twelve disciples minus Judas, a common iconographic element in early modern art; and if we count Pegasus as the twelfth, then Cavendish may be subtly shown as a Christ or God figure over human and animal life. While Cavendish was in no way trying to offend his readers, and while this image can seem to negotiate a fine line between shameless self-promotion and heresy, Cavendish represented himself as a Hobbesian god, as "a secular God" secure in his governance.[78] Cavendish is shown to embody all of the qualities necessary for Hobbes's sovereign person, the one who could covenant at will and who represented the most influential men in society. Cavendish is depicted as a man who, through his skill in discursive horsemanship with rational horses, has become more than a noble of the realm, more than human, more than his peers; he has become his ideal masculine governor and virtuous gentleman who is worthy of being honored by his subordinates. He has left the earth through his divine horsemanship and become a sovereign god himself who is worshipped as a right reigner (reiner) by his mounts, who are arranged in homage around him and "Worship him as God and author of their skill" (L'adorer comme Dieu et auteur de leur adresse).[79]

POWER AND HONOR

The public accolades given to horsemen for their skill were of no account if they did not generate an image of masculine power over the rider's social inferiors. For Hobbes, man by nature pursued participation as a political animal in the body politic, not for any altruistic desire to help the nation but through an entirely selfish drive to gain glory and honor. As such, there was "a generall inclination of all mankind, a perpetuall and restlesse desire of Power after power, that ceaseth onely in Death." Man did not undertake this search for endless power and status simply for its pleasurable attainment but "because he cannot assure the power and means to live well, which he hath present, without the acquisition of more." Power was society's driving force because it could do two things: maintain the social hierarchy and generate honor. These interwoven and mutually informing concepts worked together to establish and maintain sovereign status. As Hobbes defined the term, "*Honourable* is whatsoever possession, action, or quality, is an argument and signe of Power." Power, in turn, was defined as the ability to "obtain some future apparent Good." This good was partially an ethical drive to improve the lives of other men, as in the building of fortifications for the defense of a stronghold, for example, but was primarily the ability to improve a man's own situation, and especially to increase his reputation and standing as an honorable sovereign. As Hobbes argued, "as the Power, so also the Honour of the Sovereign, ought to be greater, than that of any, or all of the Subjects. For in the Soveraignty is the fountain of Honour." Indeed, "the Obligation of Subjects to the Soveraign, is understood to last as long, and no longer, than the power lasteth."[80] Without power, there was no honor and could be no sovereignty. It was for this reason that honor was absolutely everything for Cavendish. As he informed his sons in the incomplete *Truth of the Sorde,* "Honor . . . Is much more then your Lives & Securers your Lives withall." It evidenced those who were worthy of governing and those who evidently were not.[81] Done through a combination of practiced sovereignty in horsemanship and the continual display of those governing skills, for Cavendish and Hobbes, all men were by nature equal, and it was only through the display of power, or honor, that hierarchy and sovereignty were established.

To complicate matters further, in addition to forming the heart of a man's reputation and his identity as a gentleman of England, honor was also one of the primary means by which masculinity was conceived and measured.[82] Some of the principal components of seventeenth-century honor were honesty, temperance, and generosity, visibly displayed. However, according to Cavendish, the most important virtues to be acquired and performed were associated with reason and rational thought, and the full managing of desires and actions. This was a somewhat ironic argument from a man who was a famous playboy within the notoriously libertine Stuart court, but without this self-bridling a man could be subject to questioning or to the impairment of his ability to influence his own, his family's, and the commonwealth's honor.[83] Without the characteristics of temperate and moderate rational behavior from the managing of the passions, the very position of an elite man as an adult within the community was uncertain. To be unreasoned, irrational, and intemperate was to be subject to connotations of ignorance, baseness, effeminacy, and inhumanity—as Cavendish vehemently argued was the case for men who insisted on entering into a duel with their restive horses.[84] Therefore, "Temperance or modestie, ought to accompanie every wise man, and chiefly him that hath authoritie over others: For no man there is that can rightly judge, howe to direct the maners of other men, that knoweth not first how to governe him selfe."[85] Unmanaged gentlemen were "brutes" who, in stations of power in the military camp or political cabinet, "having prostituted their reason, and inslaved themselves to their passions," contributed nothing beneficial to king or country. Thus, "when in man passions are exalted above reason, nothing follows but disorders, mischiefs, and unavoidable ruine both within and without."[86] Those who could not govern, did not know how to, or were ignorant, and "those that know ignorance, can neyther purchase Honour nor weild it."[87]

Cavendish, and other horsemen of the seventeenth and eighteenth centuries, functioned within, and sought to belong to, an elite and highly selective social group constructed according to shared interests, gender, economic and hereditary status, and the possession of honor. This organization was similar to what Mervyn James has termed a "community of honour," to which all men belonged to some extent, but that was expressly multispecied in conception.[88] By the time Cavendish produced his manuals on horsemanship, this community revolved around the central figure of the monarch, and membership in it was dependent not only on acknowledgment by the monarch for honorable or virtuous actions in service to the state, but also on a man's adherence to a regulatory "code of honour" and the collective opinion of the other members. Of course, lineage, the older measurement for community membership, was still very much a part of the conveyance of honor, but in the early seventeenth century its importance in a man's community status was accompanied, and almost supplanted, by honors for actions to the benefit of the state. It became the ideal for honor to be composed both of natural lineage and of virtue, wisdom and "civill and political" involvement, according to Thomas Milles, writing in 1610.[89] Indeed, as Francis Segar wrote in his 1557 *Schoole of Vertue,* men who were born with innate virtues—which led to the display of natural honor—were considered blessed, but men who gained honor through virtuous actions in service to the state were "double happy and counted most wyse."[90] Through civic action for "the good of the community," a man could be reputed to be useful, supportive, and honored for fulfilling his duty to his sovereign lord and the wider commonwealth.[91]

These components of the code and community of honor applied to horsemen of the seventeenth century as well as to men who did not interact with the animal on a regular basis; however, horsemen were subject to similar but more stringent codes and discourses of honor within the wider community. Horsemen were members of the community's most elite social organization, closest to the body of the king, and hence the one that allowed "the performative effect of preferment and autonomy within a patriarchal society in which" all humans, including other men, were under the power of other men. According to Thomas King, this power structure, one form of which was Hobbes's commonwealth headed by a sovereign, created a "male entitlement" that "was therefore tenuous, limited to certain spaces and times, a privilege to be exercised and not a bond defining men as psychologically and ideologically equivalent."[92] Horsemen of the seventeenth century functioned within a hierarchical social structure that was central to the larger community of honor, and, like the community of honor, the horseman's community was classed and predicated on power; however, the horseman's community was also determined by the display of sovereign power, and hence the performance of honor, with horses.

Nicholas Morgan of Crolane first introduced this power structure in his 1609 *Perfection of Horse-manship, Drawne from Nature; Arte, and Practise,* but it was not until Michael Baret's 1618 *Hipponomie, or The Vineyard of Horsemanship* that the complexities of horse-human interaction within it were discussed in detail. One of the more lengthy treatises on the subject in the seventeenth century (well over four hundred pages), Baret's *Hipponomie* was dedicated to James I and was intended for an elite audience well grounded in horsemanship principles; although it only had one print run, the *Hipponomie* became a central text for seventeenth- and eighteenth-century English horsemen. For example, Richard Berenger favorably referred to it in 1771, and in 1802 John Lawrence went on at great length about the continued usefulness of Baret's tome (he was more admiring of it than of Cavendish's work).[93] Lawrence even went so far as to say that readers of Baret's manual would "find great store of important and useful observations, by no means inapplicable even to the present enlightened period," and that Baret "ought ever to be mentioned with honour and respect."[94] As for Cavendish, while he does not mention the *Hipponomie* explicitly, he does follow the social organization outlined in Baret's manual. He also boasts that he has "Practised, and Studyed Horse-manship ever since I was Ten years old; Have Rid with the Best Masters of all Nations, heard them Discourse at Large, and Tryed their several Wayes: Have Read all their Italian, French, and English Books, and some Latine ones; and in a Word, All that hath been Writ upon that Subject, Good and Bad."[95] Cavendish probably read Baret's work, and if not, it is highly likely that he was introduced to Baret' theories by other horsemen who also understood his social organization.[96]

Expressing his ideas through the early modern propensity to discuss morality through gardening imagery, Baret and Cavendish both conceive of the horsemanship community, or "Vineyard," as one among many other vineyards in operation during the seventeenth and eighteenth centuries. Like the larger community of honor, Baret's and Cavendish's vineyard was "self-selective and self-authenticating," excluding those who did not visibly exhibit the required class, virtue, or honorable reputation.[97] Karen Raber and Treva Tucker argue that a horseman only needed to be "noble and male" in order to be considered a horseman (in principle at least); horsemanship "helped to create a sense not just of group identity but also of group superiority. Those who fell outside the 'right' categories (noble and male) were not merely forbidden access to certain types of horsemanship"; such men were "also deemed incapable of performing these mounted activities, or at least of performing them properly if somehow they managed to obtain access to them, because they lacked what accompanied noble manhood." According to Raber and Tucker, only those of accepted "rank," "gender," and the "characteristics that accompanied that rank and gender" could become horsemen.[98] As such, and as a microcosm of the larger community of honor and Hobbesian society in general, the vineyard of horsemanship was highly competitive in its very essence.

Baret's and Cavendish's vineyard was based on "practises" and "endeauours" that "worke by the rule of reason" to ensure the prosperity of virtue, honor, and masculinity (the vineyard's "fruits") of the vineyard's members ("Vines")—and by extension of the vineyard itself. According to Baret, through reason or self-governance, horsemen "will make such a firme and sure fence, that the wild beasts of the Forrest shall not breake downe their hedges nor spoyle their grapes, that is their wills and affections shall not so ouercome them, that they shall passe the bonds of reason, and fall into either of the extreames of violence or lenity, and so confuse their labours and discourage their practise."[99] A horseman produced "fruits" only if he adhered to tightly controlled bodily and mental conduct that kept out beastly irrationality while displaying "discreet bearing, moderation, bodily strength, and even-headedness."[100] A gentleman, but especially a horseman, was required to govern not only his mount but himself through reason, experience, and patience to avoid appellations of ignorance and irrational animality, and the eventual destruction of his own, the vineyard's, and the state's honor through extremes of behavior toward his mount.[101]

We can see this in plate 3 from Cavendish's *General System of Horsemanship* (fig. 3). Here, Cavendish is not mounted but is depicted as a monarch making a triumphal entrance before the worshipful gaze of his adoring subjects. He is illustrated sitting in a stately carriage reminiscent of those popular in masque enactments, with a monarch's crown on his head. Both he and his carriage are decorated with royal lions, and he gestures imperiously to the surrounding circle of worshipful horses of the manège with a switch. Cavendish is portrayed as a muscular man in the prime of his life, even though he was in his sixties by the time this print was made public, as Elaine Walker has pointed out.[102] He is shown as a "genius" and as ultimate ruler over both horses and humankind through his art of horsemanship, but as a conqueror over centaur status as well. The carriage is drawn by literal centaurs who are willingly, joyously, obediently, and with pride pulling (*en lavade,* in accordance with the teachings of the manège's haute école) Cavendish on his triumphal arrival. Through his own visibly kinesthetic governance and successfully complete unity with his mounts, Cavendish has proved himself to be an elite vine among other vines; he has been able to "triumph over the knights," and through his "Philosophizing" on horseback, he has come to possess the "power to tame the spirited, and the wise." As a result, "all together make tribute" and bow down before his awesome majesty.[103] Cavendish, through his art, has become a centaur among centaurs, a governor among governors, and a cavalier among other military cavaliers. He is shown as the embodiment of those who are "triumphers both in Camps & Courts," and as an elite man capable of perfect personal, equestrian, and commonwealth governance.[104]

The absolute necessity of temperance and passion control was further contained within the image of centaurism itself. While I have discussed the centaur as an ideal or positive figure of animality, as a symbol of embodied human-animal governance, and as the epitome of horsemanship skill, the image of the centaur also contained elements of the Platonic tradition. This centaur was a dangerous dual-natured creature from myth—where the human-animal being was a "peculiarly mixed creature, capable both of extraordinary wisdom and equally remarkable depravity."[105] Representing humanity's tendency to fall into moral baseness and unchecked desire, the classical centaur was certainly not an ideal to covet.[106] To avoid becoming

FIGURE 3   Abraham van Diepenbeke, plate 3 in William Cavendish, *A General System of Horsemanship* (London: J. Brindley, 1743). Photo: Yale Center for British Art, Paul Mellon Collection.

this centaur, then, a man's "Reputation" or "stampe vpon Nobilitie" was to be preserved through *"Temperence"* and *"Moderation* of the minde" or passions, according to Henry Peacham. Horsemen, and seventeenth-century men in general, were to "bridle," "curbe," and "breake" the "ranke and vnruly Passions," of themselves and their horses, signified by the classical centaur of myth, in order to maintain their "Reputation and honest Fame, without which, as one saith, we *are dead long before we are buryed.*" From that base of guarded moderation they became a base of guarded moderation to become a "true" horseman's centaur.[107]

Merging one's identity with that of one's horse in order to become a centaur required long study in horsemanship, and a man's skill in all components of the art determined his position in the vineyard and even whether he was worthy of inclusion there at all. According to Baret, youths, who could not yet claim the title of men and who were beginners in the art, were able to enter into the vineyard's elite ranks on the strength of their own reputations, but they could not be considered influential or honorable members therein.[108] While these "Impes" must continually be drawn to the vineyard to prevent the imperiled art, and the vineyard on which it was based, from becoming corrupted, dishonored, or destroyed, it fell to the "Vines," the experienced, practiced, "true" horsemen who were able to rule themselves, other men, and their mounts with reason and virtue, to "preserue" the "fruits" of the vineyard and to "merit great fame" for themselves.[109] Only horsemen (vines) were able to claim the title of honorable, manly, and "true" horseman, and were able to enforce the member's adherence to a vineyard-defined code of horsemanship-based honor.

As the keen sportsman and accomplished horseman Philip Herbert, fourth Earl of Pembroke and first Earl of Montgomery, made clear in a letter to Cavendish dated May 20, 1631, it was only after a man gained skill and experience with horses and in horsemanship that he could be invited by other vines to join the vineyard. Herbert argued that it was for the benefit of the "whole Commonwealth of horsmen" (to which both he and Cavendish belonged) that one Henry Babington (who was "industrious & honest, a good improuer, & a most affectionate seruant to" Cavendish) receive "accommodation" in "very faire & honourable Conditions," and tutelage in horsemanship and general tenancy from Cavendish in order that he be brought "to perfection" in his riding and self-governance and eventually come "to performe with" Cavendish feats of horsemanship.[110]

The vines were also responsible for determining which riders were to become members, as Herbert's letter implies. Only those who were practitioners of the vine's ideal of normative horsemanship were eligible. According to Baret, for the vines to flourish in society and for the vineyard itself to remain a strong and influential element within civic arenas, first the ground (art of horsemanship) must be "laid out" and "weeded and drest from the errors of ignorance, and after that be made formall, by a good decorum and order."[111] The social appropriateness and normatively acceptable practices of horsemanship, the ground of the vineyard, needed to be "drest" or solidified by established vines in order to ensure the continued purity, use, and prosperity of the true art—the reason why Babington was seeking Cavendish's instruction. As a "community," the vineyard was self-authenticating, but it also was defined by the type or form of horsemanship practiced. Cavendish's vineyard was that of the most elite, dedicated, and knowledgeable horsemen, and primarily practiced continental and "classical" horsemanship.

The vineyard, through the level and type of horsemanship practiced, distinguished the elite members of the honorable community from the socially and virtuously inferior chaff. It was composed of the elite of the elite, the visibly true and perfect horsemen, not the community-defined false riders from other horsemanship communities or nonequestrians who continually sought to invade the vineyard's closed ranks through their own forms of horsemanship. As a result, honor required a man to continually seek power through virtue, coupled with lineage, and to do so before other vineyard members. A man's honor was determined by public visibility and spectacular performance before other vines. For Hobbes, the more adept a man was at an art, the more honor he could attain from it through the "admiration" and "flattery" of his spectators for his "excellence in . . . art."[112] For Cavendish, the most beneficial "art" for the creation of honor (besides swordsmanship) was that of spectacular horsemanship.

SPECTACLE

However, the spectators were not simply looking to the human in their viewing. As the centaur was composed of two species working together as one body and one will, they were also observing the horse for clues to his rider's honor, status, and sovereign horsemanship abilities. Rider and horse were one dual-natured being and were viewed and reviewed as such. Thus, for horsemen, not only were physical indicators and their associated meanings interchangeable between species, but the characteristics

FIGURE 4
Giambattista della Porta, *De humana physiognomonia libri IIII* (1586), 83. Photo courtesy of the National Library of Medicine.

and epistemological status of the man could be made visible through the performing body of his horse.

This visibility was frequently expressed through the dual practice of pathognomy (the study of bodily movement) and physiognomy (the study of static physical traits), which as a pseudoscience suffered fluctuating popularity over the course of the seventeenth and eighteenth centuries.[113] With pathognomy and physiognomy, there were many correlations between the physical features of humans and animals—primarily between men and apes, elephants and horses. For example, according to Giambattista della Porta, at the end of the sixteenth century, and Johann Caspar Lavater, at the end of the eighteenth, these physical similarities allowed for further understanding of the masked elements of a person's character. Lavater was the more forthcoming on the subject, and argued, quoting della Porta's *De humana physiognomonia* (1586), that "no proposition, undoubtedly, is more certain than this: 'The resemblance of forms [man and horse] supposes a resemblance of characters'" (fig. 4).[114] He illustrated this point when discussing the various signifying elements of equine physiognomies found in hog-necked horses: "The neck above and below is alike broad; the head hanging downward; the middle of the nose is concave, in profile; the ears are long, thick, and hanging; the eyes small, and ugly; the nostrils small; the mouth large; the whole body round; and the coat long, and rough. These horses are intractable, slow, and vicious; will run the rider against a wall, stone, or tree. When held in, they rear, and endeavour to throw the rider. . . . I leave the reader to apply these remarks to the human countenance."[115] If a rider shared a conformation similar to that of his mount, people thought he possessed the same characteristics, passions, and temperament symbolized by those physical features. In this case, a man who was built like a hog-necked horse would also be prone to harming others (running the rider against a wall, stone, or tree), being unreasonable (obstinate and restive) and violently irrational, and being unwilling to take direction (rearing and endeavoring to throw the rider when held in) in contravention to a properly functioning civil society.

Horsemen built upon these discourses in their understanding of centaurism. Baret argued that both the virtuous and the monstrous elements of the rider's interiority were magnified through the horse's mediating influence and, as a result, were made far clearer to a spectator than if the rider had appeared on foot. He wrote, "for the least disorder in the gesture of the man, causeth a greater in the horse, not onely in his teachings . . . but also in the grace of his show, for the least error that a man doth commit in the government of himselfe [mentally and physically], is encreased in the horse, in a double proportion."[116] Likewise, Thomas de Grey wrote in his physiognomic theory of horsemanship from 1639, "For *the countenance is the true Index of the minde: And a lewd looke prognosticateth a lewd condition:* And again; *a deformed countenance doth delineate a wicked and deformed disposition and manners.*"[117] Every man could be judged by his actions when dismounted; however, for a horseman, it was not only his actions and self-government that were visible; his success in virtuous bridling could become a spectacle through his horse. Not only could a horseman's bodily actions divulge "the secret fantasies of the minde," a horseman's reason and control of his passions, but the actions of the horse could (even more) as well.[118]

Horsemen performed these "fantasies of the minde" self-consciously, intentionally, and determinedly before audiences primarily composed of men, albeit men of varying education and ways of seeing differentiated by class, economic standing, horsemanship knowledge, and variances in normative horsemanship practices. Even though the vast majority of training and riding a horse took place within the confines of a "private" environment, such as a nobleman's manège, riding house, or fallow field, horsemanship was an essentially "public" calling. In the seventeenth and eighteenth centuries, the "public" and "private" actions of a man could greatly influence his honorable reputation within society. Historians of gender have shown, for example, that sexual behavior and patriarchal control of the household could equally influence a man's honor in more "public" activities, such as political involvement. As most scholars of gender argue, to enact governed and rational actions within the "private" household greatly influenced a man's "public" honor, reputation, and social standing.[119] In Richard Cust's words, "The 'public' and the 'private' are, and were, constantly intertwined, particularly in the early modern period when the family was routinely perceived as a microcosm of the commonwealth."[120] To generate honor, reputation, and power, a man could perform his masculinity both in his "private" home or in "public" to enhance his community reputation as a horseman.

Even when men practiced horsemanship in "private," there were family members, household servants, grooms, and visiting apprentice riders there to see. As Lucy Worsley and Tom Addyman argue, Cavendish made it a habit to ride before others in his riding house at Welbeck Abbey on a daily basis before and after his exile. For example, his servants John Booth and Andrew Clayton recorded that "the horses were a Rideing and we present as usually."[121] While riding before uninitiated servants or grooms did help to uphold patriarchal norms within the "little commonwealth" of the home, and did convey honor to the horseman to some extent (it did elevate him over nonriders), performing before nonhorsemen did not produce the requisite honor for being a member in good standing within the equestrian community.[122] For a man to define his status within the community, to be "publicly" reputed and viewed as an elite horseman, it was not the opinions of the uneducated that he must win but those of other equestrians. As Anthony Dent argues for sixteenth-century riders, "ideal horsemanship" "had everything to do with display," with "magnificence," and was "above all theatrical," with necessary "presentation either to a select audience of the Prince and his court or less frequently to the eyes of the vulgar."[123] As in the sixteenth, so in the seventeenth century, for Cavendish and his predecessors, only fellow horsemen who were themselves knowledgeably capable of conveying honor were worthy of witnessing spectacular performances and bestowing honor in turn. According to Baret, "they are not Horsemen which are set on practice, and haue the applause of the common people, but hee which knoweth how to gouerne and teach his Horse aright, and so to bring him to true obedience." There was "no credit in the vulgar applause" of the nonhorseman, but only in the display of a horseman's knowledge in the true governing of himself and his horse before other masters of horsemanship.[124]

These masters, or "Vines," to continue the popular garden metaphor, must further, according to Baret, "bee set so that the Sunne may nourish them, that is, they must direct all their worke in such sort that they may be ripened with the heat of the truth, and so they shall the more easily obtaine their desire" to be perfect horsemen and complete members of the community. They must learn to identify and adopt in all of their actions the "true" or community-defined methods of (continental) horsemanship, not "traditional" (English), and visibly "*species infinit*" (infinite beauty) within themselves and other horsemen. They must gain the truth of sight and judgment—and the "higher that they grow by the frames aforesaid," by practice and experience, "the more shall bee their knowledge in the truth" and their ability to identify and see beautifully governed horsemanship. The ability to know truth, to see, increased with knowledge and practice (as did, conversely, the opacity of a horseman's visible governance of his horse). In turn, the more a horseman could see, the more he was able to understand the goal of horsemanship (graceful perfection), and the methods and time needed to "obtaine" perfect horsemanship.[125] As Gervase Markham recorded in his 1607 *Cavelarice,* a true "Vine," or "euen the finest eyde beholder must hardly perceyue the motion [of another vine's leg aids], otherwise it is grosse and vncomely." Markham agreed with Salomon de La Broue—another of Pignatelli's pupils—that horsemen who made visible their communication with their mounts, displaying "farre fetch motions with the legges, these flancke spurrings, and vniversitie riding, euer digging in a horses sides," were guilty of "the most preposterous motions that can be seene in a horseman." Such elementary, nonperfected riding illustrated a man's ignorance, "the roote of all euils and disorder," and his nonhorseman identity.[126] The more a horseman/spectator knew and practiced the "true" or normative horsemanship, the more he was able to see, to understand and recognize, exceptional horsemanship and—by extension—exceptional honor in other horsemen. The level and quality of honor extended to men of the equestrian community, like the "community of honor," was of different quality and amount depending on the honorable or knowledgeable standing of the bestower. The higher the status, the more honor could be conveyed; thus the further a man traveled down horsemanship's path, the more he would contribute to keeping the community weed-free by furthering the proper horsemanship methodologies and ideologies, and by identifying and selecting other men who were visibly worthy of membership while excluding those who were not.[127]

Cavendish followed these tenets of the equestrian community and consciously sought out honor and reputation from other highly ranked horsemen throughout his horsemanship career. When Cavendish was exiled in Antwerp and living in the former home of Peter Paul Rubens, for example, he had Rubens's painting studio converted into a small manège.

This "famous riding house" was graced with a viewing gallery for the comfort and enjoyment of his many notable equestrian guests, among them the Marquess of Caracena, the Marquess of Seralvo (master of horse to Don John of Austria and governor of the castle of Antwerp), and Don John of Austria.[128] Cavendish recorded in his *New Method* that he had ridden "three *Horses*," and his "Esquire five," before "many Noble-Men of *Flanders*, as the Duke of *Ascot*, and others," who reported to Don John that Cavendish's horses were such "that they wanted nothing of Reasonable Creatures, but Speaking." The Marquess of Caracena was "civilly earnest to see" Cavendish ride, and upon completion of his performances, "some *Spaniards* that were with the Marquess cross'd themselves, and cried, *Miraculo*." In addition to these great men, Cavendish's manège attracted "Many *French* Gentlemen, and Persons of the greatest Quality of that Nation," including "the Prince of *Conde*," and his fame as a horseman brought even the "*Landgrave* of *Hesse*" from Germany. Cavendish received so many people to his manège that "it would fill a Volume, to repeat all the Commendations that were given to [his] *Horses,* and to [his] *Horsemanship,* by several worthy Gentlemen, of all Nations, *High* and *Low-Dutch, Italians, English, French, Spaniards, Polacks,* and *Swedes,* in my own private *Riding-House,* at *Antwerp;* which though very large, was often so full, that my Esquire, Capt. *Mazin,* had hardly Room to *Ride*."[129] Through his spectacular horsemanship, his skill on horseback, Cavendish's reputation as a great man grew to the extent that the social, political, and equestrian elite of the continental courts traveled from all across Europe to witness the miracles he could perform with his reasonable creatures.

The interior of a riding house, possibly a French school, similar to Cavendish's is illustrated in his *General System of Horsemanship*. This image (fig. 5) by Charles Parrocel appears on the first page of the first chapter and clearly illustrates the diverse classes of men within the equestrian community who would have been present at a riding school at any one time.[130] In the foreground, the master of the school directs his pupils and provides supporting aids from the ground to help the training of the horsemen. The horsemen themselves are shown performing the advanced movements of the manège and haute école, the actions so important to Cavendish's system of masculine equestrian spectacle, such as (from left to right) the capriole, trot or *passage,* curvet or *pesate,* and *piaffeur*. In the background are unoccupied "palsrenier," or grooms, invited audience members, and other horsemen waiting for their turn to learn from the master.[131] The exact identities of the spectators remain unknown, as do those of the riders;

FIGURE 5   Charles Parrocel, *A Riding Academy*, in William Cavendish, *A General System of Horsemanship* (London: J. Brindley, 1743), 15. Photo: Yale Center for British Art, Paul Mellon Collection.

however, the continuous spectatorship of the audience and admirable performance by the horsemen are clear. Having other horsemen witness honorable horsemanship had the potential to elevate the rider within the equestrian community, and Cavendish certainly was attempting to do just that by inviting spectators to his manège.

While performances in a riding school were essential to the display of power and honor within the community, the ideal arena for performances of horsemanship and subjective obedience of a horse to the sovereign power of the rider for personal gain was the jousting field. Not only emphasizing the all-important connections with warfare (connections under continual attack from others of competing horsemanship methodologies) and masculine education, jousting also had traditional connections to the court and chivalrous virtues in honorable service to the state. Therefore, Cavendish recommended to Charles II that he should "ride" his "Horses of manege, twice a weeke, which will Incourage Noble men, to Doe the Like, to wayte of" him and to "to make matches, with the Noble men, So many of aside, to rune Att the Ringe, for a supper, & a play, or Some Little Juell." On the king's coronation day, Cavendish wrote, it would be beneficial to his power and the security of the commonwealth if the king were "to have, a Tilting by your young Lordes, & other Great persons."[132] Such virtuous exercises were no longer performed at Charles's masque-loving court, a change that

Timothy Raylor shows was due to Charles's desire to be viewed as the focus of all court entertainment. In a tournament, Raylor argues, the focus was on the horsemen, not the king (unless he personally participated in the tourney, an activity Charles did not practice), who become spectacles to further their own honor. In the more popular theatrical masque, by contrast, the representation of the monarch is not that of a ruler who depends on his nobles for prestige, but one upon whom the nobles depend.[133] However, even in light of these changes at court, Cavendish still felt, incorrectly perhaps, that tournaments were necessary to entice other nobles to the activity and to make visible to "the Lordes And the Ladeies" the honor, power, and sovereign horsemanship of the participants and the English monarchy.[134]

One tournament account evidences the practice's essential connections to masculine honor and political strength. Cavendish hosted a tournament as part of the festivities at Welbeck Abbey during Charles I's visit there in 1633. John Westwood recorded his impressions of the visit and presented a copy of the finished Latin text to Charles Cavendish (William's brother) in 1634. When the king arrived at Welbeck, Westwood reported, there was a vast crowd consisting of the local ruling elite, including "knights" who "rush in from either side upon their stout racing mounts," present to welcome him to the Cavendish estate. Once the tournament itself began, the men, who "the sacred hunger for renown has goaded" and who "demand ... the high honour of men," jousted or tilted before an audience.[135] Equestrian performance in the tilt yard, frequently accompanied by displays of manège and haute école horsemanship, constituted "the most Glorious Sight That can bee seen, & the most manlyeste" activity available to a horseman because of the visible displays of governing ability, and hence power and honor, that the public activity afforded. A horseman must make visible his sovereignty. According to Thomas Slaughter, "Both Hobbes and Newcastle emphasized that the basis of regal authority was power, that the important consideration was not who the sovereign was but whether or not he could maintain order among his subjects and retain his throne."[136] Therefore, to publicly display sovereignty on horseback was to bolster the horseman's own fitness to rule.

The activity was also ideal for the display of centauric horsemanship similar to that illustrated in Rubens's earlier work, in which the horse seemingly joined his will with that of his sovereign in a transspecies drive toward the generation of honor and power. An example of this again comes from Westwood's account: once the tourney itself has begun, the "knights rush in from either side upon their stout racing mounts," and "all at once you could view the rivalry of both knights and steeds." In this scene, "Everything is aglitter, decked out with rare art, and in rivalry each steed displays his new embossed trappings. This one shows off his mantle; and that one, his sleek neck wrapped with a collar, struts his limbs in close array. Another wears golden accoutrements, a many-layered collar; another floats on high a crest with varicoloured plumes. Wondrous splendour shines on every side."[137]

In Westwood's account, the horses display the same rivalry as their riders. Here, the one body and one will of the horseman as covenanted centaur takes center stage. The horses do indeed share the wills of their riders, and are understood to be working with them in their riders' perpetual search after power and honor through spectacle. The horses intentionally choose to fulfill their covenanted obligations to their sovereign riders by enhancing and performing themselves in the same way that their human-animal partners do, in order to gain honor and reputation. They purposefully allied themselves with their masters in order to create and maintain a particular (normative) masculinity, visible social status, and spectacle for themselves and for their riders.

CEREMONY

Jousting and running at the ring, however, were decidedly archaic practices by the time Cavendish recommended them to the king and when he hosted a tournament at Welbeck, as Peter Edwards illustrates.[138] However, for Cavendish it remained ideally useful because the activity was ceremonial, and ceremony was the means of ensuring obedience from man and horse through "a habitual acceptance of status which is affirmed . . . in ritualistic display."[139] The display of equine obedience and human sovereignty made visible the sovereign's ability to maintain superiority over both his horse and his people. Nostalgically using Queen Elizabeth's court as his example, Cavendish argued at length that "Seremoney though itt is nothing in itt Selfe, yett it doth Every thing." Indeed,

> for what is a king, more than a subiecte, Butt for seremoney, & order, when that fayles him, hees Ruiend,—what is the Church, without Seremoney, & order, when that fayles, the Church is Ruind,—what is the Lawe without Seremoney, & order, when that

fayles, the Lawe Goes Downe, . . . what is a Lord more Then a footman, without Seremoney, & order,—A Dispised Title,—what is parents, & Childeren, masters, & Servants, officers in all kindes, in the Comon wealth, without Seremoney, And order, nothing at all,—Nay what is an Armey without Seremoney, & order, & there the strictest Seremoney, & order, for hee that Continues Longest in order, which is In Bodyes, wines the Battle. . . . So that Seremoney, & order, with force, Governes all, both In peasce, & warr, & keepes Every man, & Every thing within the Circle of their owne Conditions.[140]

According to Lynn Hulse, Cavendish "believed that Charles's failure to maintain ceremony and degrees of honor had ultimately weakened the nobility and brought them into contempt."[141] This contempt, in turn, eventually resulted in the destabilization or full destruction of the people's covenants with their sovereign. When this occurred, man degenerated back into a state of nature, a process that Cavendish and Hobbes had witnessed in the English Civil Wars. Therefore, the public display of ceremony, and ceremony coupled with the performance of secure sovereignty with a horse, was essential to maintaining a civil society. "To be seen to have power was to have power," and as such horsemanship was "an exercise that is very noble." It makes "Kings, Princes, and persons of quality" "appear most graceful when they shew themselves to their subjects, or at the head of an army, to animate it." The "pleasure" of the manège and haute école was "as useful as any thing else, besides the glory and satisfaction that attends it."[142]

Early modern monarchs were well acquainted with this advice, as men for whom right reining of all mounts was theoretically most important, especially in light of Hobbes's controversial theories of contract, which allowed for covenant with any ruler, not just the legitimate king.[143] James I, for example, wrote to his son Henry (Cavendish's fellow horseman), "It becometh a Prince better than any other man to be a fair and good horseman," as it was only those who had resigned themselves to "study horsemanship," those who intimately had intra-actively communicated with horses, and who had gained the skill and experience needed for correct decisions on the duties of their social inferiors, who could protect the kingdom from further rebellion and social unrest while preserving their social position as powerful sovereigns.[144] Cavendish clarified this advice to sovereigns in a letter to Charles II, arguing that Charles should not "lose your dignity and set by your state." Instead, Charles should practice "the contrary: for what preserves you kings more than ceremony"? Indeed, "the cloth of estates, the distance people are with you, great officers, heralds, drums, trumpeters, rich coaches, rich furniture for horses, guards, martialls men making disorders to be labored by their staff of office, and cry 'now the king comes'; . . . even the wisest though he knew it and not accustomed to it, shall shake of his wisdom and shake for fear of it." For Cavendish, these elements of ceremony on horseback, so essential to the jousting ring or the triumphal entry *en passage,* ensured the all-important development of fear among the sovereign's subjects. By publicly performing the "mask" of indivisible sovereignty through the spectacle of a living, breathing, and obedient Leviathan as centaur, a horseman created awe or fear. These emotions in turn, like the fear of a horse, resulted in the solid covenants of the multitude to their sovereign king and the security of the "Common Wealth." As a result, for Cavendish, "authority doth what it list," and as such Charles as absolute sovereign (or any sovereign for that matter) "cannot put upon you too much king."[145] Kingship or the ability to be a good governor, like honor, was adopted; it was hard won through rational experience and practice in government of the self and others (human and animal), and it was only of use if it was put to use through fear-inducing ceremony.

Therefore, if the labor of sovereignty was not undertaken, a true system of government as a Hobbesian commonwealth could not be established or continue to prosper. Cavendish discussed this requirement most clearly in his *General System of Horsemanship,* where he argued that it was through an inability to understand the rationality of man and horse, the often superior nature of horses, and the necessity of a horseman to learn horsemanship as a sure method of self-bridling, that gentlemen were unable to practice political governance, or their sovereignty. In a somewhat ironic, and entirely Hobbesian, attack against men of learning—especially those of the universities—Cavendish complained, "The learned will hardly be brought to allow any degree of understanding to horses; they only allow them a certain *instinct,* which no one can understand; so jealous are the schoolmen of their rational empire." The "scholasticks" of the kingdom (presumably a label that did not include either Descartes or Hobbes, even though both men evidently were not keen horsemen and neither acknowledged the possibility of animal intelligence) "degrade horses so much," which was the result of "nothing else, but the small knowledge they have of them, and from a persuasion that they themselves know every thing. They fancy they talk pertinently about them, whereas they know no more than they learn by riding a hackney-horse from the University of LONDON, and back again. If they studied them as horsemen do, they would talk otherwise." These "men of letters, tho' they study, they don't study horsemanship," and as a result turn their studies "to better account, by procuring themselves to rule over the rest of mankind, till such time as they are subdued by the sword."[146] They did not dedicate themselves to an active life but to intellectual contemplation and reading. Thus their horsemanship ignorance, and their interest in alternative forms of government, resulted in continual attempts at leaving "the circle of their own conditions." This attempted social mobility was "the roote of all euils and disorder" and should be avoided at all costs.[147]

Unlike the increasingly vocal parliamentarian proponents of mixed government, for Cavendish and Hobbes, sovereignty was indivisible. There must only be one legislator, one governor in war and peace; a "government" that has power shared between the commons, lords, and king "is not government, but division of the Common-wealth into three Factions." Thus, for Hobbes, republicanism, mixed government, or "*a Kingdome divided in it selfe cannot stand.*"[148] Similarly for Cavendish: "Monarchy is the Government In cheefe of the whole body Politick, In all its partes, & Capaseties by one person only So that if eyther the whole Body Poleticke bee under Any pretennce governed in cheef by more then one severally Itt is no monarchy." As for horsemanship, the physical embodiment and enactment of a commonwealth as "an Artificial Animal," if a ruler or horseman failed to maintain his sovereignty over his social inferiors, both horses and humans, through balanced reward and punishment, his power to rule would be completely lost and society thrown into chaos. Without checks and rewards in place, or a balance between love and fear, the monarch's inferiors (and Cavendish's) would be allowed to run riot; they would gain power over their legitimate governors, causing civil unrest, or at worst another "horid rebellion." Those who were not horsemen, those who did not "study," "understand," communicate, or govern correctly would again spend their time "medeling" in state affairs, which in turn would "much disorder the Comon wealth, for their perticuler Gayne." The nonhorsemen of the world would "breed" "confution, & the king, & the Comonwealth" would be "ill served."[149] For sovereigns within the body politic, truly communicative horsemanship as centaurs visibly distinguished the social and political elite from those who were not capable or worthy of their honors. Certainly, "for the dignity; and order of the Common wealth there ought to be degrees of Honour [and horsemanship], Lest the Common people and the nobility, private men and magistrates . . . a King and a Captain should be all of one Accompt."[150]

To be a horseman with the obedience of a horse was to be honorably masculine, visibly noble, and evidently capable of governing oneself, one's horse, and one's subjects. Cavendish expressly summarized these interconnecting benefits and necessities of horses, horsemanship, sovereignty, and commonwealth in a dedicatory letter to Charles II contained in the first edition of *A New Method* (in French, 1658). A horseman, especially a king, must never allow any man other than himself to ride his horses (or, Cavendish implied, share his seat as head of the commonwealth) because of the live body politic that horse and man created when together. "Others should not be allowed to ride them too often nor to harass them," Cavendish stated. Instead, "they should be kept for Your Majesty's saddle alone, that is to say in his private affairs and those of the public." It was feared that these subjects would not only lack the skill of horsemanship necessary for the governance of an animal who frequently took it into his head to rebel against the sovereign master and rider, but would also not possess the riding skill necessary to subdue the brave beast once he did decide to resist the rider's will, an entirely expected step in the covenanting process. From this situation, many concluded that these men were also not capable (mentally or physically) of governing the multitude expressed within the horse's body:

> One should always be moderate in passions because the capricious multitude is a many-headed beast, to the extent that it has several bridles but not several spurs; because many heads should have many bridles, but the Republic, having but one body, should have only one pair of spurs and those should be those of Your Majesty, against which they will never rebel, but will always obey and will regard them as an Aid rather than a Chastisement. They will rebel against the spurs of Your Majesty's subjects, and to the extent that they ride them without spurs, like foals, nevertheless they will throw them to the ground and will perhaps act badly with them, to the extent that Your Majesty may be in danger when you mount again yourself. But Your Majesty is an excellent horseman as I desired that You should be and I am assured that You are; which makes Your Majesty glorious and Your subjects happy.[151]

If these men were allowed to ride the king's horse, or to share governance of the nation (a notion that was one and the same), they would corrupt the multitude. They would not be able to create fear and love in the king's mount, and "where there were no common Power to feare; by the manner of life, which men that have formerly lived under a peacefull government, use to degenerate into, in a civill Warre."[152] The horse/multitude would revert to its nature and give in to a growing and restless desire for power over these riders/courtiers, which in turn would lead to the full overthrow of the sovereign and the devastation of the commonwealth.

Civil war and the destruction of the sovereign body was a very real possibility in this situation (as Charles's father had found out). Thus learning to ride, to govern a horse/multitude as absolute sovereign, and performing one's hard-won skills before other horsemen not only made visible the honor and masculinity of the rider within the equestrian community; it also demonstrated the capability of the horseman to create and maintain power as an honorable and powerful sovereign over a happily covenanted multitude. As Cavendish explained to Charles II, "when you appear, to shew your Selfe Gloryously, to your People; Like a God, for the Holly writt sayes, wee have Calld you Godds—& when the people sees you thus, they will Downe of their knees, which is worshipp, & pray for you with trembling Feare, & Love."[153] This letter, so similar to fig. 2 in its ruling discourse, illustrates that to see a horse perform obediently within the horse-human relationship was to see the security of the commonwealth within a live body politic, and to see that body politic disintegrate through fraction and discord was to see the loss of sovereign power and honor, and the resulting destabilization of the entire commonwealth. As a result, and to return to Cavendish's rhetorical question, with which we started this exploration of political horsemanship, what indeed could be more glorious than to ceremonially perform and live the Hobbesian material-discursive centaur? What could be more beneficial to kings and princes than to run at the tilt or to joust? And what on earth could be "of more Use than A Horse of Mannage; nor any thing of more State, Manliness, or Pleasure, than Rideing"?

TRANSITIONS

While Cavendish's manuals cover a period that witnessed the English Civil Wars, the Cromwellian Interregnum, and the Glorious Revolution, they show little alteration in their conception of honor or their discourses on politics and masculinity. They were to be read in conjunction with each other, and were intended as two halves of one entire treatise. However, the continuity in Cavendish's manuals does not reflect a wider cultural trend in discourses on horsemanship embodiment. When the haute école was first introduced in England in the late sixteenth century, there were debates about its role in producing useful horses for war, but these controversies tended to recede in the manuals as the haute école became more established and was increasingly lauded as an elite activity. An example of the early resistance to the activity comes from Thomas Bedingfield's 1584 *Art of Riding*. Bedingfield argued that "the Gentlemen of this land have studied to make horses more for pleasure than seruice," and that "the principall use of horses is, to travell by the waie, & serve in the war." Although he understood the ceremonious and spectacular necessity of such activities for horsemen, he argued that "whatsoever your horse learneth more [in the haute école], is rather for pompe or pleasure than honor or yse."[154] However, while Cavendish was quick to point out that honorable men such as the king, the Duke of York, the Duke of Montmorancy, the Prince of Conde, and the deceased king of Spain were "Good *Horsemen*" of the haute école who considered the long practice and now arguably impractical art (owing to the demotion of the horse in warfare to a secondary role) "an Honour, and no Disgrace," such discourses of distrust and disbelief in the haute école as a profitable way of spending one's time continued to be used within the various equestrian communities.[155]

Throughout the seventeenth and eighteenth centuries, the discontent with manège horsemanship as an art form continued to grow alongside other forms of horsemanship and human-animal being. This trend accelerated after the 1660s, a change that Giles Worsley sees as evidence that the practice of haute école itself underwent a distinct decline in popularity from the outbreak of the Civil Wars until the accession of George III, mainly as a result of the absence of royal patronage.[156] According to Worsley, haute école horsemanship was practiced by an elite group that frequently was attached to the courtly circle of a reigning monarch, and when the monarch was disinclined or unable, as during the wars, to practice the art, its popularity suffered. As Worsley points out, there is no indication that the haute école was promoted under Cromwell (though Cromwell was a keen horse breeder and stock improver), and it was only with George III's ascension in 1760 that it again became popular among the social elite.[157] For Worsley, somewhat overarguing his case, haute école horsemanship as practiced in the manège followed the prewar enthusiasts (of which Cavendish was arguably the best known throughout Europe) into exile on the continent and stayed there. He does acknowledge, however, the few attempts to establish riding academies in England during this decline. For example, Sir Balthazar Gerbier had an academy in Bethnal Green from 1649 to 1650, and Henry Foubert founded one that operated from 1684 until 1743, when it was taken over by his nephew Solomon Durrell, under whom it became a riding school, finally closing in 1778. These later attempts at establishing academies, however, do not point to any large-scale interest in the haute école; instead, they emphasize its tenuous survival in a climate of "marked decline in interest" in the activity, which as a result witnessed only one "non-military riding house" built between 1660 and 1740. For Worsley, who does not discuss alternative enactments of horsemanship or the continuing militarism of the manège in England, horsemanship retreated to the European academies and only reemerged alongside royal patronage in the mid-eighteenth century, with a veritable proliferation of riding houses built in England (fourteen private manèges built between 1750 and 1780).[158]

However, instead of a strong decline in interest or a full-blown retreat to the continent, what we see in England is a continuing and strengthening divergence between men of the elite and militaristic haute école, practiced by horsemen such as Cavendish, and advocates of other emerging riding disciplines and discourses of the manège. Furthermore, the republication of Cavendish's and William Hope's work in the late seventeenth and eighteenth centuries illustrates a continuing and wider interest in these practices than has been previously noticed. Supporting the notion of a changing but continued existence of the manège and haute école throughout the period of the Restoration and Glorious Revolution are the horsemanship manuals themselves. During this time (Worsley's decline phase), there was a veritable proliferation of publications that covered the subject solely or in addition to other manège, sporting, or farrier subjects. These included Joseph Blagrave's *Epitome of the Whole Art of Husbandry* (1669, 1670, 1675, 1685), Thomas de Grey's *Compleat Horseman and Expert Ferrier* (1670 reprint of the 1639 edition), E. R.'s *Experienced Farrier* (1678, 1681, 1691, 1720), Richard Blome's *Gentleman's Recreation: In Two Parts* (1686), A. S.'s *Gentleman's Compleat Jockey* (1696), William Hope's translation of Jacques de Solleysel's *Compleat Horseman* (1696, 1702, 1706, 1711, 1717, 1729), Robert Howlett's *School of Recreation* (1701), an English translation of Georges Guillet de Saint-Georges's *Arts de l'homme d'epee* (*The Gentleman's Dictionary*) (1705), Josephus Sympson's *Twenty Five Actions of the Manage Horse* (1729), and an English translation of Claude Bourgelat's *Nouveau Newcastle, au nouveau traité de cavalerie* (*The New Newcastle, a New System of Horsemanship*)

(1754), to name a few. While these publications differ substantially in content and targeted audience, they all are either dedicated in full to or contain a section on the haute école—the practice that Worsley argues quite suddenly disappeared from English horsemanship practices between the 1660s and 1760s.

The continued popularity of the haute école is further illustrated in Josephus Sympson's *Twenty Five Actions of the Manage Horse* of 1729. For Sympson, there were "already many Treatises on all the Parts of Horsemanship, sufficient to form the compleatest Rider" in existence. He was only publishing the work to improve the current state of horse portraiture, which was inaccurate according to the terms of manège or the haute école in either "shape" or "action."[159] Sympson did not publish to instruct in the art of horsemanship, as there were many other manuals circulating among riders to make such work superfluous. Manuals dedicated to the haute école were widely available, were continuing to be produced, and were purchased not only by the prewar enthusiasts, as Worsley asserts, but also by new generations of horsemen.

2.

RIDING HOUSES AND POLITE EQUESTRIANISM

LIVERY STABLE and RIDING-HOUSE. TO be LETT, a good LIVERY STABLE, containing upwards of 40 stalls, with 100m to build more, with a large riding-house and good yard, and a very good dwelling-house, situated in Worship-street, Moor-fields. Enquire at No. 71. Corchill.
—*Gazetteer and New Daily Advertiser*, 1777

Let us jump ahead for a moment to 1797 in order to explore the trials and tribulations of taking the air in Hyde Park. A frequent pastime for many Londoners, promenading on horseback was a sure method of gaining notice from the most fashionable people; however, the trick was to be noticed for admirable equestrian ability on a horse suitable to one's status. It was this last bit, the careful selection of a mount, that one rider found especially difficult. As he did not have the luxury of owning horses from which to choose, he was forced to take advantage of one of the many livery stables around the city happy to rent horses for the day. Having gone to a stable and been given a mount, the man was in principle set to confound the fairer sex with his riding prowess. This dashing man of fortune, however, was not overly comfortable with the stable owner's selection of his horse: "Why Ostler . . . your Master [could] have Mounted me on any thing but the dam'd pye ball! he knows I'm a Constant Sunday customer, the People in the Park will take me for a Mad Man astride on a Cow," he complained.

The stable lad, in his master's defense, told the man that the ostler "was sure your Honor would like him best as he knew you wish'd to attract the notice of the Ladies. And he thought it would match your honor's Scarlet Coat to a T." However, for this man, the piebald was uncomfortably showy and worryingly unlike a horse in appearance. Coupled with his dubiously flashy scarlet coat, this man would certainly be able to attract the notice of others in the park, though probably not for the reasons he wished.

Isaac Cruikshank's *Sunday Equestrians or Hyde Park Candidates for Admiration,* a graphic illustration of the difficulty of choosing a proper horse for a day out in the park and the necessity of distinguishing oneself from the multitude of riders there, provides a glimpse of the many changes English equestrianism underwent during the eighteenth century (fig. 6). Our scarlet-coated horseman and many others illustrated in Cruikshank's caricature differed remarkably in class, equestrian ability, economic standing, self-display, and performance of gender from the world of Cavendish's cavalier manège. No longer were the country houses of the nobility the premier spaces for the instruction or performance of horsemanship; instead, London's entirely urban environment became the home of horsemanship in all of its wonderfully new variety.

The many and wide-ranging political, social, and economic changes experienced by Englishmen in the late seventeenth and early eighteenth centuries drove these differences. Paul Langford and Julian Hoppit show how, during the tumultuous time after the Civil Wars, England was increasingly tied to business enterprise, commerce, and mercantilism. According to Langford, most eighteenth-century social commentators were aware "that they lived in a commercial age, an era in which the processes of production and exchange had dramatically increased the wealth, improved the living standards, and transformed the mores of western societies." Because of the rapidly expanding international character of British trade, English people were wealthier and more socially mobile than ever before, and they lived in a competitive mercantilist era that encouraged the production and consumption of both old and new products from around the world. The global eighteenth century witnessed new forms of social interaction and normative behavior, and became increasingly concerned about the effects of its own success on society. With the relative decline in royal patronage and of the court as the site of social trends, it predominantly fell to the gentry and nouveau riche to provide the means and impetus for cultural changes and definitions of proper taste, changes and definitions that were often solidified through homosocial interaction in public gathering places such

FIGURE 6 Isaac Cruikshank, *Sunday Equestrians or Hyde Park Candidates for Admiration*, 1797. Photo courtesy of The Lewis Walpole Library, Yale University.

as the increasingly popular coffeehouse. It was there that men of diverse backgrounds, social positions, and political leanings came to discuss affairs and socialize, and it was where men discussed normative and divergent forms of display. However, the period was also an era of politeness and social refinement; socializing with the fairer sex was equally central to the development of a properly commercial and masculine man.[1]

As this chapter will show, the late seventeenth and early eighteenth centuries saw the development of a horsemanship community that embraced men who placed more emphasis on emergent codes of manners than on the older ones of the Cavendish horsemanship community. Men of both the elite and middling sorts, in keeping with wider trends in masculine behavior, turned their backs, to some degree, on the militarism, honor, and self-bridling that was so important before the Civil Wars. Instead, they displayed themselves on horseback as polite, commercial, and liberal in their governing and political views. As Donna Landry argues, "As Britons transformed themselves into the 'polite and commercial people' suited to administering an empire, a new language of free forward movement and equine initiative developed" alongside a "new language of horsemanship." The new language of horsemanship was one of liberty and "silken-thread" communication, instead of the strict control of both man and horse in the Hobbesian sense.[2] These men looked to horsemanship methodologies and forms of display that were decidedly uninterested in spectacle, simplified, and barely grounded in the manège. Their community was one where only the rudiments of horsemanship were practiced, where inclusion within its confines was open to anyone (men and women) who rode on an English or common saddle, and where politeness, conversation, and commercial endeavor were mandatory. However, even here, the older forms of masculinity, and the associated militaristic discourses, did not disappear completely. It was the increasing craze for sporting riding that took over the haute école discourses and self-displays of military might as beneficial to the nation.

A NEW MASCULINE DISPLAY

The eschewing of older traditions of display was a trend that, ironically enough, began while Cavendish was still a member of Charles II's court. It began in conjunction with a monarch-mandated simplification of personal display, and almost a renunciation of spectacle and ceremony for personal profit. In 1666, driven by the Restoration court's unstable political position and a desire to distance itself from the perceived decadence, luxury, and effeminacy of Charles I, Charles II, influenced by Ottoman fashion, introduced the three-piece suit.³ As David Kuchta argues, Charles's sartorial decision "inaugurated a new and essentially modern era of masculine aesthetics, one that reversed a long-held association between elaborate display and high social status." It instead fell to "debauched upstarts" of the middling sort and effeminate fops at court to continue displays of luxury and personal splendor. "Noble simplicity was, in essence, the absence of display, the absence of pomp and ceremony," Kuchta writes. However, the sartorial changes of Charles's court were short-lived. There was a relapse from the 1670s to 1680 due in part to the increasing political stability of the Restoration court and its renewed ties to France. It was not until the overthrow of James II and William and Mary's Glorious Revolution that simplicity of display again became the dominant form of performing political masculinity. Kuchta argues that the gradual adoption of simple, humble clothing in place of conspicuously luxurious wardrobes by both the elite and middling sorts was not an example of the "embourgeoisement" of the aristocracy—the usual argument for changes in elite modes of self-expression. Instead, Kuchta argues for a "common language" of masculinity between the classes. "Just as middle-class men had appropriated an originally aristocratic critique of luxury and effeminacy in order to help define middle-class masculine identity," Kuchta summarizes, "aristocratic men used that middle-class critique of aristocratic luxury and effeminacy to redefine their own class and gender identity."⁴

The renunciation of sartorial splendor and spectacular personal display saw parallel developments in the practice of horsemanship, but with some significant differences from Kuchta's argument. In 1639, for example, Thomas de Grey argued that a man

> shall be known to be exquisite in Horsemanship, whereby to cause his Horse to shew himselfe in his Pace, Menage, and all other his postures like as well becomes a right good Horse, perfectly mouthed, delicately borne, obedient to the hand, and to answer the Switch and Spur, will not (I say) that Gentleman be highly commended, and have more eyes upon him as he passeth along than are commonly cast upon a Comet or the Sun eclipsed: yes undoubtedly. For if we due but note when a handsome Horse passeth along, we may observe the people not onely gaze upon him as he commeth towards and against them, but to turn themselves

and looke after him so long time as he continueth within their view and sight: Mans love of the Horse is generally so great.⁵

If he was on a good horse and could handle him with skill, a man could draw the gaze of spectators to him quickly and without much effort. It was this effect, and the boost in reputation that Cavendish sought through it, that men of the eighteenth century also looked to cultivate, even in a time of a masculine aesthetic that discouraged spectacle. Many horsemen continued to follow de Grey's notion of masculine display on horseback throughout the century, but there was a parallel middling critique of elite display in the Cavendish mode, and a corresponding attempt at the adoption of a simplified, less spectacular, and seemingly less frivolous riding style by both the elite and middling sort.

As the list of manuals from the last chapter indicates, the manège and haute école specifically were gradually becoming a part of new practices and discourses in horsemanship: racing, hunting, and riding for utility. Even after the publication in English of Cavendish's *General System of Horsemanship* in 1743, and the reintroduction of his theories into the equestrian community, the branching and classification of horsemanship continued to grow. This diversification of communities eventually resulted in the creation of two distinct but interconnected schools of horsemanship practice: one that was interested in mechanistic riding for pleasure, industry, and the performance of these virtues, and one that continued to look upon it as an art form to be learned for the conspicuous display of skill, nobility, and gentlemanly greatness in the Cavendish vein. The horsemen of the elite Cavendish community continued to practice older traditions of display while engaging with new developments of masculine and horsemanship practice, and horsemen of the new communities looked to simplified horsemanship while arguing, against common practice, that some education in spectacular riding was still useful.

While Kuchta argues for a complete sharing of discourses between classes, and the gradual melding of display into one homogenous form—the three-piece suit—horsemen were aware of, and adopted aspects from, one another's horsemanship, but they remained remarkably tied to "traditional" and classed equestrian hierarchies. According to Charles Thompson's *Rules for Bad Horsemen* (1762), for example, the manège is "looked on as of use to military people only; or to those, in whom a shewy appearance is made proper and becoming, by their rank in life." In addition, "all managed horses are taught motions for parade only; and their paces are spoiled for the road and hunting. Hence riding in the manage is called *riding the great horse;* and the common opinion is, that nothing of this art can be applied to general use."[6] According to Thompson and other authors like him, young men were no longer becoming, or even wanting to become, students in the manège community. For them, the manège was suitable only for those who were interested in parading before a military assembly, and those who wanted to make a "shewy appearance," as was natural for them because of their social rank or title.[7]

Such men, as more traditional critiques of the elite often pointed out, were indulging in an activity that was essentially for their own gain, not for that of the nation, regardless of their arguments to the contrary.[8] This civic-humanist critique, where the benefit of the nation rather than the self was central, was, as J. G. A. Pocock argues, a strong force in English political debates at the turn of the eighteenth century.[9] Within this discourse, men considered the cultivation of personal pleasures such as horsemanship to be increasingly luxurious, vain, and damaging to civil society. For example, although Cavendish's horsemanship was designed to display through ceremony a man's fitness to govern as sovereign, and as such was an ideal method of helping to ensure the continued stability of the commonwealth against the proponents of republicanism and mixed government, some men now considered it entirely useless. During his own lifetime, and increasingly afterward, Cavendish was not always considered the hallmark of ideal masculinity and embodied interspecies honor, regardless of how well he rode as a horseman, nor was he thought to be a useful or beneficial citizen of the body politic as a result. In this discourse, a civically useless man was an effeminate man, and a useless man was the "very Thing . . . of Perfume and Compliment," as one anonymous pamphleteer described him.[10] Similarly, for Alexander Pope (voicing an alternative sentiment to the popular position that argued that consumption and luxury only led to self-love, and hence corruption, rather than to love of the state), while the pursuit of personal pleasure was in theory beneficial to the nation, such pursuit still needed regulation and management so that the moral and political vices associated with it did not come to predominate.[11] As Pope explained:

> *In Days of Ease, when now the weary Sword*
> *Was sheath'd, and Luxury with Charles restor'd;*
> *In every Taste of foreign Courts improv'd,*
> *'All, by the King's Example, liv'd and lov'd'.*
> *Then Peers grew proud in Horsemanship t'excell,*
> *New-market's Glory rose, as Britain's fell.*[12]

For Pope, staunchly antiestablishment and a firm supporter of the Stuart dynasty under James II, horsemanship was yet another example of the unmanly weakness and corruption associated with Charles II's court and William I's Hanoverian accession.[13] Working from a perspective on personal economies later adopted by Adam Smith, Pope argued that the pursuit of luxury, if regulated, "produced social harmony"; for him, "private vices" would beget "public benefits," but only if they were not allowed to become extravagant.[14] In Charles II's court, men were free to pursue luxury for their improvement, expand their horizons with knowledge of foreign customs and ideas, and live a life of peace and prosperity, but these pursuits did not last. Men, in their love of luxury and self-glory, became ungoverned and began to pursue unmediated prosperity at the cost of everything masculine. The courtiers and soldiers in that court spent their time in horsemanship, in striving "t'excell" in the spectacular art, at the cost of Britain's glory and strength. These horsemen, exemplified by the prime example of the whole, or "The Duke of Newcastle" and his "Book of Horsemanship" (as Pope clarified in an accompanying footnote to his poem), were not the honorable and courageous men described in chapter 1. They were not the ideal governors of the commonwealth. Instead, they were "soften'd," "yielding," "melting," and "enervate[d]" players in a society where "all was Love and Sport," and they came from a time when eunuchs on the opera stage were celebrities at the cost of everything noble and manly.[15] Charles's court provided the setting for men to display themselves as spectacle, as Cavendish had done, for social advancement as horsemen. However, horsemanship, to Pope, was associated with the unmitigated pursuit of pleasure and personal gain, and with a loss of masculinity to effeminate luxury. The manège was no longer the ideal embodiment of honorable masculinity but a symptom of unregulated consumption and social corruption. By the time Pope was writing, in the early eighteenth century, the court culture of Charles II—and its associated popular activities, of which horsemanship was arguably one of the most ostentatious and luxurious—was outdated and firmly effeminate.

However, this discourse of effeminacy and the destructive power of luxury was not confined to only one side of the political spectrum. Instead, it permeated all elements of society, from class to national identity and political ideology.[16] We see this aversion to luxury and conspicuous display in Cruikshank's *Sunday Equestrians or Hyde Park Candidates for Admiration,* introduced earlier (fig. 6). This time, it is the figure second from the left on the top row, the dashing military man *en piaffe,* that is our focus. This caricature has taken up the discourse directed toward men who sought to perform themselves in the Cavendish manner, while illustrating a keen dislike of the Stuart dynasty in favor of the new Hanoverian republic. This man, shown as exaggeratedly elegant and refined, is on a horse who is obedient, light, and highly trained in the manège and haute école manner. But the rider's clinging to past traditions, further emphasized by the manège horse type with the long tail, has prompted the artist to point out the superficiality and uselessness of the horseman's civic and equestrian abilities. The horse, rather than ridden by a master, is in the ideally collected frame suited to the manège, shown in the tie down that runs from the chinstrap of the bridle to the girth. It is not a gentle *appui* or discursive contact from the rider's hands that is keeping the horse obedient but his training by previous masters of horsemanship; between this training and his tack, the horse simply cannot do anything otherwise. The rider—displaying a seat that would have horrified Cavendish—seems content with the situation and proud of the image he displays. He says, "There is something so dignified in the Grad Pas, that if I am not admired there is no true taste existing. *One is standing stock still all the while you are moving* as the Irishman says, why I scarcely move faster than the black Man at Charing Cross." Like the equestrian statue of King Charles I (the black man at Charing Cross, also *en piaffe*), this rider is "standing stock still," even though he is moving as an ideal *piaffe* was to be performed.[17]

This rider is as stationary as the inexperienced, ignorant, and foolish Paddy Bull during his crossing from Ireland to England ("one is standing stock still all the while you are moving" was a line from the popular song "Paddy Bull's Expedition," which was reprinted in the many song collections sold at the end of the eighteenth and into the nineteenth century).[18] For Cruikshank, the manège and its elite militaristic practitioners were, like statues, stuck in the nonparliamentary and absolutist past of Charles I, and as a result were unable to move forward into the new republican era. For commentators who adopted more "traditional snobberies," or a distrust of luxury and display, and for those such as Pope, who considered commerce civilizing, horsemen of the manège were useless to their country, unpatriotically continental, associated with the stereotypically rebellious and unintelligent Irish, a drag on the nation, and simply focused on image and public appearance rather than on the cultivation of practical and useful qualities beneficial to the community.[19] That said, more traditional display, where assumptions that only "military people," or those in "whom a shewy appearance is made proper and becoming, by their rank in life," could or should practice the manège, was maintained even here. This figure is the most "shewy" of the group represented, although one that, for this artist, emphasized his centauric and civic uselessness rather than his ability actively to participate for the nation's benefit.

A NEW SCHOOL OF HORSEMANSHIP

Following a timeline similar to that of the three-piece suit and of changes in courtesy literature noticed by Jacques Carré, which emphasized utilitarianism over ornament, the perceptible decline of the haute école was indicative of an increasing simplicity of the manège and a redefinition of what it meant to be a horseman.[20] For example, Gervase Markham, in his 1610 manual *Markhams maister-peece,* defined "a compleat *Horseman*" as a man who "shows, / That *Rides, Keeps, Cures,* and all perfections knows," that is, someone well versed in all aspects of horse care and interaction.[21] This behavior of a horseman, somewhat followed by Cavendish and other seventeenth-century men, gave way in the Civil Wars to a rider who was increasingly interested only in the rudiments of riding and not at all in other areas of equine care, interaction, or even training. One Civil War tract, John Vernon's 1644 *The Young Horse-man, or The Honest Plain-dealing Cavalier,* which differed greatly from its predecessors, exhibited a new aversion to everything spectacular or ceremonial in riding, favoring plain simplicity and practicality in horsemanship. Vernon wrote his manual so that "every ordinary Souldier might easily purchase [it] with his money or weare [it] in his pocket, to be his continuall advisor, and prove no hinderance unto him in the expedyating of his service."[22] Like John Cruso's *Militarie Instructions for the Cavallrie,* also of 1644, and David Leslie's *General Lessley's Direction and Order for the Exercising of Horse and Foot* of 1642, Vernon's manual was the beginning of a gradual shift away from the spectacle and self-display so central to Cavendish's construction of the masculine self, and toward a new practice and visual aesthetic of horsemanship that was simplified and designed to make the management of a horse "easy to an indifferent rider."[23] Although there were exceptions, there was a growing trend in horsemanship manuals to provide only the information necessary for the beginner rider who sought merely his safety and a modicum of gentility while mounted.

We can trace this new trend in horsemanship language and performance primarily through a string of mid-eighteenth-century manuals by Charles Thompson, J. L. Jackson, Charles Hughes, and Philip Astley. These authors look to one another—frequently quoting one another verbatim—as well as to the sporting, racing, and husbandry manuals of the sixteenth and seventeenth centuries (such as John Astley's *The Art of Riding* of 1584 and

Joseph Blagrave's 1669 *The Epitome of the Whole Art of Husbandry*), rather than to the longer tradition of the manège manuals favored by Cavendish. Thompson's 1762 *Rules for Bad Horsemen* was the first of the new manual types. A practitioner of the manège, to some extent, Thompson, following the manège-in-decline discourse of his equestrian predecessors, was writing to correct the lack of *"just taste"* in horsemanship and to reintroduce it as a worthy art to be learned by the nation's youth, who were preoccupied by their love of hunting and racing to the detriment of their equestrian abilities. "If a young fellow can ride a fox-chace, or a horse-race, he immediately considers himself, and is considered by others, as a good horseman," Thompson complained. "If he has a horse which he cannot manage, he will tell you, he designs to tame him by hunting: that is, if he can but get him to go forward, he will tire him. But what end does this answer?" he asked. "By a week's rest the horse becomes as ungovernable as ever; and surely, if a man cannot manage his horse in full spirits, he cannot well be said to manage him at all."[24] With the decline in manège participation, and the increasing involvement by those who did not have access to or inclination for proper horsemanship instruction, there was a corresponding decrease in horsemanship ability; it was this decline that Thompson was hoping to correct by reintroducing the manège as a necessary part of a man's education.

Like Vernon, Cruso, and Leslie before him, however, he presented a language of horsemanship to the new generation of horsemen that differed substantially in content, goals, and practice from that of Cavendish. For Thompson, as for J. L. Jackson in his *Art of Riding, or Horsemanship Made Easy* (1765), horsemanship remained an art, but an art that did not require the development of a close, reciprocal, and interspecies relationship, or even knowledge beyond the basics necessary for the general operating of the horse. It was an art that had become mechanized, an art that became a defining characteristic of the new horseman's community. Jackson argued that manège horsemanship in the older style was useless to the new, modern horseman interested in hunting and travel. No longer was a general practitioner of horsemanship to strive for perfection, to perform his horsemanship as high art as Cavendish had done. Instead, "indifferent" riders, those who simply wanted minimal hassle and difficulty in riding, looked to the new breed of manuals and instructors to "be taught all that is necessary to ride with safety, ease, and pleasure, and to make their horses perform chearfully."[25] The manuals were intended, as Jackson's title indicates, to make horsemanship "easy." Appearing during the age of turnpikes and increasing traffic congestion on the roads, congestion that mandated a new focus on personal safety when traveling, these manuals were something relatively new in the lineage of works on horsemanship.[26] For Thompson, "Books in which the art of riding has been fully and completely taught" had been the norm in England, but these manuals had "not been calculated for so *inferior* a part of a horseman's education. What is said here, is not therefore designed for those who ride *well,* but for those only, who are liable to difficulties and accidents for want of *common* cautions."[27]

However, this is not to say that participation in a riding house was not theoretically beneficial to the sporting and pleasure sort. According to Jackson, riding in a riding house "would be practicable, if the masters would teach the art of riding on the *hunting* or *common saddle;* or, if a person unacquainted with the rules prescribed there, would initiate himself in the riding-house, and make himself master of some general principles, which he might occasionally apply to another manner of riding. In the mean time, our present business is, to give such rules, whereby an unskilful horseman may be instructed to ride with more safety and ease than, otherwise, he can."[28] Within this new lineage of horsemanship manual, riding in the "traditional" manège riding house would theoretically be beneficial if the conventions and goals of the hunt field and business traveler were taken into consideration, or if the riders entered there to gain only the rudimentary skills common to all equestrian communities early in a gentleman's education. It was only the more precise, the increasingly difficult and specialized, actions that should be avoided as ostentatious luxury and spectacle, not the basic introduction to riding and horse-human relationships that all men required. It was up to Jackson and the other authors who shared his riding discourse to provide these new riders with the instruction.

This instruction differed significantly from that provided by Cavendish, who presumed that his readers were already in possession of a solid equestrian education prior to reading his manuals. The new authors invariably spent a large amount of time—and ink—discussing the basics, such as the ins and outs of how to stop a horse, or how to direct it where a rider wished. The greatest effort, though, was instructing the reader simply how to get on. Philip Astley's first manual, *The Modern Riding-Master* of 1776, was the most detailed on the subject, dedicating well over half the text and eleven of the twelve illustrations to the topic (fig. 7). Astley's figures 2 through 10, for example, are dedicated to the step-by-step process of mounting, with figure 11 showing the newly seated novice having his first lesson in horsemanship—on the lunge. He is not in control of his mount— the instructor in the center of the ring is the man directing the speed and direction of the horse, with the aid of another man who is driving the horse

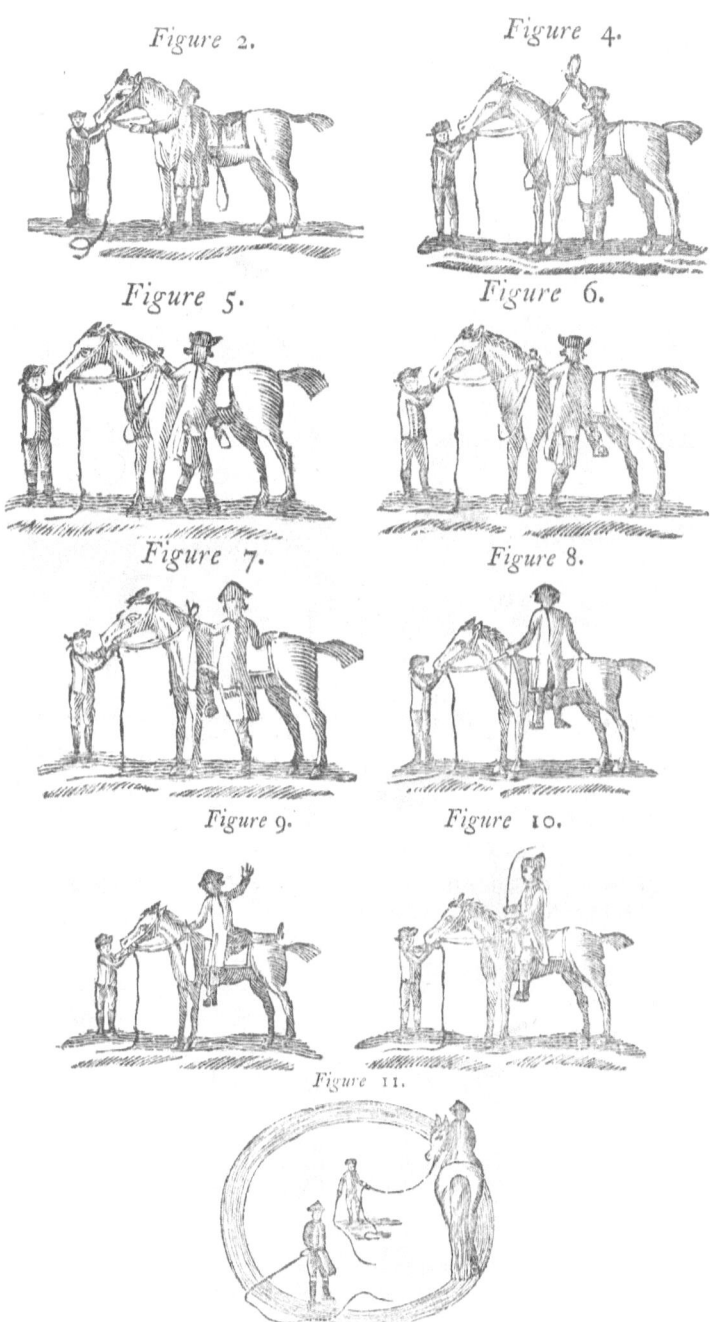

FIGURE 7 Philip Astley, figures 2, 4–11, in *The Modern Riding-Master, or A Key to the Knowledge of the Horse, and Horsemanship* (Philadelphia: Robert Aitken, 1776), 23–28. Photo courtesy of the American Antiquarian Society.

FIGURE 8   William Austen, *The Lucky Mistake, Or the Buck & Blood Flourishing Macaroni L^d—playing a Solo on the Jelly Glassez,* 1773. Photo courtesy of The Lewis Walpole Library, Yale University.

forward—the rider is simply learning how to sit there, as all raw beginners must. Astley was concerned with the rudimentary elements of riding and with providing the minimal abilities of kinesthetic communication that allowed for positive public display of possessed or desired rank. There was no discussion of human-horse mastery, and Astley did not show the men in his first manual as the source of the animal's rationality, training, or submission to patriarchal authority. While his later manuals and his own riding performances speak to alternative conceptions of self-display and masculine virtue, his first manual was very much in keeping with the time. It was a time when the definition of horsemanship was now that of an easy, inexpensive, and not overly time- or effort-consuming practice.

This easy horsemanship and simplified masculine display make the black man of Charing Cross an obvious individual of outdated, ostentatious, and frivolous spectacle. Likewise in William Austen's 1773 *The Lucky Mistake, Or the Buck & Blood Flourishing Macaroni L^d—playing a Solo on the Jelly Glassez* (fig. 8). Here we have the haute école figure of the horseman *en levade,* one of the traditional poses favored by royalty and the elite for equestrian portraiture, shown as having just ridden over a man, with a now broken wooden leg, and his jelly wares. The horseman is depicted as a macaroni, in all of his flamboyant, old-school masculine aesthetic and big-wig glory, and is shown brandishing a lash whip with which he has hit either his horse—to effect a showy appearance—or the merchant as he passed. This image, from an illustrator who was a supporter of individual private virtue enacted by commercial activities, effectively ties the extravagantly uncontrolled love of luxury and consumption, effeminacy, and unpatriotic Italian interests to the elite horseman returned from his grand tour. Macaronis, known for their unusually large wigs, ostentatious clothing choices, effete behavior, and affected Italian fashions, were considered foppish and were associated with vanity, cowardice, self-absorption, irrationality, physical weakness, and femininity.[29] As James Boswell complained of Samuel Johnson, who was increasingly reluctant to complete their tour of the Scottish highlands: "I said, 'Why sir, you seemed to me to despond yesterday. You are a delicate Londoner; you are a maccaroni; you cannot ride.'"[30] Macaronis bent gender boundaries to the breaking point and were of ambiguous and unclear sex as a result. They were "of the double Gender" and thus incapable of following the normative masculine and civic pursuits so necessary to horsemen. However, macaronis, even with their missing physical and rational masculinity, were not often discussed as figures of social or civic unrest. Instead, they remained benignly comic and devoid of true civic impact for much of the eighteenth century.[31] That said, they remained uncomfortable figures of satire, since "Display was the most consistent and most disapproved element in the recreations of an age of . . . extravagance," and it was the macaroni, here depicted as a haute école horseman, who embraced it.[32] The flourishing horseman, with his expensive, glitzy, and useless symbol of unnecessary consumption (his horse), has trod upon the properly industrious, independent, and English figure of the portly merchant and nationalistic everyman war hero.

WILL, LIBERTY, AND THE ENGLISH HUNTING SEAT

For Cavendish and other men of the eighteenth century, ideal horses, like those ridden by the flourishing macaroni and black man at Charing Cross, were "the best and rarest that were to be found," or those generally from breeders abroad and usually consisting of horses from Spanish, Barb, Turkoman, or Arabian breeding (the macaroni's horse was clearly an Arabian, with

FIGURE 9   Sawrey Gilpin, *Set of Eight Horses—The Managed Horse*, 1786. Photo © Trustees of the British Museum. All rights reserved.

his dished face, elevated tail, and delicately pointed ears).[33] This horse was an import, exotic, foreign, and in keeping with horse-purchasing trends in the late seventeenth and early eighteenth centuries.[34] However, in *The Lucky Mistake,* Austen caricatured the Cavendish type, like his big-haired rider, as something ridiculous, unnecessarily luxurious and equally hairy. Although the horse's sex is not in doubt, and his overt maleness is exaggerated through his posing and impossibly large neck (stallions possess larger necks than geldings or mares) in a fashion similar to more traditional equestrian portraiture, his and his rider's usefulness, and hence their masculinity, is questionable. Like his macaroni rider (who was at heart always artificial, according to Amelia Rauser), this horse, because of his breeding, conformation, and training, can physically do nothing but prance, preen, and make a showy appearance. He can only perform the artificial movements of the manège. He cannot perform with any aptitude the duties required by the new ideal and quintessentially English breed, the Thoroughbred.[35]

FIGURE 10 Sawrey Gilpin, *Set of Eight Horses—The Hunter*, 1786. Photo © Trustees of the British Museum. All rights reserved.

The history of the Thoroughbred is complex, with a substantial amount of scholarship from diverse disciplines (genetics, history, sociology, anthropology, and literary studies), and it will not be discussed in detail here.[36] For my purposes, it is enough to say that this new and increasingly desirable breed of horse was of a different body type from those cherished by horsemen of the past generation. The Thoroughbred was of a rangier, more sloping-shouldered physiology designed for covering ground at speed rather than for collection and the carrying movements of the manège—the specialty of the short-coupled and upright conformation common to the macaroni horse and his predecessors. Sawrey Gilpin's sketches *The Managed Horse* and *The Hunter* of 1786 illustrate the two body types, while again labeling each as suitable for its own unique form of horsemanship and masculine display; only the manège horse was suited to a man of the military, while the hunter type was of use to the sportsman in the field (figs. 9 and 10).[37] This new conformation, and the Thoroughbred's celebrated

FIGURE 11
John Vanderbanck, *The Capriole*, in Josephus Sympson, *Twenty Five Actions of the Manage Horse* (London: Printed for and Sold by J. Sympson and Andrew Johnston, 1729), 25. Photo: Yale Center for British Art, Paul Mellon Collection.

FIGURE 12
John Vanderbanck, *A Hunter upon full Stretch*, in Josephus Sympson, *Twenty Five Actions of the Manage Horse* (London: Printed for and Sold by J. Sympson and Andrew Johnston, 1729), 26. Photo: Yale Center for British Art, Paul Mellon Collection.

sensitivity, independence, and bravery, in turn "demanded" a new style of riding and horse-human interaction. Riders, now in the lighter, closer-fitting common saddle (like the one favored in Astley's illustrations) rather than the deep manège saddle, were thus beginning to participate in what Landry has called "the making of the English hunting seat."[38]

This change is readily noticeable in the manuals of horsemanship published at the time, but not more so than in Sympson's transitional *Twenty Five Actions of the Manage Horse*. Even though this manual was expressly about the older horsemanship tradition, much of the text is dedicated to discussing the hunting horse and the practice of hunting itself. For Sympson, it seems, the Thoroughbred and sporting riding were novel enough to warrant extensive discussion, and contentious enough within manège communities to necessitate the glorification of their benefits. He wrote of the seat, for example, that "the *Hunting-Seat* has its Advantages; I mean for Ease, both to the Horse and Rider, which is principally to be considered in Hunting." This seat was "like the *Seat* of the *Asiatick* Nations, who are much on Horseback, with *short Stirrups* and light *Saddles*." Also, unlike popular horsemanship thought, "Neither is this *Seat* so easily obtain'd; and tho' it may not appear Graceful, as that of the *Manage,* it is found very necessary in our fine Hunting Counties, upon a long Chase, *viz.* to sit light, and humour the Horse's Motions, by inclining the Body; and save his Wind by pulling the *Reins,* more or less, according to the Ground he runs over, which will greatly help him to last the Day; whereas one that is ignorant of this Method, will soon blow his Horse, and put an End to his Sport."[39] Accompanied by images, shocking in their stark difference from all of the other manège illustrations (figs. 11 and 12), this section of Sympson's book shows not only the Eastern ("Asiatick") tradition of what was to become the quintessentially English hunting seat but also the changing embodiments and discourses of political horsemanship.

Jackson, though he declined to treat the manège in any detail because of its apparent uselessness for most men, recorded that some horsemen "are of a different opinion, and imagine, that what is taught a horse in the manage, will not spoil his paces; and that by his discipline there, he is accustomed to have *no will of his own,* thereby he becomes more manageable and easy to an indifferent rider."[40] As we have seen, this was in essence the ideal state of horse-man interaction expressed by Cavendish and other horsemen of the seventeenth century, where the horse tied his will to his rider's through covenant to create a human-animal centaur. What Jackson pointed to in mentioning the continued Cavendish ideal were competing languages of liberty developing in the late seventeenth century and early eighteenth—one, to put it simply, "negative" or Hobbesian in origin, and the other "positive" in conception.[41] In Hobbes's theory, as Cavendish enacted it, a person, state, or horse continued to possess will and liberty if able to live in the "absence of Opposition."[42] Even though a horse was constrained by riding technologies and laws/aids of the sovereign, and completely subject to the ruling will, he willingly obeyed through fear and love as a subject in a state of covenant.

However, for the new horsemen of the eighteenth century, Hobbesian thought was more tyrannical than liberating. Similar to what Rosanna Cox sees in Milton's view of liberty, where "to be free . . . is essentially to be independent, not to be subject to, or dependent upon the arbitrary will of anyone else," not just subject to physical impediments as Hobbes contends, eighteenth-century liberty discourse emphasized a freedom from external impediment to the will of an individual and the freedom to enjoy it.[43] As John Locke summarized, "the *Idea* of *Liberty,* is the *Idea* of a Power in any Agent to do or forbear any particular Action, according to the determination or thought of the mind, whereby either of them is preferr'd to the other"; however, "where either of them is not in the Power of the Agent to be produced by him according to his *Volition,* there he is not at *Liberty,* that Agent is under *Necessity.*"[44] An agent must be free to act as he chooses, without the apparent heavy-handedness of government interfering in the independent lives of its subjects. Liberty now connoted a freedom to live life as a man chose.[45] The discourse and discussions of liberty were center stage for the majority of the century, and were hotly debated for much of it. Adopted and altered by civic humanists, and tied to the unshakeable faith in the ancient English constitution—especially under Walpole—liberty discourse (in all of its forms) was the motivating and attention-grabbing ideology of the eighteenth century.[46] The Stuart courts had started the destruction of English liberties, but the Hanoverian succession would right the wrongs. This Whig discourse—Tory and Jacobite ideology being its opposite, as we saw with Pope—would later come to include a language of deep distrust over the initially egalitarian and liberty-bestowing Hanoverian regime.

These early discussions of liberty picked up steam in the 1760s and 1770s. The 1760s was a decade of political instability that saw increasing distrust over George III's ministers—especially John Stuart, Earl of Bute, and others in the third, unofficial political party, or the "King's Friends," as they became known.[47] Bute, after stepping down as prime minister in

1764, continued to enjoy the ear of the king, and was thought to wield an alarming amount of power in English politics. There was increased opposition to his attempts to control the empire through standing garrisons in far-flung corners of the world, and to the high taxation needed to pay for them and for the astronomically expensive Seven Years' War, Bute's brainchild. Such resistance to government interference was particularly marked in the American colonies, where increasing discontent with the continued taxation of colonial trade goods and networks as a means of raising British capital played a defining role in the causes and outcome of the American War of Independence.[48] Through the influence of the King's Friends, as Kathleen Wilson argues, many feared that the government was gaining more and more influence in the daily affairs of the English people. The government, it was thought by opposition radicals such as John Wilkes, following a practice of despotism that cut out the voice of the people, and that hearkened back to the courts of Charles I and James II.[49]

This liberty discourse—especially as espoused by Wilkes and his radical followers—sought to uphold the people's traditionally English constitutional rights. Against everything foreign, apparently corrupt, and effeminate in court culture, Wilkes "and his supporters' virulent journalism ... upheld an amalgam of patriotic qualities that linked the preservation of empire, liberty and the constitution with the hegemony of English customs and culture in the polity."[50] One of the most "English" of these customs was, of course, horsemanship in the "traditional" manner, or, as Cavendish put it, in the manner of making "a horse trample with a snaffle and martingal the old English way."[51] Cavendish was referring to the vernacular English horsemanship traditions commonly practiced prior to the introduction of the continental manège and haute école. This tradition heavily relied on the use of the snaffle bit, the ancient Celtic bit, rather than the continental curb, and survived, it seems, beyond the page of the horsemanship manual. It survived among those who did not practice, or potentially even read, Cavendish's methods of horsemanship, and among those who were not of a class acceptable for horsemanship practice. Riding in a snaffle was the prerogative of men who did nonmilitary riding in the sixteenth century, and of those who trained young horses who would eventually transition over to the curb as their proficiency in the manège increased. This transition to a more sophisticated and often harsh bit from one that was thought unsuitable for a finished horse or for a gentleman was absolutely essential to the horsemen of the seventeenth century. Charles I even went so far as to issue a royal statute in 1627 that prohibited the use of snaffles for any horse used in the military and, by implication, prohibited anyone not of the required social rank from entering into civic office.[52] For Cavendish and other men of the horsemanship community, riding in a snaffle was at best not suitable for their ongoing quest for full obedience and displays of honor, and at worst illegal. It was not until the fall of the Stuart dynasty and the introduction of new, republican horsemanship practices that previously marginalized or excluded men began to enter into horsemanship communities, and snaffle bits, on their own and later as a part of a double bridle (curb and small snaffle, or bridoon, together) became the dominant method of riding in England.[53] Horsemen, influenced by the revived language of English liberties under the traditional constitution, looked to their past, to the nonmanège equestrian community and its snaffle-using practices, for their equestrian education and normative horsemanship. They looked to a glorious past free from continental influence, and free from heavy-handed government bridling, while embracing free, forward movement in their political thought and riding practice.[54]

Reflecting these political changes, beginning in the late seventeenth century and gaining popularity throughout the eighteenth, horsemen practiced, in its ideal form, a "silken-thread" control over their mounts—as illustrated by Sympson's two hunters and explored by Landry—where a light, sensitive, and noninterfering hand was the method of governance. As Landry observes, "What was at stake in English self-representations on horseback, beginning in the later seventeenth century when the importation of Eastern bloodstock burgeoned, was an image of liberty, of free forward movement of horse and rider with a minimum of restraint. This was an image with undoubted political significance. Liberty became a political watchword. Racing fast across country became its embodiment, its most euphoric, adrenaline-fueled bodily reenactment. Taking a ride on the wild side became synonymous with being English, with enjoying the liberties of the free-born Englishman or Briton."[55] In this nationalistic discourse and in Sympson's images, the men have lifted themselves out of the saddle and inclined their bodies to allow quick shifts of balance and weight as needed, to help their horses over rough ground and obstacles, while allowing their horse's heads and necks to stretch forward and down. It was this allowance for a more "natural," less contrived and artificial way of going, that the use of the snaffle bit was especially suited, and it allowed the horse to perform his duty as quickly, efficiently, and happily as possible. Instead of the Cavendish method, where the rider dictated every nuance of the centauric relationship as the will of the dual-natured creature, for riders of the hunting seat, their cry was for liberty, and their duty was to help the horse perform his. For example, Jackson argued that horses had a will of their own and should be able to express it for the benefit of both man and animal, while Sympson thought that it was the rider's duty to "humour the Horse's Motions," in order to "help him" perform his duty with ease, strength, and safety.[56] Such independence of thought and action from the horse was especially marked in the writings of Robert Smith Surtees, who depicted his horses as the dominant partners in horse-rider relationships.

Writing in the mid-nineteenth century, Surtees satirized the country sporting fraternity and its social, political, and visual quirks, while also depicting the various relationships between horse and man frequently experienced on the hunt field. One of the most frequent of these human-animal interactions emphasized the necessity of allowing a horse to "take care" of the rider, especially when negotiating difficult terrain at speed or when leaping challenging obstacles—where the micromanaging of the manège was simply not possible and where many decisions must be left up to the horse for the safety of both parties. In Surtees's novel *Ask Mamma, or The Richest Commoner in England,* for example, the character of Mr. Billy Pringle, of cockney descent and hopeless horsemanship ability, must rely on his mount, a seasoned hunter, to see him safely through the chase. The horse was cried up to be "a very nice oss . . . a perfect 'unter—nothin' to do but sit still, and give 'im 'is 'ead." Billy is assured that the horse will "take far better care" of Billy than he could "of 'im," which was certainly the case. Billy is unable to direct the horse where to go, leaving the horse at liberty to make his own decisions—which he does on numerous occasions, "after waiting in vain for an intimation from his rider" on what to do. The horse was able to be a full agent in the story of Billy's first day hunting, but it was a liberty and freedom taken to extremes.[57] The new language of horsemanship required horsemen to have silken-thread control, to practice riding and government styles of minimal intervention, but not to allow the horse complete mastery. The horse was still not to master the man, as Billy's did him in a reversal of proper governing hierarchies.

SPORTING MASCULINITY

Taking their impetus from the social and political interest in liberty, horsemen increasingly looked to sporting riding as a further aspect of ensuring the survival and revival of traditional English pastimes, cultures, and morals—as the example from Surtees's work and the widespread adoption of the common saddle and snaffle bit indicate. Cavendish, however, was a predictable naysayer when it came to the sport. For him, "In Hunting, Hawking, Bowling, Shooting, Cocking, Cardes and Dice, and many such things, there is no Use at all, but meerly Pleasure: But in A Horse of Mannage, both Use and Pleasure."[58] Even with this perspective, many men of the seventeenth century considered riding to hounds after hare, stag, or fox to be a traditional part of a masculine upbringing; they practiced it as just another facet of the manège and haute école. In his *Gentleman's Recreation* of 1686, Richard Blome argued that hunting had been practiced throughout history by "all Degrees and Qualities of Men, even by Kings and Princes," just as manège horsemanship had been.[59] However, by the beginning of the eighteenth century, sporting riding was increasingly separated from the manège as a unique pastime of its own, complete with identifiable riding methods, styles, technologies, and discourses. Although riding the great horse still influenced the practice, and sportsmen frequently argued that it was an essential grounding upon which they could build their specialist knowledge, the development of a hierarchical categorization that would solidify over the eighteenth century had begun. Sportsmen quickly became separated from the horsemanship community as men who learned the manège only as a necessity for their true joy, hunting, while many men of the manège frequently participated in learning to leap at the bar, spent many hours happily on the chase, and took great pride in their ability to do so while retaining the appellation horseman rather than sportsman.

A later example comes from the 1830 *Reminiscences* of manège practitioner Henry Angelo, who recalls a rather amusing outing where a mischievous friend tested his prowess on horseback to the utmost. "I fear that, like many another vain boaster in his cups, I had been bragging of my feats of horsemanship, in my father's *manège,* recounting my wondrous leaps over the bar, and my prowess in shooting flying, at the head of the grand Turk," Henry lamented. However, his friend, "Parson Bate, delighting in a frolic, and determined to try my mettle, kept me to my engagement, and mounted me on a horse, such another as that *harum scarum* beast upon which Smollett placed his hero, Commodore Trunnion."[60] Trunnion, from Tobias Smollett's 1751 *Adventures of Peregrine Pickle,* was a man of the sea, not a horseman by any stretch of the imagination, and was given the use of a horse (who was supposed to look after him, as Billy's did him) in order to travel to church to get married. But Trunnion never did reach the church that day; just as he and his lieutenant had "almost weathered the parson's house that stood to windward of the church," both horses took off after hearing the musical notes of a hunting pack. The horses were seasoned hunters who galloped off at full speed and, regardless of the hedges and ditches in their way and heedless of all efforts to "anchor" them, joined the merry chase. The lieutenant managed to abandon ship before too long, but Trunnion, wishing to preserve his gouty foot, chose to stay aboard. After all was said and done—a "long chase that lasted several hours, and extended to a dozen miles at least"—Trunnion ended up "the Lord knows whither" at the death of the stag and far away from where he had set out to go.[61]

This scene was remarkably similar to Henry's outing with Parson Bate:

> I pleaded headache, and invented all the ingenious excuses, of which fear is so prolific, to be off my engagement; but in vain. The parson swore I was hoaxing him; the view halloo was given; and away I was carried, through bog and fen, over hedge and ditch, scratched by bramble and briar, and worse bumped than a city apprentice at the Epping hunt. I contrived to hold on, as the sailors say; and many an ox-fence, and many a five-barred gate, were between me, my horse, and the earth. The woods hurried by with the swiftness of the wind, and the dreaded scene before, ere I could say Jack Robinson, became the scene behind. The beast, as if conscious of my dismay, rushed at the most break-neck leaps; and the dare-devil parson, close at his crupper, helped him over with a loud crack of his whip, crying, "Go it, my Nimrod! pelt away, Harry, my boy!"[62]

While Henry was able to finish the day unharmed, he was not left a favorite of the sporting pastime—unlike Parson Bate—even though he had spent many hours in his father's manège, practicing his leaps over the bar and perfecting the security of his elegant seat. He even "vowed never to follow the hounds again, and sacredly kept my word." This dislike of the chase was not due to any inability successfully to participate; on the contrary, Harry performed his feats of horsemanship spectacularly, and "Bate for ever after used to say, that 'the elder Angelo was a capital horseman—but that Harry, his son, rode like a Centaur!'"[63] His dislike was, it seems, the result of the breakneck speed at which the chase was carried out, his tenuous ability to direct or control (communicate with) his mount, and the potential loss of masculinity that these lapses in horsemanship ability could entail. For Henry, any association—even a feared association—with Commodore Trunnion and his horse was unacceptable. Smollett depicted Trunnion as a fool, a figure of ridicule, and a person of highly suspect masculinity, but also as someone who had experienced first-hand the new language of horsemanship that afforded the horse increased levels of liberty and agency. Therefore, while not handled well by Trunnion but apparently navigated without mishap by Henry, sporting riding was becoming a pastime with its own discourses and embodiments of power, agency, and performance. Henry, regardless of the hours he spent practicing his hunting seat in the common saddle, was still at heart an elite man of the old-school manège, not entirely comfortable with alternate forms of equestrian sovereignty. Henry was not a sportsman.

This is not to say that the zeal of Parson Bate was misplaced, or even overtly caricaturized. Many eighteenth-century sporting discourses self-consciously and often excessively asserted that hunting, especially the increasingly popular foxhunting, was a surrogate practice for masculine warfare and was necessary for the participants as citizens. This was the same discourse attached to Cavendish's horsemanship, but now it was couched in the overwhelming influence of liberty, nationalism, and commercial Englishness. One example of this trend comes from Robert Howlett's 1701 *School of Recreation*. Howlett argued that "Hunting being a Recreation that challenges the sublime Epithets of Royal, Artificial, Manly, and Warlike, for its Stateliness, Cunning, and Indurance, claims above all other Sports the Precedency," while Peter Beckford argued in 1781 that "fox-hunting is a kind of warfare; its uncertainties, its fatigues, its difficulties, and its dangers, rendering it interesting above all other diversions."[64] However, it was the georgic poem *The Chace*, by William Somervile, that was the most militaristic in tone. Somervile associated the hound pack with the "battalion" and the huntsman with both the "captain" and the "general," who was to keep his "troops," or the hounds and hunters, in proper military formation, arms at the ready.

> *Be thou our great Protector, gracious Youth!*
> *And if, in future Times, some envious Prince,*
> *Careless of Right and guileful, shou'd invade*
> *Thy* Britain's Commerce, *or shou'd strive in vain*
> *To wrest the Balance from thy equal Hand;*
> *Thy Hunter-Train, in cheerful Green array'd,*
> *(A Band undaunted, and inur'd to Toils,)*
> *Shall compass thee around, dye at thy Feet,*

Or hew thy Passage thro' th' embattled Foe,
And clear thy Way to Fame; inspir'd by thee,
The nobler Chace of Glory shall pursue
Thro' Fire, and Smoke, and Blood, and Fields of Death.[65]

Hunting, the sport that mimics warfare in all of its physical toil and its ability to produce fame, honor, glory, and companionship with fellow warriors, was for the benefit and protection of the commonwealth, England's commercial endeavors around the globe, and the continual profit of balanced justice. By rising early, enduring cold, hunger, and fatigue, and becoming strong in both mind and body, Somervile didactically argued, a sportsman became the "great Protector" of English liberty and a hero on actual or metaphorical "Fields of Death." It was through hunting that men learned masculine and business-saving skills, such as reason, competition, and strength.[66] Without such instruction, or with solely alternative education, such as scholarly work—for Blome, echoing Cavendish's ideas on the subject—young men would be "inflamed" with "roving Ambition, love of War, and Seeds of Anger."[67] Instead, skills that benefit society, like good business practices and management of money (middling ideas increasingly joined with traditionally elite notions of loyalty, benevolence, and courage in battle), were advocated in the manuals to promote a strong and peaceful country with a prosperous commercial economy.[68]

With the escalating importance of commerce and industry, and with the rising numbers of the increasingly rich commercial class, the realm of the noble hunt was also influenced by large numbers of wealthy men who began to self-identify, and be identified, as gentlemen in their own right. As Stephen Leonard and Joan Tronto argue, "chief among the various effects of the growth of commerce was the erosion of systems of ascribed status, and the concomitant rise of new opportunities for social mobility."[69] This social mobility, in turn, was accompanied by an all-consuming quest after "gentility"—"the most prized possession of all in a society obsessed with the pursuit of property and wealth."[70] More men (increasingly of the middling sort) sought to increase their social standing and sought inclusion in the new sporting community. For example, the *Encyclopedy,* as other eighteenth-century authors of sporting manuals called Blome's *Gentleman's Recreation* (1686), was dedicated to Charles II and James II, and was written for "all the Nobility and Gentry of Our Kingdoms." The work also contained a list of contributors to the manual, which included Charles Seymour, Duke of Somerset; Henry Herbert, Earl of Pembroke; and Arthur

Stringer, author of *The Experienced Huntsman* (1780). The expanded second edition (1709–10) begins to show this leveling trend in hunt participants, and its list of subscribers included one "Duke" and one "Lord," but the majority of subscriptions came from men of esquire or untitled status.[71] Beckford hinted at this development in foxhunting when he discussed his view of the reasons for sporting in a man's life: "Hunting is the soul of a country life: it gives health to the body, and contentment to the mind; and is one of the few pleasures that we can enjoy in society, without prejudice either to ourselves or our friends."[72] According to Beckford, English sportsmen of elite status were free to interact with whomever they wished without fear of "prejudice" from peers for associating with those of inferior social station, and those of the middling sorts could comfortably interact with their social superiors without being accused of masquerade, falsehood, dishonesty, or ambition. In book 4 of *The Chace*, for example, Somervile ridiculed the unhealthy and false atmosphere of high society, where all apparent favoritism from the "Prince" is short-lived and ultimately a lie. For him, social climbers who lacked landed status were left friendless and with their reputations ruined. In contrast, the hunt field was a multispecies and transclass arena in which all men could interact as equals. On the field, men's "social Cups / Smile, as we smile; open, and unreserv'd, / We speak our inmost Souls; good Humour, Mirth, / Soft Complaisance, and Wit from Malice free."[73] The hunt field was a space for conversation, for the easy interaction between (some) social groups, and a space that mandated the masculine virtues of truth and honor.

However, this apparent freedom of interaction was not without its critics. Mirroring wider discussions about social mobility, especially regarding the increasing popularity of socially mixed spaces such as coffeehouses, the increased interaction between groups was encouraged by some, while for others it was a worrisome cause for concern.[74] Many feared that a lessening or loss of differentiation between people from upper and lower society—on or off the hunt field—would jeopardize the elite's social and political position of power, along with that of the nation itself.[75] Therefore, when men of diverse social backgrounds and artificially constructed gentility participated alongside elite men on the hunt field (or on the racecourse, for that matter), they created a situation where the visual markers of rank—clothing, deportment in the saddle, and riding ability—could be blurred or erased.[76] However, following the discourse of display and the eschewing of rigorous ceremony in personal interaction, discussed by Kuchta, such blurring and erasure had, by the early nineteenth century, become an object of pride for English sportsmen like John Hawkes, author of *The Meynellian Science* (1808). He argued that "the Field is a most agreeable Coffee-house, and there is more real society to be met with there than in any other situation of life. It links all classes together, from the Peer to the Peasant. It is the Englishman's peculiear [sic] privilege. It is not to be found in any other part of the globe, but in England's true land of liberty—and may it flourish to the end of time!!"[77] Only in a true land of liberty, where silken-thread horsemanship on the hunt field was expected, could all classes come together. For Hawkes, only in England did sporting riding allow for discourse between classes, and let both man and animal live in freedom.

The developing sociability and coffeehouse mentality of the hunt field was also indicative of the new London riding houses. There were new men riding, and advertising themselves as instructors or masters of horsemanship, who differed substantially from Cavendish's model of elite horsemen. These men, like Gervase Markham in the sixteenth century, were often of the middling sort and catered to men of any social group who could afford their tuition. This broadening of horsemanship audience, instruction, and textual production, or the corruption of it, for men such as Cavendish, was exemplified by one Mr. Carter. Providing instruction for horses and equestrians in his riding house on "Charles-street, Berkley-square," Mr. Carter advertised that he had studied for three years at "the Great Manége at Versailles, then in its highest zenith," and had "near twenty year's experience, with constant study and indefatigable labour" in the art of the manège. Although he was trained in the European tradition, like Cavendish before him, Carter embodied the new commercial horseman adept at riding both in the deep manège seat with the curb bit and in silken-thread communication with the snaffle. One of the most prominent commercializers of horsemanship practice, especially through his prolific advertising campaigns, Carter was willing not only to train horses and riders at his riding house—for a price, lists of which were detailed in London newspapers—but also to ride "horses standing any where in town, or short distance from it."[78] These were all actions carried out by horsemen of the older generation when hosting at riding houses other than their own, but certainly not actions that were advertised for sale to anyone who could pay. Carter's model of publicity and willingness to work with anyone, anyone's horse, and in any location (within reason) for a fee was typical of the new type of riding house that sprang up in London in the mid-eighteenth century, and was indicative of the growing inclusion of the middling sorts and lower gentry in the once securely elite confines of the Cavendish equestrian community. At Carter's, a pupil did not need to possess the requisite social position, virtues, or community status to attend (as with the seventeenth-century European academies); he simply had to be rich enough to afford it. Men like Mr. Carter were "Cavendish's nightmare," as Karen Raber puts it. They had "transformed the arts of horsemanship, the title of horseman, and the experience of riding the advanced movements, into consumable objects, circulated for profit," instead of holding the art up as an entirely elite activity that could only be taught by equally elite horsemen.[79]

Mr. Carter, it seems, was not entirely oblivious to the lingering worries that his profit-making endeavors would generate. His advertisements betray a level of discomfort about his expertise as a riding instructor, given his own lower social status, his ongoing efforts to commercialize riding, and his target audience. Apart from ensuring that his impeccable equestrian lineage and upbringing within the equestrian community were apparent in his advertisements (he was "brought up from his infancy in the profession by his father," Captain Carter, who was equerry to the Duke of Cumberland), he also argued that "Ladies and Gentlemen may be satisfied, that not withstanding the very moderate terms, the accommodations at his house, and improvement of his scholars are equal to any others."[80] Because his terms were affordable to a wider audience (it was thought, or he was concerned that it was the case), his services were substandard compared with those on offer to the country's elite, who still practiced in the more "traditional" or European-style academies springing up across the city. However, Carter may have been especially worried for another reason. Most riding houses and academies were for men only, while Carter's riding house catered to both men and women of all ages. He actively sought out a noncitizen, female clientele, and in 1783 he published the first manual of horsemanship dedicated exclusively to women.[81]

Michèle Cohen argues that "eighteenth-century social spaces . . . were spaces for the mixed company of the sexes, since their conversation was one of the conditions for the refinement and self-improvement at the heart of politeness."[82] Finding a home in the coffeehouses, tearooms and, to some extent, clubs, mixed company also arrived in the new riding houses, which provided sites for interactions between the sexes and were environments where gender categories were explored. Women participated in horsemanship activities and voiced their opinions of their experiences in diaries and prose for much of the early modern period, but their participation within the horsemanship community was usually bound to sporting pastimes rather than to the "traditional" confines of the manège riding house.⁸³ Cavendish pointed out this gendering when he disparagingly remarked that he had "seen many Wenches Ride Astride, and Gallop, and Run their Horses, that could, I think, hardly Ride a Horse Well in the Mannage."⁸⁴ Indeed, it was not until the mid-eighteenth century that women became increasingly visible as active participants in the commercial London riding houses and as consumers of their literature.⁸⁵ While even general numbers of participants are unknown, this increased visibility and public voice suggest that more women were participating in riding than ever before, and that interaction between the sexes was gaining legitimacy within the masculine confines of the horsemanship community at a time when women's presence on the hunt field was increasingly problematic.⁸⁶

An example of this gendered diversification of participation and consumption can be found in the popular manual of horsemanship by the master of the horse to George III, Richard Berenger.⁸⁷ Published with the aid and advice of his close friend and actor David Garrick, Berenger's *History and Art of Horsemanship* of 1771 had a subscription list that included the king, William Pitt the Elder, George Lyttelton, and George Grenville. These men rode within a politically charged community of horsemanship that also included women.⁸⁸ Hester Pitt, Baroness Chatham (Berenger's cousin, a skilled politician and keen horsewoman) was reported as adding "her best thanks for" Berenger's "obliging Comm'cation of this valuable Institute of manly Accomplishment," while another riding companion of Berenger's, the bluestocking leader Elizabeth Montagu, waxed chivalric in her glowing—yet tongue-in-cheek—praise for the manual.⁸⁹ According to Montagu, the "learned & Courteous Baron Lyttelton, skill'd in love of chivalry, much commends thy book, & as I trust thy Courtesy will on some milk white Palfrey put in side saddle for use of Damsel Errant, I do insist on being a Subscriber." However, she was worried that "as yᵉ gentle name of Elizabeth might disgrace thy perilous adventure in litterature," she instructed Berenger to "put down Sʳ Guyen the red cross Knight . . . under which name I will pay the Squire thy bookseller on demand." Like "Don Quixote," Montagu (jokingly claiming the title of the female Quixote and in so doing reaffirming her own status as a skilled horsewoman secure in her femininity) was going to "ride & seek the second volume" "at yᵉ hour of Dawn" because of the manual's expected usefulness and its potential to make Berenger more famous than "the renouned Amadis de Gaule[,] Palmerin of England, & all les preux Chevaliers of antient times."⁹⁰ Elizabeth Montagu purposely sought out Berenger's expensive publication for her own use, and presumably as a sure method of improving her own equestrian abilities. She not only consumed the products of the male horsemanship community but engaged with popular literary heroes and chivalrous traditions inherent in the community's discourse, history, and mythology as a key aspect of her own gendered equestrian performance.[91] Even though she complained of not spending enough time riding "that excellent animal the horse," she averred that "two hours a day spent on his back gives one more spirits, cheerfulness, and fortitude than twice the time passed with a moral philosopher or stoic," and it seems that she did manage to enjoy "constant riding on horseback" on a somewhat regular basis.[92] However, expressing herself in the discourse of masculine chivalry and purchasing manuals intended for a male audience were certainly not the ideal behaviors of a woman during the eighteenth century. Women riders were arguably one of the most worrying features of the ongoing leveling trends of the eighteenth-century riding houses, and they were frequently the target of some of the century's most vehement critiques of (masculine) femininity as a result.

PONIES AND PETTICOATS

In 1790 Edmund Burke famously wrote: "a queen is but a woman; a woman is but an animal; and an animal not of the highest order."[93] Burke's polemical statement was inflammatory for Mary Wollstonecraft, but was not a new idea at the end of the eighteenth century. Women often were represented as closer to animals in their passions, thoughts, and rational capabilities than men, and were popularly believed to rely more on instinct, imagination, and emotion in their understanding of the world.[94] Wollstonecraft acknowledged the general acceptance of this thinking, and thought Burke's ideas were "All true, Sir, if . . . [women are] not more attentive to the duties of humanity than queens and fashionable ladies in general are."[95] For Wollstonecraft, women were compliant to a society that mandated ideal femininity as weak, soft, frivolous, uneducated, and sexually pure. Associated with the lack of reason and rational thought and the domestic sphere, these feminine "attributes" could only be remedied through education, changes to social understandings of ideal femininity, and equal rights between the sexes.[96] Only once these social and personal changes had come about, Wollstonecraft argued, could women work to improve their rational and practical abilities as strong and virtuous educators of the nation's young in their own right. Only then could they become attentive to the nation as equal and rational beings secure in their humanity.[97] For Montagu, this was precisely what riding could achieve. Riding a horse could provide more fortitude, enjoyment, and high spirits than time spent discussing the latest philosophical controversy with the greatest minds of the age. Riding was a cherished pastime that allowed the inclusion of women in traditionally male social circles, and it was one avenue open for female empowerment—as Montagu's reference to the female Quixote, Arabella, indicates.

However, when we take a closer look at horse-woman interaction, interacting with animals had direct consequences for the rider's gendered performances. In some instances, the performativity of riding worked to uphold the social conventions and normative notions of femininity that Wollstonecraft squarely rejected. In others, the association of women with riding and horse-human interaction served as worrying transgressions of the gendered norm, and as a further means of reinscribing the similarities between women and animals by betraying hidden animalistic passions and unchecked desires. However, even though riding was and is usually considered a transgressive activity through which women could establish new (and frequently scandalous) forms of gendered behavior, of which Montagu's letter to Berenger is an example, very few women of the eighteenth century were able to use the act of riding and interspecies communication to challenge established gender hierarchies and categorization. Instead, social convention, horsemanship instruction, and the presence of a horse itself closely regulated the practices, expectations, performances, and representations of female equestrians.

Mr. Carter's manual for women was expressly published for the feminizing of the gender-bending associated with women riders, and his riding house opened to bring those teachings to fruition. Frequently given lessons in a closed house—where "no gentlemen are admitted while the ladies are riding but their friends"—the women were instructed in the necessities of mounting, how to sit and hold the hands at all paces, the tack required for riding sidesaddle, how to arrange the petticoats while stationary and at speed, and how to elegantly dismount.[98] Women increasingly participated in riding for exercise and entertainment, but at no point were they instructed in any of the more advanced manège movements.[99] At no point did the language of female equestrianism allude to the firmly masculine performance or embodied co-becoming with the animal. For women, according to Carter, there could be no centaur status, no absolute perfection in human-animal communication. Instead, riding for a woman was ideally about grace, beauty, and ease—all quintessentially feminine attributes—which were made possible not necessarily by her expertise in the saddle, as with men, but by her horse.

While safety, elegance, and ease of travel were also important objectives when purchasing a mount for a man, with women these were the only objectives. A "horse intended for a lady's use, should be the most perfect of his kind, every point essential to her safety, ease, and elegant appearance, depends on it," Carter emphatically argued. The horse should have "spirit," "wind," "beauty," and "swiftness," but above all he should have "docility" and "steadiness." For the safety and ease of the rider, the horse must be "steady to mount," instant in his obeying of commands, and "not jarring" in his movement. He must be a joy to interact with and by nature careful of his rider; he must protect not only her appearance but also her physical self.[100] These animals, always to be expensive and well-bred horses (of mixed Arab, Persian, Barb, and Spanish pedigree, in keeping with fashionable breeding practices), were generally trained by Mr. Carter prior to being mounted by a lady, or by another horseman (sometimes in a lady's riding habit, to accustom the horse to flowing skirts that might otherwise spook him).[101]

Through this training, a lady's horse (usually a mare or a gelding rather than a stallion) was prepared for her role in the human-animal relationship, while also coming to embody the patriarchal power of the male trainer. Through training, the horse would learn obedience in a fashion similar to that espoused by Cavendish, but without the overt Hobbesian leanings. This obedience, and hence shared will to support whatever the rider wished, was further extended beyond the body of the rider by Carter. In this understanding of riding, the horse came to embody the will of the rider even when separated from her centauric other half. In this formulation, Mr. Carter's instruction and protection of ideal femininity on horseback transferred to the horse, who would in turn fulfill Carter's objectives. Here, the horse symbolically came to belong to the trainer, even though materially she may have belonged to the rider. According to Carter, women did not receive instruction in training their own horses during any stage of their education and were unable to establish their own mastery as centaur as a result. That is not to say that all women abided by Carter's attempt at gender control, but the behavioral and epistemological boundaries encompassing women's lived realities on horseback were part of a feminine ideal upheld within popular culture.

The ideal role of the patriarchal centauric man and the suitably delicate feminine equestrian is illustrated in the intricate *Mr. and Mrs. Thomas Coltman,* painted by the couple's friend Joseph Wright of Derby between 1770 and 1772 (fig. 13). In this image, the newly married pair are about to depart on a ride and seem to be in the midst of discussing their route for the day. Mrs. Coltman, in fashionable equestrian garb, is already mounted on her mare, while Mr. Coltman nonchalantly leans against his wife's leg while waiting for his charger to be brought to him.[102] Positioned at the center of the canvas, Mr. Coltman is immediately shown to be in a position of power over not only his wife but also the mare, the dog, the groom leading his horse, and the wider estate. The slight contrapposto positioning of his body, along with the possessive and domineering leaning on his wife and her mare illustrates Coltman's mastery over both human and equine subjects. There is no need for Coltman to be shown mounted in order to convey his status as a capable horseman secure in his skill; this is instead shown in his easy and relaxed mastery of his human and animal servants and partners. Even when seemingly doing nothing, he is still in complete and perfect control.

This easy control is also evident in the intimated product of Mr. Coltman's training—Mrs. Coltman's mare. The mare is the key to reading the gendered and power relations of the human and animal actors depicted. It is the mare who not only embodies the patriarchal training authority of the husband but ensures the continuing femininity of her rider and the contradictory, and species-crossing, role of the horse when mounted by a woman. The mare is painted by Wright in an uncharacteristic pose for most mounted equestrian portraiture of the period, with her right hind leg resting and head lowered.[103] This position connotes relaxation and unconcern in a somewhat chaotic environment composed of people, a potentially dangerous dog, and another horse (a stallion) approaching from behind, all distractions that many horses would notice. This almost exaggerated relaxation and unconcern speak directly to the disciplinary skill of her trainer (and also to her temperament, aligned with Carter's ideal). A horse that was excitable—as Mr. Coltman's apparently is (prancing and making the groom's job of leading him to his master difficult)—was potentially dangerous to his rider and required intense self-control and self-bridling on the rider's part and extensive training for the horse in the manège. The excitable horse was perfect for a man but entirely unsuitable for a woman. The mare, in contrast, is unflappable and at ease in her mastery over the dog, whom she is driving away from the young couple (she is

FIGURE 13 Joseph Wright, *Mr. and Mrs. Thomas Coltman*, 1770–72. The National Gallery, London. Bought with contributions from the National Heritage Memorial Fund and The Pilgrim Trust, 1984. Photo © The National Gallery, London.

clearly warning the dog to keep its distance through her pinned-back ears and direct eye contact).

As such, this mare does the double duty of embodying the protection and patriarchal dominance of Mr. Coltman and Mrs. Coltman's own determination to remain faithful, chaste, and devoted to her husband. In much the same way that a horse could manifest the internal qualities of his male rider through his behavior and obedience (or lack thereof) to his rider's aids, in *Mr. and Mrs. Thomas Coltman,* the ideal breeding and calmly obedient disposition of the mare directly reflects and protects similarly feminine qualities in her rider. Mrs. Coltman is the ideally feminine wife to an equally masculine husband. She is a "charming," "beautiful," and "delicate" practitioner of Carter's ideal horsemanship.

Such imagery and the equine embodiment of human characteristics and selfhood were similarly used by the anonymous artist of *The Favourite Footman, or Miss well Mounted* of 1778 (fig. 14). Taken directly from Wright's portrait of Mr. and Mrs. Coltman, this caricature mercilessly lampoons the ideal of feminine chastity and proper decorum made visible by that practitioner of Mr. Carter's equestrian ideals. Depicting an alternate relationship, and for some critics a much more truthful one, between women and animals, in this caricature Mr. Coltman has been replaced by a footman (the woman's apparent love interest), while Mrs. Coltman has been replaced by a woman who is gazing at her assistant not with tenderness and devotion but with a wanton smile. Similarly, Mrs. Coltman's mare has become the embodiment of the woman's innermost base desires instead of a cherished protector of virtue. The mare still has her head lowered, but now lowered in submission and invitation to the advances of the footman's stallion. Instead of looking to the cowering dog (symbolic of her desire, and in this image sitting at attention, ready to spring into action), the mare is shown with her ears forward, her gaze locked on the face of the footman's horse and her tail raised in sexual invitation. In this caricature, the woman is associated with the antithesis of ideally correct deportment and with untamed and unchecked animality. She, like many other women, wanted "to join the ranks of the horsey set through new modes of aspirational recreational riding," but instead of her actions being "validated" in print and in society (as was usually the norm), her lack of innate femininity—and the gendered moral transgressions it entailed—were exposed, found wanting, and judged by the truth-telling animal.[104] Thus, the woman's mare and her insistence on riding reaffirm the position of women as near to animals on the chain of being, so objectionably expressed by Burke.

This anonymous caricature, however, was not typical—like the original it lampooned—in its representation of unchaste female equestrianism. Instead, falls from normative femininity, secure social status, and chaste reputation were typically illustrated and discussed as literal falls from horseback. Falling from a horse instantly reaffirmed normative gender categories and behaviors for both men and women, and functioned to reassure social commentators worried by women who were actively pushing against their positioning, in relation not only to irrational brute being but also to masculine domination, that order had been reestablished. This may be one reason why Carter instructed his ladies behind closed doors and in a single-sex environment. If a woman did try to ride beyond her gender category (one method available to her for showing an intellect and rationality superior to those of her mount and of adopting male horsemanship methodologies and skills), she could enjoy "admiration and praise" from spectators if she performed her horsemanship well. However, by doing so she rode a fine line between admirable delicacy and skill and the potential for loss of femininity, destruction of her reputation, and suspicion of her morality.[105] If at any point she fell from her mount or encountered other problems in control, her credit and reputable virtue immediately became suspect. Carter, for example, tells the story of one female equestrian who declined the assistance of a helper when dismounting. Because of this breach in female decorum and reliance on patriarchal codes of behavior enshrined in the practice of dismounting, the woman was so "unfortunate as to dislocate her ancle and break her leg." The injured party, according to Carter, "desired this [incident] to be made public as a caution to others." Having ridden "upwards of thirty years without meeting with the least accident" (most probably by following Carter's instructions), this woman suffered bodily injury and, although Carter does not explicitly mention it, injury to her reputation as a genteel horsewoman, only when she dared to dismount without assistance.[106]

John Collet's *Soft Tumble after a Hard Ride* (1780) is another expressive example of riding and falling, while making visible the connotations of suspect female sexuality that Carter was too polite to mention but was seemingly well aware of (fig. 15). In this image, the man suggestively raises his lash whip toward the woman sprawled invitingly on the ground after tumbling from her horse during a sporting accident. She had cut "a ridiculous figure" in her riding habit and "had the misfortune to be thrown on her back," much like a "French Equestrian heroine" who captured the attention of the *Morning Post* on April 28, 1778, for riding each morning

FIGURE 14 *The Favourite Footman, or Miss well Mounted*, 1778. Photo courtesy of The Lewis Walpole Library, Yale University.

FIGURE 15
John Collet, *A Soft Tumble after a Hard Ride*, 1780. Photo: Yale Center for British Art, Paul Mellon Collection.

in Hyde Park in masculine style.[107] Riding, or an inability to ride, in this case, exposed both of these women's baser, animalistic instincts. Both had failed to procure suitable mounts and to bridle not only their horses but themselves. As Amanda Gilroy argues, mental and physical skill in control elevated some women over others of lower social status—who were thought unable to practice self-bridling—but also made visible their own internal worth.[108] Both women failed in this endeavor and were suggestively thrown on their backs as a result, one to be ridiculed in a national newspaper and the other to be associated with untamed sexual desire, symbolized by the hounds frolicking around her.

Like the spaniel that has attracted the ire of Mrs. Coltman's and the lady's mares, the dogs in Collet's euphemistic caricature are visual allusions to unchecked animalistic desires and passions (one of them is set to run up the fallen lady's titillatingly flowing skirts). However, unlike Collet's image, in which the sportsman's mare has also fallen, in a mirror image of his future rosy-cheeked conquest, or the satire on Wright's portrait, in which the mare enacts her mistress's desire, Mrs. Coltman's mare protects her rider from both "real" canine rambunctiousness and its connotations. Unlike women who attempted to contravene normative femininity codes and equestrian rules, to their physical, moral, status, and gendered cost, Mrs. Coltman adheres to normative and minimally subversive horsemanship practices, along with the accepted femininity and reliance on patriarchal systems. Even though she is an equestrian, she maintained her femininity alongside the delicacy, softness, and submissiveness of body advocated by Mr. Carter. She did not attempt to adopt male riding practices, and did not distance herself from her alliance with animals and their perceived shared limited rationality, intellect, and reliance on instinct. Mrs. Coltman remained a woman strong in her mastery of her mount and her gender, but secure in the protection offered by that same mount and by her husband.

Social convention dictated that women ride but that they do so in a manner that redoubled gender categorization and even enhanced their femininity. The epistemologies of the riding house and the ontologies of being on horseback reflected social anxiety about women as possible agents in the performance of their mastery over their own animalized selves, over animals as rational beings, and alternatively "masculine" femininities. Women were taught to interact with their mounts (themselves purposefully selected guardians of feminine delicacy) in a way that allowed for their control over brute being, while emphasizing the presence and continued power of the male trainer as patriarchal guardian of woman's physical and moral self. Like the sidesaddle, "a social machine for producing gender and for managing anxieties about masculinity and femininity during the very period in which modern gender difference was being formulated and then formalized," the horse also functioned as a highly mediated and man-made intermediary of social management that made visible the femininity—or its deviations and absences—of the rider, while allowing for the continued presence of masculine guardianship and control.[109]

ANGELO'S ACADEMY, SOHO SQUARE

Unlike Carter's female equestrians, elite horsemen in the Cavendish mold continued to perform the ceremonially spectacular haute école alongside the new masculine aesthetic in a somewhat contradictory mix of old- and new-school masculine display. An example of this comes from Claude

Bourgelat's *New System of Horsemanship,* translated by Berenger (1754), which provided English readers with the heavily edited teachings of their "illustrious Countryman, *William Cavendish,* Duke of *Newcastle*," who "has the highest Claim to our Praise and Acknowledgments," without the "Imperfections" of his work. For Berenger, in the translator's preface to the manual, "It would be needless to describe his [Cavendish's] Excellencies; his Character, as a Horseman," as they are "universally known, and universally admir'd. The Truth and Soundness of his Principles, and the Extensiveness of his Knowledge, have opened to us an easier, a shorter, and more certain Way to Perfection in the *Art,* than was known before." Indeed, "His Precepts have accordingly been adopted by all succeeding Professors, and his Writings consider'd as the Oracle of Horsemanship," even though "the *ornamental* Part [of horsemanship] . . . is not so requisite to be known: It can only be called an Accomplishment, and placed among the superflous but refin'd Pleasures of Life."[110] Now, there really was no practical use to the haute école or of ceremonial riding in tournaments, but this did not mean that it should be neglected by horsemen, especially elite horsemen of the community, whose position in it continued to be dictated by their proficiency in the art.

Henry Angelo, who again provides a useful example, records how he enjoyed an afternoon riding "*en cavalier*" with his friend the Chevalier d'Eon and his guest "Omai, the Otaheitan" (who arrived in London on July 1, 1774, from Tahiti aboard the *Adventure* after Cook's second voyage to the South Pacific), up the Oxford road in London.[111] Henry, who also enjoyed practicing leaping the bar in the common saddle as preparation for hunting, in this instance intentionally adopted the visual persona and riding habits of the seventeenth-century cavaliers, the riding habits of William Cavendish. Henry, d'Eon, and Omai, in doing so, intentionally placed themselves on public display as spectacle; they had "cocked hats, long-tailed horses, and *demi-queue* saddles" of the old style, and accoutered thus went on to "prance up" the road "to the delight of a number of lookers on." This particular outing did not end well for Omai, the inexperienced horseman of the group, whose horse "made a full stop" at the Pantheon and could not be persuaded "to move an inch forward. The horse's capers afforded much amusement to the people, although in action he was stationary the whole time, whilst we were hailed with shouts of laughter, D'Eon the whole time calling out to us in French." Henry found the situation as funny as the spectators did, and the telling of the tale "contributed very much to the amusement of my mother; not so of my father, who was angry with me for not telling him which rein to use"; "poor Omai," in contrast, was "trembling from head to foot" by the end of the ride.¹¹²

Henry's amusing anecdote is loaded with Orientalist imagery—the inept, fearful, innocent, and inelegantly Other, Omai—but it also provides a unique insight into gentlemanly display and public performances of the self during the late eighteenth century.¹¹³ These three gentlemen were seemingly not ridiculed for attempting to show themselves *en cavalier,* as one would expect in light of the new horsemanship aesthetic, but for the failure of that display. They paraded in the Cavendish mode (not walking or trotting but *en passage*), and performed the associated masculine traits of self-command, ceremony, honor, and militarism that traditionally accompanied such riding. However, even though Omai was apparently doing fine on one of Angelo's impeccably trained horses, and was described by Frances Burney as having an "appearance & behaviour *politely easy, & thoroughly well bred*" when in society, the decision of a nonhuman to refuse the inexperienced and incorrect communication from Omai managed to make all three men, two of whom were accomplished horsemen, into public figures of derision.¹¹⁴ They became, Omai most of all for his lack of manège schooling and Oriental Otherness, figures similar to the "Buck & Blood Flourishing Macaroni" and "black man at Charing Cross." Their intentional and, according to the new horsemanship community, useless performance of the manège as a parade designed to draw in the approving gaze of an audience was betrayed yet again by the truth-telling abilities of the horse.

However, it does not seem that Henry suffered socially because of their outing (there is no record of d'Eon's or Omai's response); Henry's horsemanship training, and presumably his continued mastery over his own mount as an elegantly refined gentleman, even when dealing with someone else's difficulty in riding, seems to have protected him from any negative effects of the public's laughter. For him, it is more than likely that the admiring gazes experienced prior to the horse's decision more than outweighed any subsequent bruises to his reputation. For him, and for other horsemen of the old school, ornamental horsemanship of the Cavendish model should be sought out, practiced, and perfected, and the sure way of doing so was through the rapidly expanding collection of academies springing up around London during the first half of the eighteenth century.

Like the Royal Academy for Teaching Exercises in Edinburgh (founded in 1763 and patronized by the gentry, upper aristocracy, and the king), these academies served to instill in their pupils "the principles of useful knowledge and at the same time exercised [them] in all these liberal accomplishments which qualify a man to appear in the distinguished spheres of Life."[115] They served as institutions where the elite came to learn normative masculinity (politeness, sentiment, honor, and military capability) from masters of horsemanship proven in their abilities and social connections. Also, it was these horsemen who successfully avoided "base effeminacy" through their interspecies and civic discourse, and who would provide an ideal worthy of emulation—much like Mr. Coltman. According to Berenger, "Such long has been the state of horsemanship in this kingdom; but since the accession of his present Majesty, the prospect has brightened, and better times begin to dawn. Since this happy event, the *Art* has raised itself a little, and given some signs of recovery; public riding-houses have been opened, which are largely encouraged, and frequented by the youth of the nation: many are *called,* and it is to be hoped, *many* will be *chose*[*n*]."[116] The governors of the nation, it was hoped, would follow the illustrious examples set by the equestrian-minded "Princes of the blood, the Nobility and Gentry; and his Majesty," who all dedicated vast amounts of time and wealth to the art, and who provided "Maneges" for the benefit of the socially worthy. These individuals, especially George III, who "cultivates, protects, and honours the Art, in so distinguished a manner," were "illustrious examples," the following of which would cause a revival of the "golden age of horsemanship," where those who lived the mixing of the centaur would cultivate civic feeling, ensure the safety and prosperity of the nation, create politely refined men who possessed friendly sentiments toward their fellow man, and, above all, again entice the elite to the noble and manly art of horsemanship. However, in a time of increased egalitarianism in society, the old-school riding academies remained sites of social and epistemological stratification where group self-regulation resulted in a continual shuffling of position.[117] Academies were the physical spaces for the horsemanship community where the lessons of the horsemanship manuals could be taught, and, like Cavendish's, Berenger's required young riders to go through a process of group-sanctioned inclusion in the community's ranks. Academies opened by true horsemen should be encouraged and frequented by the "youth of the nation," but though "many are called" to the practice because of the horsemen's bewitching abilities to discourse, to appear as one with the noble beast, only a select few would be "chose[n]" as suitable members of the elite group.

The most famous academy along these lines was founded and managed by Henry's father, Angiolo Domenico Maria Tremamondo (1717–1802), or

Domenico Angelo, as he was popularly known in England. Angelo was among the top horsemen of his day, having studied under "the celebrated master of equitation, Talligori, the most scientific horseman in Europe," and having been a pupil (along with the Chevalier d'Eon) of François Robichon de La Guérinière (the avid admirer of Cavendish). Better known today as the preeminent fencing master of his time, Angelo was master of horse for Henry Herbert, tenth Earl of Pembroke, at his Wilton estates and London townhouse, and was the master of his own academy at Carlisle House, Soho Square, where he taught horsemanship of the haute école and manège. According to Henry, whose *Reminiscences* provide scholars with most of the information concerning the Angelo family, Angelo "had been educated with care, and at vast expence," and his father had provided "masters to teach him those accomplishments which were common to the forming a well-bred gentleman of the last age; hence, it was a general observation, in speaking of the elder Angelo, that he was quite the gentleman of the old school." He was an expert, as Cavendish was, in the military arts. He regularly taught the royal princes and the boys of Eton to fence, hosted a famously hospitable table, and most important, was a horseman in the truest sense.[118]

These men, and the men under Angelo's care, were instructed in two methods of riding: the "style of riding the '*great horse*,' as practised according to the system of the continent," or the "old school," and that of the new horsemanship community.[119] This mixed instruction reflects not only a generational gap (Henry, not his father, practiced leaping at the bar) but also a clear hierarchy of equestrian proficiency and horsemanship artistry. Like Mr. Carter, who ensured that his pupils and readers knew about his Versailles equestrian instruction in the haute école while proceeding to teach in the common and sidesaddle, Angelo's continental equestrian heritage was requisite for his reputation as a master of horsemanship and able instructor in both the haute école and the leaping bar. Angelo practiced a horsemanship system that came from non-English schools, and, mirroring what Thomas Blundeville did for Federico Grisone in the sixteenth century, he (re)popularized a form of equestrian expression and personal display that had struggled through the Stuart Restoration and early Hanoverian reign of the first two Georges. He imported the teachings of his own Italian instructor but married these practices with the great English masters of the haute école.

Another one of Henry's anecdotes provides a good example of this mixture. At the invitation of George III to show his horse, Monarch, Angelo

FIGURE 16
John Kay, *Angelo Tremamondo, Riding Master*, 1788. Photo courtesy of The Lewis Walpole Library, Yale University.

rode him first in the continental tradition and then in the anglicized Cavendish tradition. "The king was pleased to express his satisfaction; talked of the manner of riding in the tournament, and of the style of riding the 'great horse,' as represented in the splendid folio work, by the Duke of Newcastle, published in the time of Charles the First. My father, who was ardent in the pursuit of knowledge, had studied these things with the most sedulous attention, . . . [and] could exhibit every style," of riding, including that of Cavendish, and proceeded to do so for the king's enjoyment. Displaying himself as an elite member of society and of the equestrian community, along with the superior stature of his equine partner, Angelo presented the horsemanship of his academy, which led the king to declare Angelo (if we are to believe the self-congratulatory memoir in which Henry recorded the event) "the most elegant horseman of his day" (1:35–36). As John Kay's portrait of Angelo (fig. 16) shows, Angelo looked to seventeenth-century horsemanship traditions, not to the popular eighteenth-century models practiced by Thompson, Jackson, Hughes, Astley, and Carter, in order to display elegance, manliness, and accomplishment. He looked to the tall-booted, long-tailed, *appui*-loving, and *levade*-practicing horsemanship of the seventeenth-century sovereigns.

It was these accomplishments that Angelo passed on to the next generation of horsemen. What Berenger hoped would be the outcome of building all of the new academies, that "we may expect to see the golden age of horsemanship revive," Angelo attempted to bring to fruition. "In the arts of riding and fencing," according to Henry, the elder Angelo "was long at the head of his profession, and, by his skill in both, brought them into general adoption, as necessary branches of education" (2:64). Angelo and his academy upheld the older forms of gentlemanly behavior and display in the face of their increasingly unstable masculinity. It was through his academy and personal influence as a horseman that Angelo ensured the popularization of equestrian pursuits—at least according to his flattering son—while ensuring that the young riders gained the social graces necessary for their position in life. As Henry summarized:

> At the time my father resided in Carlisle-street, young men of fashion boarded there, where riding, fencing, and dancing, were included in the terms, one hundred guineas per annum; an adequate sum then, (fifty years ago). In addition to these necessary accomplishments to give the exterior of the gentleman, he was ever attentive to their manners. Numerous advantages they must have derived, being in company often with some of the first characters of the day, whom his table was always open to. Those boarders who at first were, "*les ours mal léché*," unlicked cubs, returned home, both in *manière* and deportment far different to the present race of dandyism, where bows, &c. &c., are exploded, their *address* keeping pace with their *dress*. (2:62–63)

For Henry, both elements of a gentleman's education, sartorial simplicity and spectacular horsemanship, were ensured by multispecies relationships and heterosocial interaction within the confines of the academy. Taught through the spectacular format of horsemanship and the visible display of interspecies interaction and physical ability at Angelo's, young riders learned to conform to the sartorial regime that dictated an austere masculine aesthetic. Through the luxurious horsemanship and personal display caricatured in *The Lucky Mistake* and *Sunday Equestrians* but enacted by Cavendish, the pupils learned gentlemanly deportment that insulated them from the accusations of effeminacy, foppishness, or dandyism so worrying for the health of the nation.

BECOMING CENTAUR

RIDING HOUSE SOCIABILITY

As Henry intimates, Angelo's Academy was home to the best that London society had to offer. The Sheridan and Garrick families, the Duke of Cumberland, the Duke of York, the Duke of Gloucester, Johann Sebastian Bach, Carl Abel, George Stubbs, George III, Benjamin West, John Wilkes, the Chevalier d'Eon, the Marquess of Granby, Joshua Reynolds, Thomas Rowlandson, Thomas Gainsborough, Captain Francis Grose, and James Barry were just some of his pupils and friends on a very long list of acquaintances whom Angelo hosted at his academy. As Henry remarked, "His house was the common rendezvous of all the ingenious, his compeers, of every country, and every profession; and, at his well-appointed table, I became acquainted with many great, good, and eminent men, whose memory I cannot cease to think of but with reverential fondness and respect" (1:6–7). The gathering place of musicians, artists, politicians, royalty, and actors, Angelo's Academy not only educated the sons of the elite but provided a space where members could come and socialize, much like the London tearooms, clubs, and coffeehouses—themselves favorite haunts of Henry as he grew up.

This was especially evident in that the pupils and family friends were frequently guests at the supper table as well as in the manège. Henry described in his memoirs many evenings spent in conversation while eating Mrs. Elizabeth (Johnson) Angelo's famously delicious macaroni with some of the most notable men in London society. Angelo had "a constant chamber for the evening *conversazione* with his numerous friends," including Garrick, "the celebrated patriot, John Wilkes, and the scarcely less well-known personage, Chevalier D'Eon." "These, with the elder Sheridan, frequently sat for hours over the bottle, in lengthened arguments upon the politics of the day" (1:55, 60, 189). Angelo's Academy, in a fashion similar to the coffeehouses, was a neutral space where men openly debated and encouraged divergent political beliefs, but regardless of the diversity of men who frequented it, Angelo's was also the home of the same stereotypes that created the macaroni craze in the 1770s.[120] In the academy, unlike popular culture outside it, macaroni eating, the embrace of everything continental, and the espousal of conspicuous display were means of developing authentic masculinity and an ideal social reputation.[121] The men at Angelo's were the same ones caricatured in *The Lucky Mistake,* the ones who sported continental tastes, engaged in continental consumption, and practiced continental horsemanship; and it was at Angelo's Academy that manly, courageous, honorable, and usefully polite horsemanship was practiced in a mixed arena, where the lines between domestic and public instruction spaces were blurred. Such mixing allowed the academy to become an ideal location in which gentlemen came to ensure their development of not only strong, athletic, sensitive, controlled, and refined bodies but also of politeness or ease of conversation and the manners necessary for urban gentlemen.

Like these mixed social spaces, the grand London riding houses were sites for the gathering and socializing of men and women from the social elite.[122] While the women at Angelo's did not ride, it seems, they were an integral component of masculine competition and personal display, as it was their gaze (disapproving or appreciative) that was sought after by the men of the manège. Placed in the viewing gallery, the ladies could listen and watch the lessons while training their knowledgeable equestrian eye to see the variances in riding ability on display and judge the riders' (physical and moral) abilities. One man who took full advantage of this feminine gaze was Captain Riddle, one of Angelo's "best riders" and an officer in the cavalry, whom Henry described as "an elegant young man, of affable disposition." According to Henry, "Whenever the gallery . . . was crowded, he was always ready to exhibit his equestrian manoeuvres," and on at least one occasion he had "promised" Angelo "that he would bring some ladies to the riding" (2:358–59). This was not to introduce them to riding itself—nowhere in his *Reminiscences* does Henry mention ladies participating in the manège, further distancing Angelo's Academy from other riding houses—but to introduce them as sounding boards against which the men would try out their performances of masculine riding. At Angelo's, mirroring the influence of women in the production of politeness, men partially established their masculinity through a knowledgeable feminine gaze. Like the scarlet-coated dandy of Hyde Park introduced at the beginning of this chapter, Riddle intentionally made a spectacle of himself before the perceptive gaze of women, but unlike the Hyde Park madman astride a cow, he apparently possessed the horsemanship abilities to make such displays admirably masculine rather than comically foppish. The Hyde Park equestrian rode every Sunday, rented a horse to do so, and sat like a sack (if his caricature is anything to go by); Riddle, in contrast, was an accomplished horseman who performed his polite, refined, and manly horsemanship before those who could judge it.

As Cohen argues, eighteenth-century social spaces, such as coffeehouses, great houses, theaters, gardens, public squares, and tearooms were "spaces for the mixed company of the sexes, since their conversation was one of the conditions for the refinement and self-improvement at the heart of politeness." These spaces allowed for the feminine conversation so necessary for civil men; conversation could soften and refine men's natural tendency to roughness, ungraciousness, and brutality in language and behavior, and as a result produce refined and polite men suitable for public life.[123] Time spent socializing with women would lead men to "further temper their conversation to avoid performances which, though perhaps acceptable in male-only company, would offend in mixed and, hence, polite society." Many also hoped that socializing in female company would result in the men's adopting some of the polite and more sensitive attributes of the fairer sex.[124] However, as an excess of refinement and politeness could result in luxury, uselessness, effeminacy, and foppishness—our Hyde Park candidate—men also understood that homosocial conversation and participation in more "traditionally" masculine pursuits were necessary in conjunction with female company.[125]

Other riding houses, however—like the majority of London's homosocial clubs and associations—excluded women entirely.[126] For example, Sir Sidney Meadows, another eminent horseman of his time (if unorthodox for his high hand positioning) and a onetime riding master at the academy in Geneva, Switzerland, was equal to Angelo in equestrian ability and served as a consultant to the Royal Academy in Edinburgh.[127] His own riding house in London was a desirable establishment for the practice of gentlemanly sociability, and while Meadows's riding house was a community space similar to Angelo's Academy, Meadows did not, unlike Angelo (a professional instructor), it seems, charge tuition. For him, the inclusion of his pupils in his horsemanship court and the instruction of them there was strictly by invitation, in accordance with acceptable behavior for one of his rank, like Cavendish before him. Henry recorded his experiences under the guidance of the great horseman as a child: While still "under my father's tuition," Henry received an offer for instruction from Meadows. Although he was already receiving instruction from a man who modeled by royal command for the figure of "King William" in Benjamin West's *Battle of the Boyne* (because "'few painters place the figure properly upon the horse, and Angelo is the finest horse-man in the world'"), Meadows's invitation "was too great an honour not to be accepted." The opportunity to join "the first amateur of equitation . . . [of] the last century" was too advantageous for Henry's social position and community status to forego (1:35–36). At Meadows's riding house, Henry could join the nobility that gathered every morning to hear the master speak, and he could engage in the enlightening conversation common among the riders. Meadows "usually . . . was visited by plenty of the nobility at his riding-house, where he constantly, every morning, took his exercise; nor, whilst riding, did it prevent his affability and lively conversation, which was much listened to, and as much admired as the command and management he had over his horses: if not an elegant rider, his knowledge may have been superior to others. His house was at the corner of Bolton-street, Piccadilly" (2:140–41). Henry's riding house experiences, under his father and Meadows, followed the maxims of the "manly . . . ancient nobility and gentry," who were "rough, bold, and handy to pursue the sports in the field, or wield the spear and battle axe against the enemies of their country," as a piece in the March 1771 issue of *Town and Country Magazine* put it, yet able to correspond with women and their mounts as polite and honorable gentlemen.[128]

However, even as Angelo's Academy was at heart one of the old-school horsemanship establishments, it was also firmly moving toward a new era in which horsemanship instruction was seen as a business, as a more egalitarian pursuit available to both men and women of all classes to enjoy at their leisure. Angelo's pupils were required to pay "sufficient" tuition, and while most of them were of elite status (he taught the royal princes to ride and George III to fence, for instance), this was not always the case. Angelo grudgingly accepted at the insistence of his wife, who was friends with Catherine Hyde, Duchess of Queensbury, the duchess's black servant, Julius Soubise, into his academy in order to teach him the arts of riding and fencing.[129] A controversial figure at the best of times, it was feared that Soubise's inclusion in the riding house would not be a welcome event for the other pupils. As Henry recalled, "At this time our house had many inmates, as I have mentioned before, the sons of persons of rank, with all whom Soubise was a great favourite. Indeed, so far from what my father had feared, that his colour and humble birth might have made him repulsive to his high-born pupils, on the contrary, these circumstances seemed to excite a greater interest in his favour" (1:448–49). Oddly enough, contrary to Angelo's fears, the pupils welcomed Soubise with open arms, an event that evidences how far horsemanship as an art had traveled from the closely guarded confines of the seventeenth-century horsemanship community. Even in an establishment that prided itself on old-school instruction at the heart of a gentleman's education, no longer was the manège reserved for the titled elite. Nor was it solely reserved as a gentlemanly pursuit of honorable status. Soubise, Mrs. Coltman, and even the madman astride a cow were just some of the many men and women who started to enter the horsemanship community, slowly redefining what it meant to be a horseman. Although his instruction at Angelo's proved corrupting for Soubise (according to Henry, it was at the academy that he unfortunately and "suddenly changed his manners, and became one of the most conspicuous fops of the town," only to be thrown out for his transgressions [1:449]), life at Angelo's was the making of other men. Philip Astley was the most famous, influential, and controversial of these men, and it is to him that we now turn.

3.

ASTLEY'S AMPHITHEATRE

He stands unrivalled,—"a creature by himself."

—POSTER, JAMES COOKE'S ROYAL ARENA

Sometime in late May or early June 1788, General George Elliot, first Baron Heathfield, gave his Arabian charger to a man who had previously served with him in the Seven Years' War.[1] As a "Serjean [sic] Major in his Majesty's Royal Regiment of Light Dragoons, commanded by Lieu. General Elliot," Philip Astley was not a likely candidate for such a gift.[2] He was not titled, rich, or even literate (if the rumors are true); instead, Philip Astley was the owner, manager, and lead performer of Astley's Amphitheatre, Westminster Bridge. Begun in 1768 as a venue for the performance of vaulting, the Amphitheatre, by the 1780s, was a well-established minor theater that specialized in a veritable "hodge-podge" of entertainments. "Dear, dear, what a place it looked, that Astley's; with all the paint, gilding, and looking-glass; the vague smell of horses suggestive of coming wonders; the curtain that hid such gorgeous mysteries," wrote Charles Dickens.[3] For Dickens, Astley's Amphitheatre was a place of wonder, childish delight, and sparkling mystery not to be missed. There one could see "rope-dancing, singing, pantomime, wire-dancing, the warbling of birds, . . . women vaulting on the slack rope, imitations of hounds, organs, and dying wild boars, stage-dancing, buffoonery, mimicry, and agility of all kinds." At the Amphitheatre, you could listen to the music, allowing "the eye and the ear" to be "amused by an incessant variety" of the strange and wondrous, while being transported away to the realm of magic and surprise.[4] But, after all, it was "the vague smell of horses," not the singing of birds or the smell of the sawdust in the ring, that suggested coming wonders for Dickens, and while all manner of life could be viewed at the Amphitheatre, the horses were the true stars of the show.

One of the Amphitheatre's greatest stars was the Gibraltar Charger, who enjoyed immediate celebrity status after his entrance into the Amphitheatre's performance program. He was the headlining act for the entire 1788 season, and his performances were so popular that one commentator projected that they would net Astley more than a thousand pounds in profit (the equivalent of roughly eighty thousand pounds today).[5] The Charger's first public appearance came "a few days" after Elliott presented him to Astley, and was carefully timed to coincide with the celebrations for George III's birthday on June 4. To commemorate the occasion, Astley devised a new fireworks display, something he did most years, though this one was more ambitious than any he had designed before. Consisting of seven "Division[s]," the fireworks illuminated various patriotic and royal images. Beginning with "A Vertigal Sun," and by division progressively adding more complex, ornate, and emblematic figures, the fireworks concluded with "a Ballustrade, $7^{1/2}$ feet long, illuminated and composed of Pedestals, Garlands, and the Emblems of Peace, supporting the gallery of Potfires, Sheaves, and Roman Candles, with six Fans in Chinese Fire, supported by Pedestals, between which will be six fixed Suns. At each end o' the Ballustrade, a grand Lustre and Potfire, and in the middle VIVAT.G.III. illuminated with Stars, and terminated by a display of Flying Fuzees, representing the Prince of Wales's Plume."[6] While pyrotechnic displays from previous years had been larger and more expensive, this time, "nothing could exceed the brilliancy of the fireworks exhibited" on the Thames, and no other celebratory "illumination" could boast the presence of an animal so unique or "courageous."[7]

The fireworks were situated on a series of barges anchored in the middle of the Thames directly before Westminster Bridge, and, as Astley needed to be close to "Messers. Cabonell and Son," the men he had hired to light the fireworks, so that they could see his "different signals" telling them when to do so, he was "placed in a barge in the front of the line." While this was not unusual, what was unique is that Astley directed the entire display while mounted on the Gibraltar Charger.[8] This was surprising enough, but what really made the Charger's presence unique was that as the fireworks were lit, it was reported that he was frequently and unconcernedly "entirely covered with fire."[9] This astonishing feat was massively popular with the audience and was immediately adopted into the Amphitheatre program itself. Throughout the 1788 season, the Charger and Astley performed the same fireworks display in miniature. In these performances, either the Charger appeared "through a Shower of Fire" or the two together would perform surrounded by a "Chain of Fire," while Astley "will salute the audience with an Olive Branch in Fire Works."[10]

What did these performances with a horse mean at a time when Britain's military might had been sorely tested (and found wanting) in the American War of Independence, a time of social and political anxiety marked by public debates about effeminacy and radical politics?[11] When Astley held his fireworks display in June 1788, Britain was in the middle of a constitutional crisis caused, in part, by King George's declining health. While the king had been ill for some time, he suddenly took a turn for the worse, and Parliament feared that he was now completely incapable of continuing his rule. The resulting discussions revolved around whether Parliament should continue to govern the nation without a monarch, or whether the Prince of Wales should be invited to sit as regent with limited power. Coupled with this crisis of national stability, already exacerbated by Britain's earlier, destabilizing defeats in America, were ever louder rumblings over the social unrest in France, rumblings that were to culminate on July 14, 1789, in the storming of the Bastille.[12]

With this context in mind, in this chapter I expand on the diversification of horsemanship schools, forms of masculinity, and associated political allegiances in order to investigate the significance of the various performances of the Gibraltar Charger with Philip and John Astley at Astley's Amphitheatre. This chapter explores what an immensely popular minor theater, a theater not licensed for spoken plays that functioned outside the Lord Chamberlain's censorship for much of its history, was saying about national politics through the bodies of its performers.[13] It also questions how the Amphitheatre's performers negotiated shifting codes of masculinity at a time when military men were found wanting, while examining the complexities of gendered performance and equestrian publications in a theatrical environment. How were horse-human interaction and Cavendish's centaurism understood, experienced, and performed at the Amphitheatre, and how were horse-human relationships influenced by a very Astleyan concept of both "horse" and "human"?

The Amphitheatre became the home of popular horsemanship and the "rememorations," to use Daniel O'Quinn's term, of national and international events designed to further a clearly patriotic understanding of beneficial gendered display.[14] In the Amphitheatre, as in theater in general, the stage "operates both as a separate space subject to its own laws, and also as an extension of the everyday." It is a place where the "performances of everyday life are themselves re-performed, and in the process changed" into something greater, something spectacular.[15] In the Amphitheatre, I suggest, the everyday—both past and present—was re-performed as a means of instructing the audience and the nation in ideal masculinities, masculinities that were at once in keeping with wider understandings of normative gendered display within the many London riding houses, while also highly exaggerated and spectacularized in form. Furthering the commercial civic-humanist discourse discussed in the previous chapter, and in the interest of promoting masculinities that would ensure the continued success and stability of English society at the Amphitheatre, soldiers were heroes, circus performers were celebrity soldiers, and astonishingly uncanny horses were the mediums through which it was all made possible. For Philip Astley, their display consisted of highly militaristic chivalry grounded in the reenactment of his and his horse's military history in a dual-species recollection of Britain's glorious past. For his son, John, beneficial masculinity was a more androgynous affair, consisting of the enactment of politeness so valued at Angelo's riding house alongside refinement, grace, and physical strength. Together, horses and humans of the Amphitheatre performed "Manly Exercises, With the Horse, from the Horse, and on the Horse."[16]

ASTLEY'S

Astley's Amphitheatre, according to scholarly consensus, was the first modern circus. An establishment to which most other circuses in England, Ireland, France, Russia, and America could trace their origins, the Amphitheatre at Westminster Bridge catered to a mixed audience of all genders and classes.[17] Immensely popular, Astley's was the first entertainment venue of its kind, while its owner and manager was the first horseman of his kind. Specializing in equestrian entertainment and feats of trick riding, especially early in his career, Philip Astley began the Amphitheatre with performances traditionally more at home in pub yards and fairgrounds. While he was not the first trick rider in London, where there was a rich history of such entertainment prior to his interest in the activity, Astley was nevertheless the first rider of any sort to take the usual cordoned-off area suitable for riding lessons or training and fence it in so that only paying spectators could enjoy the performance. He was the first to stage public equestrian performances as a commercial business, and he certainly was successful in doing so. Astley had erected nineteen amphitheaters in Britain and Europe by the time of his death in 1814, including the Olympic Pavilion (opened in 1806) and the Amphithéâtre d'Astley in Paris (opened 1783), where his troupe spent their winters prior to the outbreak of the French Revolution.[18] Like Mr. Carter and many other enterprising horsemen of the eighteenth century, Astley was a businessman, but unlike any of his contemporaries, he combined horsemanship languages and practices with the masculinities of different classes and equestrian traditions to create a theater tradition that was entirely new.

Astley's Amphitheatre (also at various times called Astley's Riding School, the Royal Grove, and Amphitheatre of the Arts, among other names) was one of the first and preeminent illegitimate theaters in London. Unlike the patent theaters of Covent Garden and Drury Lane, illegitimate theaters were not permitted under London's theater-licensing acts to stage legitimate forms of drama (such as Shakespearean plays) or drama with spoken parts. Illegitimate theaters were known instead for the sheer variety of entertainment on offer and the amazing generic mixing such entertainment provided.[19] Astley's Amphitheatre, which was often advertised as leading the vanguard for the new and unique, continually incorporated novelty acts, theater, other traditional circus acts, and clowning into its program, which was itself continually altered to cater to audience demand—sometimes as frequently as once a week. A typical show, lasting up to five hours, was simply described as "a hodge-podge" by one reviewer. At Astley's, an audience could expect to see everything from the Learned Pig—the most famous animal on the London stage for a time—humans with "unnatural" physicalities or deformities, such as the Monstrous Craws and their goiters, who played a few nights at Astley's while on their tour of entertainment venues in the capital, athletic trick riding and vaulting (the primary claim to fame for Astley and the only acts he performed in the first year of his Amphitheatre), and even, in the late eighteenth and into the nineteenth century, grand equestrian spectacles, or hippodramas.[20]

Immensely popular, illegitimate theaters were frequented by spectators from all walks of life. Often considered "miniature parliament[s] of the nation," as Jane Moody argues, "this social inclusiveness also endowed [their] dramatic performance with a special kind of influence and power."[21] They were sites of generic upheaval and redefinition, institutions that blurred the demarcation between legitimate and illegitimate forms of entertainment (especially since performers and performances appeared in both theatrical environs), and places eminently situated to engage with the period's many, often controversial social debates.

However, while many illegitimate theaters could boast a similar theatricality, influence, and diversity, Astley's Amphitheatre was not a space entirely dedicated to the stage. Instead, it was a strangely hybrid establishment that merged the more traditional forms of horsemanship instruction found in London's riding houses with popular entertainment. Emerging directly from the schools of horsemanship discussed in the previous chapter, specifically from Angelo's Academy, Astley's did double duty as one of London's many riding houses when not preoccupied with stage productions or rehearsals.

Domenico Angelo, while seemingly focused on the old-school spectacle and self-display inherent in horsemanship practice, did at times emphasize the purely practical side of riding. He, along with the Duke of Pembroke, took a lively interest in the reformation of the English cavalry, an activity that Astley himself spent a great deal of effort to achieve. Apparently suffering from incorrect training methods, to the detriment of the troops, horses, and the army in general, the cavalry's institutional ills inspired Pembroke to publish his manual of horsemanship and Angelo "to introduce a new and superior method of riding." As Henry Angelo remembered, "This was a favourite object with [his father], even to a late period of life—one, indeed, which was recommended by some of the first military characters of the age, to the attention of the Government, which, though admitting its utility, never could be persuaded to adopt it." Such setbacks did not deter Angelo, however, and he sought out men whom he could instruct in his superior methods as examples of how beneficial his teachings would be if the nation's cavalry units would adopt them. "This, I may be permitted to remark, is the more extraordinary," Henry wrote, "as my father had made several experiments, by selecting certain men from two or more cavalry regiments, whom he instructed gratuitously, and whose superior skill in the management of the horse, consequently, was sufficiently manifest to procure them applause, from every master of equitation in the kingdom." Taken from "Elliot's light horse," or the Fifteenth Regiment of Light Dragoons, which was at the time under the command of Pembroke as lieutenant colonel, these were not socially elite men.[22] They were not titled, wealthy, or brought up to horsemanship from childhood, and in general they were not the men who usually frequented Angelo's Academy.

Henry considered his father's experiments unusual and, unlike his thoughts toward Julius Soubise, whom he seemed to think was eminently respectable regardless of his background and ethnicity, was worried about the inclusion of lower-class men in the academy. Regardless, the elder Angelo's decision to instruct such men, to make them examples of ideal military and equestrian training, gave Astley the equestrian education necessary for both his subsequent stint in the Fifteenth Light Dragoons and his later career in the Amphitheatre. Eventually becoming his regiment's "rough rider, teacher, and breaker," after Angelo's instruction, Astley absorbed the teachings of the manège and haute école while making a few riding experiments of his own in preparation for the stage.[23] As the titular character at his Amphitheatre, he was a quintessential social climber from an environment that allowed for "unparalleled social mobility." Self-styled a "Professeur d'Equitation," Astley frequently displayed the arms of the French monarchy on his tunic—he was given the right by royal ordinance in 1782—and enjoyed the patronage and friendship of some of the greatest nobles and celebrities in England and Europe.[24] His experiences at Angelo's Academy, along with the patronage and seeming friendship of Pembroke and the Duke of York, introduced Astley to the elite London horsemanship community. However, unlike other horsemen before him, Astley was not interested in establishing a history or lineage of equestrian practice. Breaking from tradition, he never advertised his time at Angelo's or under any other instructor of horsemanship. Instead, he developed his own form of equestrian practice and performances at the Amphitheatre that were the result of his personal experiences as a military man.

At the beginning of his career, Astley's horsemanship and allegiances were closer to the discourses found in the new-school horsemanship manuals than to those of Angelo or Cavendish. In the first manual he wrote, in 1775, Astley did not aim to teach the manège or haute école, nor did he attempt to perform either practice onstage. Instead, his work was expressly practical in its simplicity. However, as his career progressed, he did cross over into the manège horsemanship community and associated language, or attempted to at any rate. Much of his career was spent in the middle ground between the "common" horsemanship community and that of the manège, practicing "His Method between the Jockey & Manage" "particular to himself" alone.[25] Pointing to an interesting correlation between celebrity status, horsemanship practice, and textual production, it was not until his much later publication, *Astley's System of Equestrian Education* (1801), that Astley, by now internationally famous, provided horsemen with a manual that closely resembled those by horsemen of the seventeenth century or those of the manège community who followed.[26]

However, the manège was not what initially interested Astley. He was not content to perform either the jockey or the manège onstage; instead, he turned to a more common, vulgar form of riding that allowed for the exhibition of the dangerous and courageous self so necessary to his performance of masculinity. Astley looked to the tradition of vaulting for inspiration. Closely associated with the itinerant vagabonds, acrobats, dancers, tumblers, and charlatans who worked with learned horses, vaulting was a popular component of the many English fairgrounds of the seventeenth and eighteenth centuries.[27] On the surface, vaulting was not readily associated with any performance of idealized masculinity, and it was certainly not associated with exceptional skill on horseback necessary for a man self-styled a professor of equitation. By the time Astley had obtained his discharge from Elliot's dragoons on June 21, 1766, however, vaulting was gaining notoriety as a potentially lucrative endeavor. The act of vaulting was practiced with "great success" by three "famous men" of the time, "namely, Price, Johnson, and Old Sampson, who had been exhibiting at the Three Hats, Islington, and other places round and quite contiguous to the heart of the Metropolis," according to Jacob Decastro, a comedian at Astley's Amphitheatre for a time.[28] Johnson, the Tartar, first performed his "dexterity in riding" in London in 1758 at the Three Hats with Mr. and Mrs. Sampson, who later moved to the Globe Inn, Whitechapel, while Thomas Price performed vaulting at nearby D'Aubigny's pub starting in 1767.[29] Astley heard about their feats of vaulting while still in the army under Elliot, and he immediately resolved to "become a rival to them all" upon his discharge. Once he arrived back in London, Decastro recalled, he sought them out and "studiously endeavoured to glean from them all their superior methods of teaching and breaking, and was not long before he was able to commence his career as a public equestrian, and rival of theirs."[30] The itinerant and lower-class practices of public equestrianism, trick riding, and vaulting interested Astley, not the careful control of the manège and the strict behavioral codes of the Angelo riding house. He wanted to make money in public performance, and he could not readily do so, at least at the outset, with an elite horsemanship practice. His manège and his horsemanship were, he avowed, the start of a new tradition and horsemanship methodology designed for the use, entertainment, and improvement of the nation.

Astley was cognizant, however, of the negative connotations attached to such equestrianism and to itinerant performances in general, those "monstrous medlies" feared for their corrupting influence on social morals and theatrical integrity.[31] As a result, and as a component of his own ongoing desire for legitimation as a serious performer rather than a simple fairground hack, Astley was careful to include an eminently respectable origin story for his knowledge of vaulting. In this instance, Astley looked well beyond the horsemanship greats of the previous century to the horsemen and historians of the classical world. Astley looked to Pope's translation of Homer's *Iliad* for this history: "when a Horseman from the wat'ry mead, / (Skill'd in the manage of the bounding steed) / Drives Four fair Coursers practic'd to obey, / To some great city thro' the public way," he is "Safe in his art, as side by side they run." As the horses race through the town, the horseman "shifts his seat, and vaults from one to one; / And now to this, and now to that he flies, / Admiring numbers follow with their eyes!"[32] This was Astley's version of vaulting history, and it allowed him to tie the dubious practice of vaulting to a noble past ideologically removed from fairgrounds, pub yards, and his own humble origins.

According to Berenger, the imitable vaulting of ancient Greece and Rome was also widely performed in Turkey and Italy prior to its introduction into England in the sixteenth and seventeenth centuries.[33] In this history, vaulting was not taken up by itinerant performers but instead became a cherished component of a gentleman's well-rounded and masculine education. Practiced alongside swordsmanship, dancing, and horsemanship, vaulting, especially in full armor, was a hallmark of a properly honorable horseman (Cavendish may have practiced the art alongside the haute école).[34] Direct reference to this tradition, or to the concurrent practices of the art among seventeenth-century university men, has not been found among surviving circus or Amphitheatre ephemera, but the discourses of masculinity, along with the actual activities performed by vaulters of this more elite history, share many similarities with Amphitheatre performances, and are worth examining in detail.

In 1652 William Stokes wrote the first English text on the subject, the fully illustrated *Vaulting-Master,* in an attempt to educate university students in the art of this ancient practice, and to convince a seemingly skeptical readership of its masculine usefulness. Suffering from a similar sentiment that argued that horsemanship, especially the haute école, was at best not beneficial to know and at worst actually dangerous, the detractors of vaulting who made their "dislike [of] the thing it selfe, nay the verie name of Vaulting," known, considered the practice "an unnecessarie and dangerous exercise, a device to breake ones neck, or limbs, or the like." There were also some skeptics who "are content to allow the thing, but

FIGURE 17
Ouer The head of the Horse, in Will Stokes, *The Vaulting-Master: Or the Art of Vaulting, Reduced to a Method, comprized under certaine Rules, Illustrated by Examples. . . .* ([London?]: Printed for Richard Davis, in Oxon, 1652). Photo: Beinecke Rare Book and Manuscript Library, Yale University.

will by no meanes have it an Art" but only "the child of an accidentall and undigested experience, receiving the degrees of its excellenceie, from blind custome only and difference of bodies."[35] Vaulting was unnecessarily dangerous and useless, and required little skill to perfect; vaulting over a horse (in this case a wooden one) was not an activity, or an art, fit to spend one's time learning. However, Stokes argued that vaulting (especially when wearing a full suit of armor) was a method of ensuring that a man maintained his masculine physicality and strength. Performing the "Pomado" over the back of the saddle or leaping over the horse's neck (fig. 17) was the ultimate test of strength, agility, and virtuous morals necessary for a gentleman, and was directly beneficial to his exploits on the battle or jousting field.

Reflecting a surprising embrace of physical animality in the vaulting man, Stokes saw vaulting as a sure way of symbolically and essentially combining the human with the animal. Here, the human ideally adopted and nurtured the animal qualities within himself through interaction with its constructed representation, in the form of the wooden vaulting horse used by performers in their quest to leave behind "the lazie and unmanly life." Vaulters were "rendred . . . equall to the most active of the beasts" by the art. As man was the mold from which animal life was created, it made sense that he also contained all of the elements of the animal kingdom within his own corporeal being. Stokes argued a man should come to understand "how in his thighs the Horse, in his heart the Lion, in his hands the Ape, in his back the Elephant are (as it were) stored up, all making one, by so much more mightie than they all, by how much he is but one." Within man there existed elements of animal life, figured as our earlier classical centaur for Cavendish, but within his frame these potentially subversively irrational elements were distilled and tamed, through physical training and practice on the vaulting horse, to create ideal humanity. Stokes insisted that a man must come to understand "that Nature is not wanting to man, but man to himselfe, and that it is not lack of abilitie, but lack of use, that has shrunk mens sinews, and enfeebled them, even to the contempt of beasts."[36] Therefore:

> *Here's that will soone restore what e're hath bin*
> *Impair'd by* ease, *or what more eating* sin,
> *Here's that will set your nerves in tune againe,*
> *And find for each forgotten string a straine:*
> *Winde up your sickly muscles, and refine*
> *Th'embased spirits to temper* Masculine.[37]

Without the strenuous and admittedly dangerous practice of vaulting, according to Stokes and the other contributors to his volume, men of the kingdom had become enfeebled, effeminate, and unfortunately practiced at "sins" harmful to society at large. A man became monstrous by not embracing his animality, and by not working with what nature had intended. It was through the refinement, the cultural education, of one's animal spirits through the physicality of vaulting that men could perform ideally controlled, improved, and tempered masculinity.

In Astley's Amphitheatre, as in Stokes's manual, vaulting was a physical pursuit in which the performer's body must become strong, agile, and flexible if he was to perform successfully. Astley performed feats of daring similar to those of earlier university vaulters, but he and other equestrian performers of the eighteenth century made one crucial change: they switched out the stationary wooden horse for a live animal traveling around a ring at "a good gallop."[38] Accustomed to vaulting on and off, sweeping the ground with his elbows, lying down back to back with his horse, standing on one, two, or three horses at once while galloping or jumping over obstacles, and standing on his head while firing a pistol, Astley pursued a physically demanding form of vaulting that became increasingly dangerous. To vault at Astley's, a performer needed to be courageous, while also performing feats of physical ability and horsemanship prowess that were abnormally great.

However, boundary transgression of the type experienced and embodied by Stokes, where the vaulter as a man was one of the animals in nature but also elevated over them through art that enabled his mastery over nonhuman elements within himself, was frequently considered impossible by the time Astley was performing a century later. Vaulting bodies in Astley's Amphitheatre reflected a more general trend toward the solidification of boundaries between "human" and "animal," a trend that was a part of a larger, scientifically driven social movement toward hardened categorization in general. According to Dror Wahrman, there was a general weakening of the doctrine of humans being unique in opposition to other animals during the last quarter of the eighteenth century, a weakening caused, paradoxically, by advances in the knowledge of animals that showed their previously unrecognized similarity to humanity—especially in the case of apes. It was precisely this similitude that resulted in a drawing away, a solidifying of boundaries, and a reaffirmation of human/animal division on the great chain of being, a division based partially on verbal speech, the possession of a rational soul, and superior rational morality.[39] In 1774, for example, Oliver Goldsmith argued that "in the ascent from brutes to man, the line is strongly drawn, well marked, and unpassable"; and William Bingley remarked in 1809 that "the barrier which separates men from brutes is fixed and immutable."[40] Within this intellectual climate, it was frequently no longer feasible or acceptable for society to entertain ideas of human-animal cross-border migration; the ideal of the dual-natured centaur was no longer a possibility, and vaulters were advertised in the Amphitheatre press as remaining firmly human.

This advertising, with its often placating overtones, evidences an ongoing perception and enactment of human-animal being that rubbed against the intellectual grain. Because the live horse was part of the vaulting apparatus, the human vaulting body was not able to divest itself of the continual co-constituting so evident in horsemanship in general. While horsemen and vaulters normally understood this animalization as unproblematic and eminently positive, within the Amphitheatre the masculine pastimes of riding and vaulting were coupled with horses who were themselves worryingly human. These animals, and the men who purported to command them, refused to conform to normative categories of either "human" or "animal" and were thus tacitly understood as both ideally masculine for their dangerous feats of vaulting, riding, and dancing, and as wonderfully monstrous.

FROM THE HORSE

Traditional horsemanship discourse argued that equine bodies functioned as material mediations of the rider's performed self. In this discourse, the physical presence and conformation of a horse could instantaneously represent the "true" interiority of the rider; riders thought that nothing about a person could be hidden when on the back of a horse. This truth-telling ability of horses remained a popular idea well into the eighteenth century, and was a formative element in writings on horsemanship and in equestrian portraiture and caricature.[41] However, this perceived equine ability was altered in the Amphitheatre because of the horses there. These horses not only could truth tell like their compatriots in the past, but, it was thought, could also perform intentionally constructed identities for themselves and their riders.

In studies of animal performance (in this instance, the physical enactment of becoming Other, or the conscious effecting of more than being), the animal is frequently ascribed a lack of understanding, a naturalness, an inability to act in the human sense while before an audience.[42] Building on current sociobiological theories of animal training and "natural" behavior, animals are seen as unable to "sustain fictive bodies and effect a consciously ironic meta-braiding of a not-self with a not-not-self."[43] They are unable to adopt other personas, to change their physical actions, in order to create a visible identity different from their "natural" state. In short, there is no culture in the natural animal; they make "lousy actors" for most scholars who have questioned the performing animal.[44] David Williams also points out the inability of most scholars to recognize the performativity of animals onstage, and suggests that instead of entertaining the idea of their possible understanding and enacting of performance or acting from an Othered, alien position with its own intelligence and ways of speaking, scholars should adopt yet another definition of performance. For Williams, building on performance theorist Jerzy Grotowski's characterization of a human actor's "psycho-physical organicity," an animal in its very beingness is "already doing." The physical presence and doingness of the animal's body, and the human's interaction with it, call up something else, something more, in both humans and animals. When communicating with a horse, the human's animal interiority is touched and called upon, while the animal comes to understand and respond to its own humanized aspects. For both Williams and Grotowski, the animal thinks "with its body, short-circuiting the gap between internal impulse and external action; being is already doing."[45]

This humanized being onstage, Nicholas Ridout argues, frequently results in profound audience unease over the acting animal body. According to Ridout, theatergoers, past and present, do not expect to witness animals onstage, and certainly not acting ones. As a result, when they were treading the boards, animals "appeared as an anomaly, and a worrying one at that." Much like the precocious child who appears as a simulacrum of an adult, acting animals, when taking on the human, are "uncanny" beings capable of upsetting audience understandings of themselves as the only rational species. Since audiences experience disquiet and even "shame" associated with the ethical problems of exploiting animal labor, according to Ridout, animals onstage overturn audience expectations of the theatrical experience and viewers' understandings of themselves through the power of the animal gaze looking back.[46] While the horses at Astley's did prompt repeated commentary in periodicals and newspapers about their fair treatment, the labor and coercion implicit in the presence of animals onstage was not the primary cause of audience concern.[47] Astley's had always been the home of acting animals; their presence was not unexpected. They were known, like the spotted pony Prince, for performing "the part of a page to his master"; Prince "delivers from him an epistle to the lady of his love: this done, he waits with all the air of one who is accustomed to good living, rings the bell, and when it is not answered, rings it again, with the impatient look of a testy old gentleman, whom it is not safe to disobey."[48] Horses like the Little Military Horse and Formidable Jack did act, and were advertised, viewed, and reviewed, as top-billed performers in their own right.[49] As such, at the heart of audience unease and enjoyment was not their physical presence but their apparently rational *acting* ability. Their ability to perform feats and identities, for themselves and their riders, not necessarily in keeping with any "true" self, was radically different from anything witnessed outside of the Amphitheatre's environs. The Amphitheatre horses could create idealized personas in a way that their predecessors and compatriots outside the theater could not, simply by being there onstage.

This was also the case for arguably the most famous acting horse of the seventeenth century. Morocco and his trainer, Joseph Bankes, traveled around the fairs and courts of England and Europe performing the seemingly impossible. The first learned horse mentioned in print, and a powerful antecedent for Astley's troupe of learned horses, Morocco could count, fetch a handkerchief, and pick predetermined people out of an audience, among other tricks. These abilities made him internationally famous and inspired periodic references in diaries, poetry, plays, and almanacs.[50] The voice of truth in a short tract of sociopolitical commentary, the 1595 *Maroccus Extaticus, or Bankes Bay Horse in a Trance,* Morocco was "a horse of wondrous qualitie, / For he can fight, and pisse, and daunce, and lie. / And finde your purse, and tell what coyne ye have."[51] Morocco was wondrous for the exhibition of seemingly abstract reasoning (counting, for example), a human ability generally thought impossible for irrational animals.[52] He was an anomaly that resisted the usual categorization and conceptualization applied to the behavior and cognitive abilities of animals, even superior ones such as horses. He certainly upset his viewers' understanding of themselves as rational beings securely superior to brute kind. As a result, people who saw him perform with Bankes frequently looked for a supernatural, a magical, explanation for the seemingly impossible. Many spectators considered Morocco's performances as an acting horse to be "vnnaturall, strange, and past reason." Contemporary understandings of animal rationality, intelligence, and ability simply could not rationalize him.

Audience unease over Morocco's uncanniness was not confined to the performing animal. The humans who shared the stage with an acting horse were as important to the performances as the animals, as Williams's articulation of animal acting indicates, and were frequently implicated in the supernatural abilities assigned to their animal charges. In the case of Morocco, he was dubbed "a deuill" while Bankes was thought "a coniurer" responsible for his devilry. As one audience member put it in 1591, "many people judgid that [his performances] were impossible to be don except he [Bankes] had a famyliar or don by the arte of magicke."[53] Only through contracts with the devil, with witchcraft and magic, could Morocco "smel a knave" or "dance and lie." Such opinions were so widespread, and the performance of a seemingly rational animal so problematic, that both man and animal were thought to have been imprisoned in Paris in 1601 for magic use and devilry (they were only released when Bankes showed the Paris authorities how the seeming supernatural feats were done). It was also rumored that in the 1630s some Roman critics may have gone so far as to burn them both at the stake for witchcraft at the pope's command.[54] While most scholars are suspicious about the validity of this event, and Kevin De Ornellas outright refutes it, some of Bankes's contemporaries found the rumor entirely plausible because of the pair's audacious performances.[55] Regardless of the manner of their deaths, the rumor of their execution makes clear "a fascination . . . with the mere potential of animal intelligence," and a deep anxiety about its presence in animal actors and about the power of the man who could make such cognition possible.[56]

However, and pointing to a similar disconnect in understandings of "animal" ability expressed by Cavendish in his refutation of Descartes's view of animal rationality, these were the responses of people who did not understand the often straightforward methods used in the training process. For many horsemen of the seventeenth century, Bankes's magic was easily understood and copied as equestrian skill. Gervase Markham, in his 1607 *Cavelarice,* for example, followed Bankes's example and provided his readers with precise instructions on how to train their horses to perform like Morocco. "Although *La Broue* do much discomment and disparise the teaching of a horse to do these vnnecessary and vnnaturall actions which more properly do be long to Dogges, Apes, Munkies, and Baboones," he noted, since "Mens natures are so apt to delight in nouelties," and "because these vnprofitable toyes shew in a Horse an extraordinary capacity, an obseruant feare, and an obedyent loue, all which are to be esteemed worthy qualities," he provided his readers with the required information.[57] Taught on the principles of horsemanship used in more "traditional" training, teaching a horse tricks was not overly difficult and was considered useful if a horseman wanted to garner "admiration" from spectators. However, the abilities of Bankes and Morocco, along with other trained trick horses, were not universally applauded, as Markham's refutation of La Broue's views indicates. Cavendish followed La Broue and typically thought that it was only "the Ignorant" that "Admire" horses "like Bankes's Horse," and that such people who "Teach Horses Tricks, and Gambals" "shall never Teach a Horse to Go Well in the Mannage."[58] Even so, Cavendish was not under the impression that Morocco and Bankes performed anything other than what all horsemen and horses could exhibit. For these horsemen, arguably among the most influential of their age, Bankes and Morocco were not that unusual; any horsemen with the inclination and understanding of training methodologies could instruct their horses to perform acts of rationality, understanding, and the seemingly magical. For these men, and many horsemen of the eighteenth century, the theory of the performing animal as uncanny simply did not apply.

However, for people not fluent in horsemanship epistemologies, it was an entirely different matter. As Barbara Benedict has pointed out, many scholars have long understood the eighteenth century to be the period when belief in the unnatural, the unseen, and the magic of nature was banished before "empiricism, secularism, and consumption."⁵⁹ In this argument, the eighteenth century was the period of increasing understanding of animal cognitive abilities and of the growing animal rights movement. "By the eighteenth century," many "intellectuals" influenced by Lockean philosophy were "claiming that animals had some degree of sentient feelings and cognitive abilities (how much exactly remained a contentious point), although at a level obviously inferior to human beings."⁶⁰ However, as Benedict has found, tracing the literature of it-narratives, the new move toward the collection and scientific understanding of things did not entire supplant older beliefs.⁶¹ As Jacques Derrida and Aaron Garrett have shown, most philosophers remained followers, to some extent, of Cartesian thought and were skeptical of animal rationality in any form—their ability to respond rather than react to external stimuli.⁶² Such views were widely acknowledged—as in Cavendish's time—but were again complicated by the position of the knower. For those of nonhorseman status, horses and what could and could not be performed with them consisted of foreign knowledge; the common assumption remained that they simply were not equipped to take on any level of human rationality.⁶³ In contrast, horsemen such as Astley, along with Cavendish and Markham before him, who subscribed to an epistemology that resisted Cartesian understandings of animal sentience, thought the horse was a reasonable animal who could reflect on his handling and easily be taught through the usual methods to perform the seemingly magical.

The horses at Astley's Amphitheatre were similar to Morocco. The Amphitheatre's first performing horse, the famous "little learned Military Horse," for example, was advertised as able to perform the "most extraordinary and uncommon exhibitions":

> This little animal will prove his abilities to be far superior to any horse in the kingdom; he readily answers various questions, tells gold from silver, and its value, ladies from gentlemen, &c. Mr. Astley borrows a handkerchief, which the horse carries in his mouth, and tells the person it was borrowed from; he strikes with his foot the hour of the day, day of the month; he pleases and deceives the eye with different deceptions—He falls lame, shams a pain in his head, imitates sickness, and, on being told he is to fight for the Spaniards, he lays down as if dead; but on the contrary, being told he is to go to Germany, with his master and Elliot's dragoons, he rises and fires a pistol, as if he understood word for word.⁶⁴

Horses like the Military Horse could tell time, sit at a table, serve tea, and through an apparent ability to act could also participate in contemporary politics of the day—in this case, the enactment of popular sentiment toward Britain's enemies and support for its allies during the Seven Years' War. These animals did more than reason the solution to a problem using methods analogous to human ones (as Cavendish's horses had done); instead, for many, they crossed the line between normative human and normative animal cognitive capability. Like Morocco before them, the Astleyan equines were able to perform "wonders" and were "surprising" in their "magical capacity."[65]

As with Bankes, Astley's critics accused him of working with and even embodying the devil. As one journalist complained, "What a wicked age this is, and likely to continue so! for no less than two thousand persons nightly walk and ride to the Devil—at Astley's."[66] Also, as a letter in the *Brussels Gazette* of March 6, 1787, related, "Astley and his troop are the general topic of conversation here in all the polite circles and assemblies; and true it is, there never was his equal seen in Brussels. . . . The surprising feats performed by his troop, and especially by his inimitable son, appear to some, to be the *ne plus ultra* of the art of horsemanship and equestrian exercises." However, "other people, of weaker minds," those who made up the bulk of Astley's audience, also "imagine[d]" Astley's feats of horsemanship to be "really assisted by a little magic."[67] Thus the performances of Astley's sagacious horses often resulted in a "delighted astonishment which is tainted by the suspicion that spectacularly visible accomplishment could readily be associated with devilry in disguise" for an audience made up of the "common" sort, who were susceptible to wonder, disbelief, and superstition.[68]

According to Helen Stoddart, these accusations of devilry leveled against Astley and the horses who worked with him contained "tongue-in-cheek humour," and resulted in "no serious moral implication" for him or the Amphitheatre (unlike the accusations leveled against Bankes and Morocco).[69] While there certainly was a comedic element in the accusations (and in the advertising that used them to advantage), the many accusations of devilry did result in the issuing of a warrant and Astley's eventual arrest in 1765. He was subsequently sent to Bridewell for trial on the charge of "dealing with the Devil" along with his "Servants, Horse and Foot."[70] Accusations of demonic involvement, of inhumanity, or of the supernatural—for man or beast—while opportune for effective advertising, did have tangible consequences for Astley's reputation and business success. As a result, Astley took great pains to maintain the surprising and spectacular nature of his equestrian work while making it clear that it was through training and practice that the animals performed the seemingly impossible. He endeavored not only to implement his methods in the ring but also to show the uninitiated common sort that what he and his horses did was not supernatural, simply the result of a lifetime of work and knowledge that only seemed superhuman.[71] As he argued in one puff, it was through his "Terrestrial Excellence" working with horses and his ability to spectacularize this ability as a showman (playing the "Devil") that he and his horses were able to appear more than human or horse,to appear as supernatural beings.[72]

However, even with the negative associations (and consequences) of such devilry, Astley's Amphitheatre could not function without that very monstrosity. Astley deliberately cultivated a public persona as a superior man through his and his horses' uncanny abilities in an attempt to use the supernatural personae of himself and his horses as influential tools of bodily instruction. Through the surprising and destabilizing nature of himself and his horses, Astley instructed his audience in ideal masculinity. Since the Amphitheatre was a minor theater not licensed for spoken plays, the acts there encompassed genres—such as pantomime, harlequinades, dance, and clowning—that consisted almost entirely of silent performances, just as at similar London theaters. As a result, both the animal and human performers tapped into what dance master John Weaver termed the "mute rhetorick" or "wit corporeal" of acting bodies to convey idealized virtues and morals.[73] Here, "in very much the terms of the Cartesian machine-man . . . the silent pantomimic spectacles that Weaver was proposing . . . 'would be a mechanick way of implanting insensibly in Minds not capable of receiving it so well by any other Rules, a sense of good Breeding and Virtue.'"[74] For theatergoers in the eighteenth century, the body language of actors—both horse and rider—could speak in a way that potentially overrode the influence, or absence, of the spoken word. Weaver further explains this theory of the mute performer when discussing what dancers were able to do onstage: the performing body had the ability to mirror the audience, where "every Spectator must behold himself acted, and see in the *Dancer,* as in a Glass, all that he himself us'd to do and suffer." In this formulation, the mute body onstage, the uncanny and devilish beings of man and horse, could recall an ideal and nostalgic past, a past where the gender anxieties and social and political ills of the current age were nonexistent, through the silence or "*manual Language*" of the performing body, and could imprint them in the minds of the audience much more clearly and powerfully than spoken words of the "traditional" English theater.[75]

The horses and riders of Astley's Amphitheatre were thus able to mirror and construct their audience, to mirror them as beings superior to them— as a sometimes uncomfortable ideal. In this way, as Ridout explains, "the moment they [animals] do look back," they excite us; they "disturb us by being just like us, or even . . . better than us in some impossible way."[76] At a time when losses during the American war frequently saw the once secure and ideal masculinity of soldiers become unstable and dubiously beneficial in the great "gender panic," discussed at length by Dror Wahrman, military men were described as "fribbles" unsuccessfully fighting a "macaroni war" in America. The Amphitheatre directly addressed this "deplorable state of masculinity" through the horse-human physicality of performing bodies, bodies that together looked to mythologized heroes and cultures of the past for inspiration and ideal gender models, government, and horse-human relationships.[77] The equestrian performers of the Amphitheatre, and the horsemanship manuals published to augment and advertise the teaching available there, looked nostalgically to a past that revolved around the horsemanship and masculinity of the sixteenth and seventeenth centuries and to a more recent past of Britain's glorious imperial expansion around the globe. In keeping with Astley's interest in vaulting and the masculinity inherent in the activity, the Amphitheatre performances recalled and performed a past that was gloriously chivalrous and ruled by virtuous knights wielding broadswords and jousting for their lady's honor, a past that was produced by men who gained their laurels through personal experience in warfare.[78] Performing animals onstage exposed audience insecurities and problematized certainties about themselves simply by being there, looking. Like the humans, the horses of the Amphitheatre were worryingly just like their spectators, and yet superior. They performed the human and exceeded it with "much more tenderness and segacity [sic] than many, very many, monsters in human shape."[79]

WITH THE HORSE

The Amphitheatre "rememorations" with the Gibraltar Charger recalled primarily two events in British imperial history: the Seven Years' War (1754–63) and the American War of Independence (1775–83).[80] Connected in Amphitheatre rhetoric and Astley's personal history with the person of General Elliot, a decisive presence in both wars, these events were recalled in the Amphitheatre performances as much-needed and famous examples of what truly British and properly masculine men on ideal horses could achieve for their king and country. Widely supported by the British citizenry, the Seven Years' War was the first world war, encompassing the Americas and parts of Africa, Asia, and Europe. It was a war that saw the defeat of France and Spain, the solidification of Britain as the preeminent imperial power of the time, and the establishment of Elliot as one of the nation's top military commanders. Becoming aide-de-camp to George II, Elliot also raised a regiment of light cavalry in 1759 that would later become the Fifteenth Light Dragoons—Astley's regiment. The "Fighting Fifteenth" was a "well-known crack regiment" "much in vogue" and highly respected for the battle prowess of its men.[81] The first of its kind in Britain, and consisting primarily of striking London tailors, the Fifteenth, along with Elliot and Astley, first saw combat on the German front at Emsdorf in 1760. The regiment "acquired immortal fame" by capturing "five battalions of French infantry, complete with their 16 colours and nine guns," in a campaign that gave them "one of the first battle honours ever granted to a British regiment."[82] Astley distinguished himself at Emsdorf, where he captured an enemy standard (which he later presented to George III) and later at Freiburg, where he rescued the wounded Prince of Brunswick.[83] He was, as Charles Dibdin the Younger grudgingly recalled (Dibdin had a turbulent relationship with Astley as the Amphitheatre's house writer), "a perfect exemplar of Industry, perseverance, and enterprise." He "enlisted in the celebrated General Elliot's own Light Horse [the Fifteenth]; to whom he endeared himself by his discipline and bravery; he served in the German War; saved the life of one of the imperial Princes, whose horse was shot under him, by bringing him off, on his own Horse, when surrounded by a score of frenchmen, through whom he cut his way with the most heroic resolution." Astley "also took a Stand of Colours; and at the siege of Valenciennes, (after his discharge) where he served as a Volunteer under the late Duke of York, he recovered from the French a piece of Ordnance and four Horses which they had taken; they were presented to him by his Royal Highness as a recompense for his gallantry." These horses he put "up to auction; expending their produce for the comfort of a company of his old comrades (Elliot's) who were in the English Army, and whom he had joined. The Cannon he brought over to England and exhibited to the audience in the circle of his amphitheatre at Westminster Bridge."[84]

Astley was a highly decorated national hero, and by taking full advantage of this reputation, and by performing through mute rhetoric, he and the Gibraltar Charger were able to idealize masculinity and patriotic service to the state. The physical presence of horse and human onstage recalled the nation's heroes. Astley sought celebrity status, and wanted to perform feats of horsemanship based on his own history that would "rival" all others.[85] Joseph Roach argues that actors and actresses of the eighteenth century cultivated a public persona that provided an illusion of "public intimacy," an illusion of knowing the true individual self of the performer, as an essential means of creating celebrity. From his earliest performances in pub yards, Astley cultivated an illusionary intimacy as an accomplished horseman and military veteran to create a simulacrum of exaggerated masculinity. As Roach argues, in the "expansion of celebrity to a wider aperture of visibility," the eighteenth-century "stage produced totemic signs, by which the intimate persons of its stars became as familiar to the public as the heraldic trappings of monarchy once were and continued to be."[86] In his own celebrity performances, Astley adopted through mechanical military arts the "traditional" totemic signs of the nobility and monarchy (horsemanship, virtue, civic duty, and honor). He used his own history in the war that helped make Britain into a global colonial power, alongside repeated references to "old English" pastimes and "manners—subjects which have an unfailing charm for the supporters of this house"—to create a stage presence that was a bodily and mythical simulacrum of ideal (and proven) military might.[87] The performance and frequent rememorations of this persona, and the illusion of intimacy between audience and performer created by "the celebrated young English Warrior," hailed into being a glorious and chivalric history, where battles were won, conspicuous consumption, luxury, and effeminacy were eschewed, and men's masculinity remained secure.[88]

Astley's performances recalled and promoted a traditional form of masculinity that would not be out of place at home with Cavendish. This masculinity upheld courage, physical strength, and success on the battlefield as central components of the Amphitheatre's "useful" entertainment.[89] As a medium for social, personal, and state improvement, Astley used "self-promotion" and spectacular displays for personal gain in the form of honor and reputation. As he argued in his *Remarks on the Profession and Duty of a Soldier* (1794), the attainment of "*honor*" should be the "first and principal task" for a soldier. A soldier should never "lose sight of" his "grand instructor, *Honor;* as that soldier who neglects discipline, may not only prove the means of seeking his own destruction by such an error, but in all probability prove the source of misfortune to his brave and valiant comrades," especially during the century's frequent wars, "when his service is mostly wanted for the defence of his country." Much like Cavendish before him, Astley saw the defense of one's country and bravery in the face of danger, along with "a competent knowledge of the *management* of his *horse, arms,* &c. in every instance," as the surest route to honor and a masculine reputation.[90] Michèle Cohen argues that "despite the stress on the martial training and heroic deeds that were part of the chivalric code, chivalry did not present models of heroic martial masculinity for late eighteenth- and early nineteenth-century military action."[91] At the Amphitheatre, however, Astley provided the model. To be a chivalrous, honorable man, Astley constructed his public persona in a way that not only highlighted his military education and the chivalrous behavior it engendered but his very real military action in war. It was "defiance of danger" and fair fighting on the battlefield in defense of his country that gained a man honor, a sentiment that Jacob Decastro sang about at the Amphitheatre during a popular reenactment of the 1793 "Siege of Valenciennes." Astley, who had reenlisted under York in 1793, was present at the siege, where he captured an enemy color and four horses.[92] Decastro received the details of the British victory at Valenciennes from Astley, and he delivered the rousing song as a substitute Astley, dressed in the uniform of the Fifteenth Light Dragoons:

> *When sent the intrenchments to cover,*
> *Each danger we boldly despise;*
> *And oft is our task to discover*
> *Where the force of the enemy lies:*
> *Still forward we dash,*
> *While bombs and balls clash,*
> *And the foe on all sides giving way;*
> *Still, still we pursue,*
> *And cut our way through,*
> *And true British valour display.*
> . . . .
> *And though hissing bullets on each side may rattle,*
> *We fearless push on while the enemy fall:*
> . . . .
> *For Britons e'er fight,*
> *Not for plunder but right,*
> *For honor's their standard at home or afar.*

During the performance of this song, where the rhythm of the verse suggests a hunting tune while conflating the military and sporting bravery advocated earlier in the century by authors like Somerville, the audience was never allowed to forget the presence of Astley, or his views regarding masculine honor and service to the state.[93] A subheading to the song stipulated that the "writer of this spirited air lays particular stress on the excellence of the discipline of a Light Dragoon, by portraying in the act of cutting his way through every impediment, in defiance of danger, rather than suffer himself to be taken prisoner by the enemy."[94] In this and other rememoration acts at the Amphitheatre, the performance of glorious military feats recalled the celebrated body of Astley while also constructing a sense of national memory and pride in Britannia's soldiers, who bravely defended "true British valour" regardless of the odds. Astley "set an example of a nature so spirited, so noble, and so loyal, in every sense of the word, as does credit to his feelings as a man, and his honour as a soldier," both on and off the Amphitheatre stage.[95] Through such Amphitheatre performances, honor became the true and indispensable marker of Britons, "at home or afar."

However, such honor and military might, as the Gibraltar Charger's own history illustrated, could not be achieved alone. The Charger came to the Amphitheatre with a known story of glorious military victory and a history intimately connected to his rider, General Elliot, now the governor of Gibraltar. Elliot distinguished himself throughout his career, but he became a national hero for his work in the American War of Independence. By all accounts a disastrous attempt to maintain British power over the American colonies in the face of united opposition, the American war had few military campaigns that went well for Britain—except the Siege of Gibraltar. This protracted siege of excessive boredom (which by many accounts the siege was for much of the time) became one of Britain's greatest triumphs, and saw not only the continued rule of Britain over the Rock of Gibraltar but also the unquestionable defeat of Spanish interests in the area during the siege's climax on September 13, 1782. Generating copious fanfare and celebratory commentary in England, the naval attack of Gibraltar (an attack that saw the Spanish fleet bombarded and set alight by Gibraltar's guns) was for many a "favorite scene of Fame, / Where Britain's Genius blaz'd in glory's brightest flame" (fig. 18).[96] Cause for national celebration, Britain's defeat of Spain and the frustration of its French and American allies at Gibraltar was achieved through battle, bloodshed, and fire. Britain's genius and fame blazed in glory's fame, but so did many attacking Spanish ships that dared to try and breach Gibraltar's walls.

FIGURE 18 John Singleton Copley, *The Siege and Relief of Gibraltar, 13 September 1782*, ca. 1783. Tate. Purchased 1868. Photo © Tate, London 2015.

While Elliot received much of the credit for the victory at Gibraltar, the Gibraltar Charger also received his fair share of the accolades. He was famed and mythologized in image and print as the horse who bore Elliot throughout his defense of the rock, and as a horse who did so with great courage and selflessness. The Charger was there, and this material connection to the siege, along with one of the siege's greatest heroes, was deliberately recalled through fire and his seemingly supernatural and bodily presence onstage. As one newspaper wag quipped, "It is a matter of doubt, whether the Gibraltar Charger has not been used to eat fire, as he seems to be so very fond of it."[97] The Charger was a celebrity, and a celebrity famed for his exemplary (even uncannily superior) service to his master while under fire. In this instance, the performed personhood and unique memories of the horse were indivisible from his rider, from the actions undertaken together, both past and present.

For many horsemen of the seventeenth and early eighteenth centuries, the embodiment and performance of the male self were indivisible from the material presence of the man's horse. However, in the past, such merging of bodily identities through the act of riding, or becoming a centaur, tended only to encompass the interacting beings. With the Charger, the spectral presence of Elliot complicated this understanding. As the Charger's performed self could not be separated from his history, it could also not be separated from the primary elements of that history, including his service to the nation and his master, Elliot. His theatrical identity, then, was an amalgamation of both his service to Elliot as a being of uncommon courage and status as the mount of Philip Astley, in a tripling of referential presence.

However, even while this was the case within the Amphitheatre, horse and human boundaries remained firmly in place. There was no becoming of the Other, or deminaturing with a brave beast, as in Cavendish's time. In Astley's performances with the Gibraltar Charger, this calling up of the Other in the self was not an enforced becoming of one entirely hierarchical transspecies being (as was the case with Cavendish and Angelo), in which the horse would essentially become the body to his rider's mind; it was more an egalitarian "becoming-with" the Charger, whereby both parties called up the glorious military past in each other to form a being proud and worthy of its triple-natured military glory. In this instance, to return to Ann Game's theories on horsemanship, riding is "the bringing to life of *the relation* between horse and rider, involving a mutual calling up of horse and rider in each other." Rider and horse call up, through their dual-natured acting abilities, the essential elements in the human that "are always already part horse," and the essential elements in the horse that are "part human" (including his association with Elliot and Elliot's heroic reputation) to create and make visible the human-animal as hybrid.[98]

Thus, to be a man of the Amphitheatre, and, for Astley, to be a man at all, a rider needed the partnership of a "high-mettled" mount who would courageously "snort in defiance of powder or ball," and with whom he could call up the horse's military might into himself, while his horse took up his masculine virtues in return. Astley argued that not only must animals be supporters of men in their labor; they must also be so to cement the status and position of their masters within the horsemanship community and for their masters' survival on the battlefield. A horse, as Astley argued in his highly propagandist and celebratory 1801 *System of Equestrian Education,* "participates with man [in] the toils of the campaign, and the glory of conquest; penetrating and undaunted as his master, he views dangers, and braves them." Horses were unique beings that possessed the "courage of the lion, the fleetness of the deer, the strength of the ox, and the docility of the spaniel," while also functioning as "both our slave and our guardian." "By his aid, men become more acquainted with each other; he not only bears us through foreign climes, but likewise labours in the culture of our soil; draws our burthens and ourselves; carries us for our amusement and our exercise; and both in the sports of the field and the turf, exerts himself with an emulation, that evinces how eagerly he is ambitious to please and gratify the desires of his master." Horses gave "profit to the poor, and pleasure to the rich; in our health he forwards our concerns, and in our sickness lends his willing assistance for our recovery." An ideal(ized) horse was "accustomed to the din of arms, he loves it with enthusiasm, seeks it with ardour, and seems to vie with his master in his animated efforts to meet the foe with intrepidity, and to conquer every thing that opposes itself to his courage." Horses lived for the fulfillment of their master's will—in this case, through glory or victory on the battlefield, or "in *single combat*, &c. in the field of honour, and in the *service* of his *country*."[99] It was the horse's ability to do all of this that ensured the chivalrous honor of both man and horse. The horse, for Astley, was ideally gendered as noble, courageous, brave, pleasing, and strong—the embodiment of Astley's ideal masculinity in equine form.

An anonymous author (probably someone connected to the Amphitheatre, possibly Astley himself) explored this interconnection of meaning, embodiment, and species in the "Ode on the Gibraltar Charger." Appearing in multiple London papers on June 16, 1788, just days after the Charger's surprising feats on the Thames, and designed to correspond with his new evening performances at the Amphitheatre, the "Ode" shares remarkable similarities with Decastro's earlier song "The Siege of Valenciennes." "Valenciennes" emphasized Astley's martial strength, courage, valor, and chivalrous tenacity as the true British soldier. In the "Ode," in contrast, the Charger fought for the nation:

> *He bore our warlike Hero round*
> *Gibraltar's Rock, while cannons sound,—*
>   *Fly red hot balls in air;*
> *Thousands has he to conquest led;*
> *His course has been o'er slaughter'd dead*
> *Impatient of the leading rein,*
> *He shakes in air his flowing mane,*
>   *Anxious the foe to dare.*
>   . . . .
> *Defiance in his eye-ball glares;*
> *His neighings fill war-wounded airs:*

> *His spreading chest for conquest glows,*
> *With which he meets attacking foes—*
> *In triumph o'er them treads:*
> *He welcomes Death, mankind to save,*
> *And no reward but Love he'll crave:*
> *His nostrils burn with warlike fire;*
> *'Till vict'ry's gain'd he'll never tire—*
> *His heart no danger dreads.*[100]

In this attempt to offset the morally ambiguous position of animals onstage, the Gibraltar Charger is represented as heroically eager to lose his life in the defense of his master and of mankind at large. "The Hero's aid and pride," with Elliot and under Astley as his partner in performing martial masculinity, the Charger was a teacher for the nation. However, like Astley, he could not teach alone. It was only with a horse as a dual-species figure of national pride and masculine surety that Astley could instruct the people of the nation. "When mounted on his beautiful grey," the *Morning Post* reported in 1807, "the veteran Astley, apparently in the flower of his age, still conserves the extraordinary example to the heads of families, civil and military, and to the rising generation in general."[101] A noble horse, like a noble, honorable man, welcomed death and worked with his partner (human or animal) to gain glory while fulfilling his duty to his master and country. Together, they could serve as a model of ideal virtue and masculinity for the benefit of the next generation. Together, Astley and the Charger could instill "wisdom, music, and heroism" in their spectators, much like Chiron, the famed centaur from Ovid's *Metamorphoses,* who bonded with "Achilles, him that afterwards grew up the maist beautifu' and dreadfu' o' a' the sons o' men."[102]

With this understanding of Astley's equestrian performances in mind, then, we can now return to the night that he and the Charger performed on the barge, and to their performances together on the Amphitheatre stage, the barge performance in miniature. The two were on the lead barge in front of the fireworks that culminated in "VIVAT G. III" and various royal emblems associated with the Prince of Wales. In this performance, the positioning of Astley and the Charger spoke to their own pasts and military might, but also to the ever-present politicization of horsemanship practice. Horsemanship was always highly political, and often served as the embodiment of the nation as a whole. In this formulation, the body of the horse could represent the nation, while the rider represented the body of the sovereign monarch. How well the two interacted, and what they did while doing so, in turn evidenced the governing abilities and general state of the kingdom.[103] For Astley and the Charger, then, who happened to be white—like George III's horse, Adonis, the white horse emblematic of the house of Hanover—their performances on the barge and in the Amphitheatre did more than illustrate ideal masculinity for the audience.[104] They also constructed an ideal and highly propagandist idea of what the kingdom had accomplished in the past and what it would achieve if it continued to be governed by a monarch or his regent rather than by Parliament. For Astley, in this instance bodily recalling the person of the king in a fashion remarkably similar to Cavendish's, the ideal horseman could never be divided from his horse; the nation needed its royal governor, and to separate them would be disastrous.

Astley engaged directly with the politics of his day and took it upon himself to provide a model of patriotism, national security, and continued peace and prosperity through his and the Charger's bodies—the metaphorical bodies of the king and his kingdom. By performing the ultimate masculinity, chivalrous and militaristic masculinity proved profitable for the nation and the self as heroic, a performance greeted with "loud and repeated huzzas" by the people on the bank of the Thames. Astley and the Charger hailed their audiences back to a time of victory and strong men who brought peace and prosperity to the imperial nation. They were brought back to a time when men rode, battles were won, and victory was achieved with a horse. Astley and the Charger were the kingly body that saluted the audience with an olive branch of peace. They became the messengers of national salvation who performed together at the end of the night with "a range of fireworks," laid "close to his nose" and forming the words "'God save the King' in letters about four feet high."[105] If the people followed Astley's patriotic lead, the kingdom, like the Charger, could stand triumphant, at peace, and "as firm as the Rock of Gibraltar itself."[106]

ON THE HORSE

The nation's papers widely advertised Astley's performances with the Charger, but the Charger also performed alongside Astley's son, John. While it is possible that the two performed in the same 1788 season as the Charger's more popular fireworks acts, it is almost certain they appeared together a year later, on the eve of the French Revolution. Almost nothing is known

FIGURE 19
William Hincks, *Young Astley, the Equestrian Hero*, 1789. Photo: Victoria and Albert Museum, London.

about their performances together, and the only reference to John's performing with the Charger comes from one of the few illustrations of him in existence, William Hincks's *Young Astley, the Equestrian Hero* (fig. 19). Printed four days after the storming of the Bastille, just as news of the event was reaching Britain, the image is not a typical eighteenth-century portrait, and is certainly not in keeping with traditional equestrian portraiture. Instead of riding on the Charger, John is depicted performing the act he was most famous for—dancing on horseback. Here he performed "several pleasing Feats of great Agility," and "in a most amazing Equilibrium whilst the Horse is on a Gallop, dances and vaults, &c. Also plays an Air on the Violin, and displays a Flag in many comic Attitudes, which have never been exhibited, or even thought of, by any Horseman in Europe."[107] John performed the same feats of vaulting and manège horsemanship that his father did, but his dancing on horseback, "commonly called rope and stage-dancers attitudes," was his unique contribution to the equestrian theater.[108]

Like his father, John used the silence, or *"manual Language,"* of the performing body to mirror the audience and to reflect an ideal masculinity for the spectator's edification. However, he also used understandings of the performing body specific to dance alongside his horsemanship to form an image of himself, of his physicality, that was vastly different from his father's. Dance master John Weaver thought that "Dancing is the Task of one that is Strong, Active, Brisk, and much Exercis'd." Weaver argued that the activity was the creator of "manliness" via a grace and beautiful positioning of the limbs so necessary for a properly commanding masculinity. A man who danced was a "*Bold Man*" who "carries his Point, by a sort of Ascendant, or Superiority of Nature above all Opposers; every thing pays Homage to him, and so he becomes indeed the Framer of his own Fortune." Dancing, especially from a young age, created a "becoming" "Manliness and handsome *Confidence*." In turn, and taking inspiration from John Locke's views on the subject, Weaver further argued that this confidence resulted in men who "might have become more serviceable both to themselves and the Publick" because of their self-assurance and ability to speak confidently before an audience. For Weaver, there was "something in the Nature of *Dancing,* that stirs up those manly Thoughts," those "Animal Spirits," necessary for the beneficial flow and ease in polite conversation. Through physical training, the dancer became more adept at personal interaction and exerting influence over those around him through his very aura and ability as an orator or statesman.[109] This theory, from a man who strongly influenced dance and pantomime for the remainder of the century, appears to have been an integral component of John's horsemanship performances and of the Amphitheatre's constructions of him as a man who, because of the "attitudes of his body," was "just and noble."[110]

John's dancing on horseback, like his father's equestrian prowess, also made him a celebrity, but a celebrity who was unique in his interaction with his audience, his horses, his masculinity, and his performances. Unlike his father, John "cultivated with assiduity every external accomplishment, and became proverbially one of the most elegant men of the age." It "was to these natural and acquired advantages that" John "owed . . . [his] future fortune and . . . fame," and through dance he was able to create a public persona as a "polite gentleman" rather than a "rude rustic."[111] John joined two of the most dominant masculinity codes of the eighteenth century, politeness and military chivalry, in a unique and gentlemanly form of gender performance.[112] By embodying the advice of Weaver and the century's many conduct manuals, John was able to make visible a movement of the body defined by "Attitudes and Motions easy, free and graceful" that allowed him to "distinguish" himself from the more mechanical, lower-class soldiering of his father.[113] He had "the manners of a Gentleman" in the way of the men at Angelo's, but the body of a fighting man handy for life as an officer (roles he frequently adopted in the Amphitheatre).[114] John was an amalgamation of both the rough and ready British hero and the refined and polished French gentleman. Spending part of each year at the Amphithéâtre d'Astley in Paris and the rest in England, John embodied the gender codes of Britain and France in an unparalleled form of masculine display.[115]

However, while the grace and elegant appearance of male dancers was considered necessary in a proper gentleman, dancing without horses frequently led to accusations of softened and overly refined manhood. These were the same accusations leveled against men thought too polished in the feminine art of conversation, itself associated with foreign (French) institutions and notions of elegance.[116] Within the Amphitheatre, John's dances on horseback usually escaped such accusations and were generally considered (in the Amphitheatre press, anyway) graceful, polite, and fantastic for their physical skill. Rival theater establishments, however, were quick to take advantage of dance's lurking associations with effeminacy and unstable gender to undermine the value of John's performances. Appearing in the column "Small Talk, or Chat on the Turf" (a column used by both the Amphitheatre and the Royal Circus to advertise their acts, usually at the expense of each other's reputation) the circus, where Charles Hughes was the lead horseman, took direct aim at the potentially emasculating effects of dancing on horses:

Lord Gallop. Pray does Mr. Hughes dance a minuet on horse-back?
Groom. Oh no, my Lord, he is too fond of manly exercise to dance a minute [*sic*] on horse-back like a *he, she, girl*.[117]

From the perspective of a rival equestrian entertainment venue, dancing minuets with horses alongside, it was implied, John's elegant and polite dances on horseback were performed by infantile and ambiguous "he, she, girls" rather than proper men "fond of manly exercise," such as were apparently performed nightly at the Royal Circus (where the acts of horsemanship were, ironically, almost identical to the Amphitheatre's).[118] In its efforts to discredit its rival, the Royal Circus fell back on the tried and true discourse of dance's effeminacy, Frenchness, and the associations of politeness's enervating dangers.

John taught the manliness of dance and the grace and beauty of confidence in bodily control to his male spectators, but, to help offset the dangers of dance's inherent effeminacy, and in keeping with wider trends in the display of the English male body at the end of the century, John added to his physicality an overt heterosexuality built into the practice of vaulting from its earlier inclusion in university life.[119] According to Richard Godfrey, a contributor to Stokes's manual, with vaulting,

> *False capers, and soft cringes, that betray*
> *Who's a French Courtier, are quite laid away:*
> *Our Gallants are growne sound, th' have learn'd a sport*
> *For men of backs, and may be lik'd at Court.*
> *He that can mount the wooden Palfrey best,*
> *And sit him as Knights Errant doe their beasts;*
> *Descend so quick, that you would sweare he flies,*
> *And were himselfe the* Pegasus; *can rise*
> *. . . You'l think a reall spirit were i' th' play:*
> *Can stretch his sinews so, to jump with ease*
> *. . . He, he's the Man! He shall applauded be*
> *'Bove the gay sutes, and Tinsell-Poetrie:*
> *Mark how the Ladies drink to Him alone!*
> *He mans them out; He's talk'd on too at home.*[120]

Speaking to the commonly perceived effeminacy of the luxuriously debauched Stuart court, the vaulting man "mans them out." He eschews the effeminacy found in those of a more delicate, French constitution within the English court; he practices mounting the wooden horse and develops an athletic, acrobatic physique so desirable to the ladies; he is agile, graceful, skillful, beautiful, sexual, and, like a Cavendish-like Pegasus, seems to defy the mortal pull of gravity as a nonhuman animal. The vaulting man becomes the ideal male figure in the eyes of both men and women of the judging court.

Philip Astley's performances of vaulting also incorporated these tropes of masculinity and bodily display, although the related discourse and newspaper advertising made no reference to any sexuality or physical desire felt on the part of the viewing audience. The "celebrated young English Warrior" was brave, acrobatic, magical, and dangerous, but not beautiful, graceful, or sexual.[121] John, by contrast, was all of these things. "Young Astley seems to attract the Ladies," while his "spirit rules the whole" Amphitheatre, recalled one female correspondent. John was a commander of both human and animal life as a pseudodeity, to the "delight" and "charm" of the female spectators.[122] John not only provided enjoyable entertainment for the audience but also literally looked back. He directly engaged the audience in a performance of male virility. He looked to the audience with such frequency, in fact, that many feared he would not be able to perform his dancing without mishap. As one newspaper jokingly argued, John "should be cautioned against admiring the ladies too much, lest he should be thrown off the saddle!"[123] His returned gaze threatened distraction and inattention in his performance, and his performance in turn caused hearts to flutter and salacious thoughts to run wild. John's performance of "leaping over the garter," for example, made some women state that "he seems an angel flying into the seats of Paradise" "when he is *above the garter*." Here, conflated with an allusive physical titillation caused by his visible male sexuality ("for he looks and performs it [leaping over the garter] so well"), the performance of angelic beauty and skill on horseback moved beyond associations of classical purity to ribaldry and rakish masculinity.[124] As one rather remarkable newspaper puff of 1786 related:

> A young Lady, whose wit and beauty has lately made her the toast at the West end of the town, having been heard several times to say, "*That young Astley was a Thief!*" her brother, an Officer in the Guards, feeling it seriously, and thinking that his Sister's delicacy prevented her from bringing *our Equestrian Hero* to justice, privately obtained a warrant against him, and under pretence of giving his Sister an airing in the family coach, actually took her to the Magistrate's house, where the supposed *culprit* was attending. The Lady no sooner perceived *Young Astley,* than she fainted away, and upon recovering, exclaimed "*Oh, there's the Thief!*" Patience, young Lady, (cried his worship)—"You shall have justice done you—but, pray, *what* has the rogue stolen from you?" A general silence now prevailed, and every one seemed anxious to hear the charge. "Come, Madam, (said the Justice again) *what* has he done?" "Sir, (cried the Lady, just bursting into tears) *he has stole my heart!*" "Oh, I am sorry for that (replied the Magistrate) but if I was to sit here, to hear such complaints against him as these, I should have nothing else to do—he is an old offender—and the best thing I can do, is to recommend it to the parties to settle the matter amongst themselves."[125]

According to this account, John had a long history of stealing women's hearts and, however unintentional his effect on women seems, his rakishness remained a glorified and almost idealized aspect of his character. As Margaret

Hunt has found, displays of "heterosexuality became a defining feature . . . of English manhood" over the course of the eighteenth century, and such displays were, as Charles Conaway argues, especially necessary for men of the theater.[126] Given emerging male types of ambiguously gendered antitheses to hegemonic masculinity, such as the fop or molly, it was crucial for many men to distance themselves from these emerging effeminacies—frequently thought the first step in unwanted associations with same-sex desire—and unstable masculinities so problematic at the end of the century. David Garrick looked for parts that theatricalized solid "masculine virtue," while John mirrored an aestheticized and almost aggressively heterosexual masculinity that was simultaneously polite, courageous, refined, and athletic as the most effective means of ensuring his and his audience's ideal masculinity. He was a fantasy figure, larger than life, and thus both men and women admired him as an ideal of masculine beauty, virtue, and virility. "Young Astley seems to attract the Ladies," noted one newspaper article, "and his manly abilities of lofty vaulting and other manœuvres on the Horses are much admired by the Gentlemen."[127] His sexuality and affective power "attracted" the women, while his mastery of the nonhuman in horsemanship and vaulting won him the "admiration" and awe of the men. Whether labelled *sprezzatura,* magnetism, radiance, attraction, aura, charm, presence, or charisma at various times in history (qualities that Joseph Roach has shown that "abnormally interesting people" possess), John Astley had "It."[128]

What did John Astley's masculinity mean for his performances with the Gibraltar Charger? While Philip Astley used his own history as a soldier to perform ideal masculinity, John did not possess any such history to draw upon. He was never a member of the military; he grew up on the Amphitheatre stage, where he began performing as early as age four.[129] Therefore, for him also to perform the message of a glorious military history so beneficial to the continuing prosperity of the nation at a time of ever-louder rumblings of social unrest in France, and their reverberations in England, he needed to adopt a fictitious masculinity joined with his interior self as a performer known for his horsemanship abilities though a mixing of theatrical genres: acting, dancing, and horsemanship.

The blending of these three genres was summarized by one London reviewer:

> The conversation of the town seems at present to be entirely upon Mrs. Siddons, Mrs. Abington, and Young Astley, who is universally allowed to be even much improved since his last trip to Paris,

and to be now the first performer in horsemanship that the world ever produced. The Beauty of his person, and the elegance of his deportment, long since acquired him the appellation of the English Rose in Paris, and indeed it is hardly possible to conceive that so much strength and agility could be blended with such wonderful ease and grace, and displayed in one and the same person.[130]

John was ranked in importance, influence, and ability alongside some of the greatest actresses of the eighteenth-century patent theaters.[131] This was quite an achievement for a horseman from a minor theater specializing in animal performances, and it spoke to the popularity of his patriotic dancing and acting on horseback. Few could boast a similar popularity, a popularity that packed the Amphitheatre night after night, and there were "fewer still, *if any*, who, like Young Astley, can *mount* the horse, as well as *tread* the Stage."[132] And they certainly could not do both at the same time.

John's dancing took place upon the "Flying Equestrian Stage," like his father's vaulting before him.[133] In these acts with other horses, the horse/stage would move around the Amphitheatre ring, at a gallop, at the behest of a man in the center of the ring directing the pace and direction of the horse. The horse was lunged, as all horses were as a routine component of their training, and as a result there was no acting animal here; there was no uncanny ability to mirror the audience and perform the human. Like the other horses who performed the part of a stage, the Charger did nothing more—or so it seems from Hincks's illustration—than move around the arena at a set pace while John danced on his back. However, his (arguable) demotion from named actor to unnamed objectified piece of theatrical technology apparently did not inhibit his ability to embody/recall his heroic horseness. The potential for the continuation of the acting animal and for interspecies masculinity creation was recalled through the fictional, seriocomedic philosophies of the characters Tickler, Shepherd, and North in the anonymous *Noctes Ambrosianae* of 1831. Discussing the transcendent abilities of Amphitheatre horseman Andrew Ducrow, Tickler argued:

> The glory of Ducrow lies in his Poetical Impersonations. Why, the horse is but the air, as it were, on which he flies! What godlike grace in that Volant motion, fresh from Olympus, e'er yet "new-lighted on some heaven-kissing hill!" What seems "the feather'd Mercury" to care for the horse, whose side his toe but touches,

as if it were a cloud in the ether? As the flight accelerates, the animal absolutely disappears, if not from the sight of our bodily eye, certainly from that of our imagination, and we behold but the messenger of Jove, worthy to be joined in marriage with Iris.

SHEPHERD. I'm no just sae poetical's you, Mr Tickler, when I'm at the Circus; and ma bodily een, as ye ca' them, that's to say, the een, ane on ilka side o' ma nose, are far owre gleg ever to lose sicht o' yon bonny din meere.

NORTH. A dun mare, worthy indeed to waft Green Turban, "Far descended of the Prophet line," across the sands of the Desert.

SHEPHERD. Ma verra thocht! As she flew round like lichtnin', the saw-dust o' the Amphitheatre becam the sand-dust o' Arawbia—the heaven-doomed region, for ever and aye, o' the sons o' Ishmael.

TICKLER. Gentlemen, you are forgetting Ducrow.

SHEPHERD. Na. It's only you that's forgettin' the din meere.[134]

Tickler apparently experienced an imaginative transcendence of the eye's tyranny over affective experience, as Moody points out, because of Ducrow's skill, while Shepherd, whose eye was more attentive, or "gleg," could not erase the presence of Ducrow's mare even if he tried.[135] For Tickler, the mare remained a "horse," an example of the "animal," whose contribution to Ducrow's performance was minimal at best and ignored at worst. However, for Shepherd and North, the animal became an identifiable dun mare who could not and should not be ignored. Her physical presence, her beingness onstage with Ducrow in a dual-species performance of an exotic tale, allowed the imagined transformation of the Amphitheatre into the hot, dry sands of Arabia. Both Ducrow and the mare were central, and it was Tickler, in his humanist view of Ducrow's vaulting on horseback, who was incorrect.

In a similar vein, the Charger was a celebrity famed for his supernatural affinity with fire and warfare. He came to the Amphitheatre with a very specific history as a courageous military horse who "carried the gallant Veteran through the glorious toils of war," and performed alongside Astley in their statements of patriotic and royal strength.[136] The presence of the Charger in John's portrait and onstage came with referential baggage that in turn may have influenced John's performance. In this instance, the Charger's physical presence within the ring, much like the dun mare's, could create sensual worlds, mythical realities, simply by being there. Thus, while the dun mare's galloping hooves stirred up visions of dusty Arabian deserts fit for Oriental narratives of heroic men, the Charger's active presence recalled the fiery ramparts of Gibraltar under siege and the glorious horse-human endeavors experienced there. His very body created, called up, the imagined realm of fire, his "favourite element," we are told, and much-needed British victory.

While with Philip Astley this gendered and nationalistic memory embodied by an animal was called up and mirrored in his performances for the enjoyment and edification of the audience, with John there was no militarism to call up. Instead, performing with John called up the nobility, beauty, and physicality of the Charger, while the Charger provided an authentic history for John to adopt as a part of his acting. In a way similar to pantomime, the dancer, both for Weaver and for John, adopted "*but one Body*" and "*many Souls*" when performing.[137] The dancer took on the character, persona, and soul of another being—in this case, the Charger and his various riders—as a central aspect of performing a character who was an "*Imitation* of Persons, or Manners and Passions."[138] In this understanding of a centauric relationship, John took on the militarism, authenticity, and willing service of the Charger (so necessary to period understandings of civility) to create a public self that joined his own refined abilities and politeness to illusionary skill in battle.[139] He also took on the all-encompassing constructions of "horse" extensively outlined by Astley and other authors of horsemanship. To be a horse was to be a slave and guardian of a rider; it was to be courageous, willing, and essential to the smooth workings of the eighteenth-century fiscal-military state. Thus John was able to adopt the specific attributes of the Charger and a reference to a single point in British history, while also taking on through his dancing on horseback the virtues and desired qualities of horses in general.

In Hincks's illustration, John's adoption of the Charger's history and equine body also becomes a direct reference to an associational chain encompassing General Elliot, Philip Astley, George III, and all other great military men who fulfilled their civic duty to the kingdom. In this act, John dressed in the theatrical version of a military coat—complete with service medals—a costume similar to those worn by these military men. In this way, John may have literally clothed himself in the guise of these men, and through dance with the Charger may have adopted their courageous souls. He channeled the heroism, status, and bravery of great men in an admirable example of pantomime at its best. Nevertheless, John did not lose sight of himself in these performances. His public interior self as conversationalist and refined gentleman shone through, and as a result his dances conjured up a new form of military hero who shared similarities to his father but was also radically different.

In John's interpretation of heroic masculinity, Elliot, Astley, and George III became not figures of brave skill at arms ready to join the fight, but above all gentlemen. They were military men, but critics also interpreted them as civilized, polite, and refined. They were idealized as General Wolfe figures (another popular character for John during his Amphitheatre career), who embodied and "valorized the national character," which was "courageous, aggressive, conquering, [and] manly," because of their interactions with a noble Charger.[140] However, they also exhibited the complementary and necessary private and public qualities that would ensure that they would be "polite, affable, gentle, free, and unreserved in Conversation," with the "extensive Spirit of Benevolence" thought necessary for the continued peace and imperial strength of the nation. These men were confident in themselves and in their oratory abilities. According to John's performances with the Charger, Britain needed something more than just the nostalgic chivalry of Philip Astley. It needed virtues beyond honor and the ability to swing the broadsword or perform well under fire.[141] The kingdom needed heroes if it was going to mend from the past war, end the constitutional crisis brought about by George's illness, and survive the impending troubles of the 1790s. Britain needed heroes who were "truly brave, truly noble, friendly and candid, gentle and beneficent, great and glorious!"[142]

AMPHITHEATRE SCHOOL OF THE ARTS

Ultimately, however, both forms of masculinity were necessary. John's masculinity and dancing on horseback, as displayed in the course of an evening's entertainment at the Amphitheatre, could not exist separately from his father's. An idea seemingly acknowledged by both men, the lessons and masculinities of beneficial patriotism and military might embodied in John's and Philip's performances with the Gibraltar Charger were needed side by side if the nation were to remain strong. And how better to illustrate the necessity of this togetherness of masculinities than through another famous Amphitheatre performance in which dancing *with* horses was the aim? As one correspondent noted, "Among the great variety of amusements which is exhibited at Mr. Astley's Ambigu-Comic, there is none . . . more truly pleasing than the Equestrian Minuet, between him and young Astley"; this was the very same minuet for which the Royal Circus had mocked John Astley as a he/she girl. The Amphitheatre's minuet with two horses was "a sight that not only entertains the attention from its excellence, but it also interests the feelings of nature, from its uniting the father and son in,—thus exhibiting their conjoined efforts to please, and their devoirs to thank the audience, of whose liberal patronage they are so much the deserved favorites." The "manliness and dignity of the one, with the youth and grace of the other, display a picture of relative performance, which certainly has no equal in any of our boasted diversions."[143] In the minuets, the horses and riders dance "with surprising grace," with "each keeping time to the music, in a manner truly extraordinary." The result was "full houses, unbounded applause, every time the horses appeared."[144] The horses, trained to move according to the beats of the music, seemed to "dance" as well as human performers on the theater stage, and with such a "graceful appearance" that it was joked in the newspapers that Astley was "engaged for the next season as Ballet-master to the Opera-house."[145] Astley's minuets were "executed with a precision and exactness of time that truly astonish," and made the performer's control, grace, and ease on horseback easily visible.[146]

Astley described the "famous minuet danced by two Horses," along with their training, in his *System of Equestrian Education,* as follows:

> In the first place, my Horses were educated to PIAFE loftily, with grace, elegance, and agility (Haydon's minuet regulated the action of the PIAFE during the salute) as also the TERRE-À-TERRE, which brought us to opposite corners. The action of the DEMI-VOLTES, to approach each other for the purpose of giving our hands (foreshortened our Horses to great animation by a corresponding APPUI and aid of the leg) in the action of the PIAFE, we came nearer each other, head and croup, continuing the PIAFE on our centre, an intire round; prior to which we gave our hands, and then let them gracefully descend to their original position. . . .
>
> Here both our Horses fronting the spectators (and precisely on the same ground we occupied at the commencement of the minuet) each by a graceful APPUI and corresponding *aids,* foreshortened and threw them well upon their hanches, [*sic*] (nearly to a balance) encouraging them into a brilliant and lofty PIAFE. . . . After

a CADENCE with a stop, we each made a PIAFE back to the same ground[,] my son to the left and myself to the right, and continuing the PIAFE concluded the minuet with the music; after which, each of us pressed his Horse's side with sharp horizontal spurs, animated him to the highest action of the PIAFE in quick time, to a sprightly air, which concluded the performance: our Horses retrograding out of the Amphitheatre by two opposite doors, croup foremost, amidst the highest applause of the spectators.

Sharing many similarities with today's popular performances of dressage set to music, known as the *kür*, or musical freestyle, Astley introduced the minuet as "the *ne plus ultra* of the MANEGE; in short, [as] the admiration of every Professor" of horsemanship, and as the ultimate proof of his method of training horse and rider either for war or for "the science of Equestrian public amusement."[147] Astley's minuets placed before a mixed audience a form of entertainment similar to the grand equestrian carousels popular in the sixteenth- and seventeenth-century courts of France and Italy, which were also a regular component of the Royal Academy for Teaching Exercises in Edinburgh.[148] This academy, open to a fee-paying elite clientele and led by Domenico Angelo's brother, Anthony Angelo Malevolti Tremamondo, each season hosted a carousel—or a choreographed ballet to music—performed by its pupils. These carousels were by-invitation-only performances by elite horsemen riding in the grand old-school style before other elites. At Astley's, they were performed by itinerant theater performers (fig. 20) before a general audience of questionable horsemanship knowledge. Even though the display of elite horsemanship in an amphitheater famous for animal performance and a history of fairground itinerancy was a clear element of the subsequent attacks against Astley's, it served a necessary purpose for Astley. He incorporated minuets to create a display of riding designed to encompass patriotism and military masculinity while serving as visible advertising for another key element of the Amphitheatre's program of events: its use as a riding house.

The Amphitheatre opened its doors for the instruction of horses and humans of all genders and ages, while providing the stage for weekly horse auctions.[149] Men were to learn vaulting and all skills in the manège, and they were to do so through a theatrical or dancer's exaggeration of the musical equestrian (horse and human) body thought necessary by most previous horsemen, regardless of which horsemanship community they belonged to. Expressed and somewhat confusingly discussed as "Cadence,"

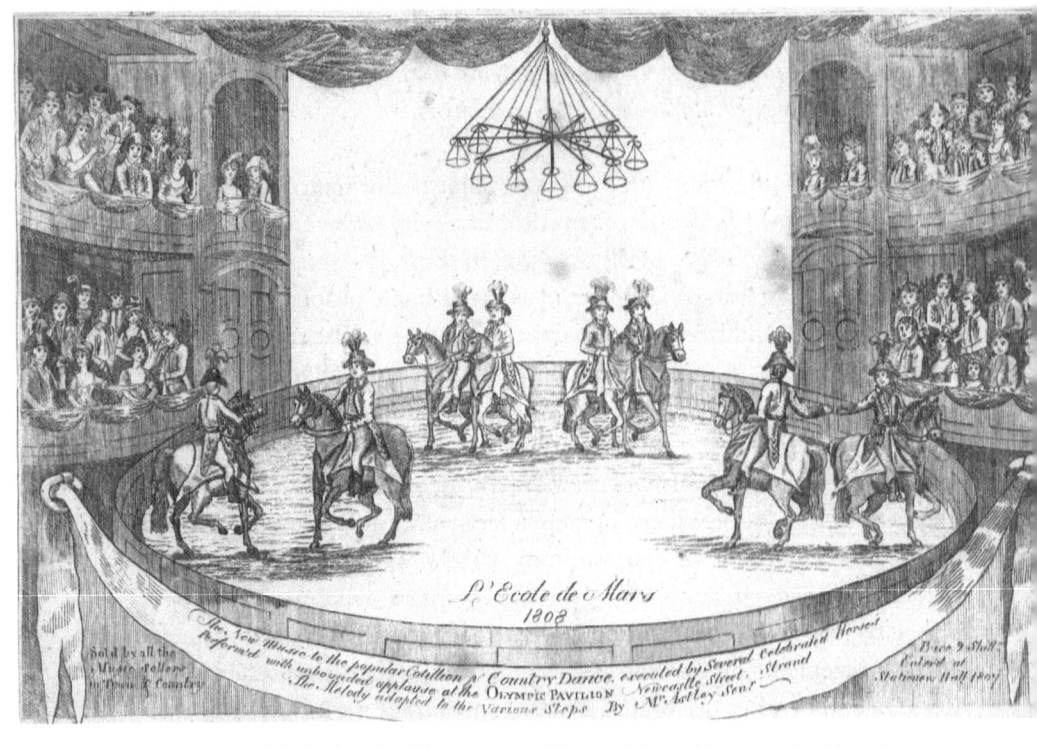

FIGURE 20 *L'Ecole de Mars*, 1808. Photo courtesy of The Lewis Walpole Library, Yale University.

a word Astley also used to describe a specific movement within his minuet, Astley's method developed musicality and rhythm in both man and horse as the foundation upon which all other teaching was built. He defined "Pure CADENCE," or true "grace and elegance," which "yields the highest satisfaction to an observer endowed with taste and discernment," as the harmonious movement between man and horse. It was "similar to such measure regulated in dancing, &c. Musical expression, or sound," which "certainly appertains to the tuition of the Horse, and which I consider as an index to direct his most willing obedience." Most important, cadence "is the very essence of regulating not only the Horse's natural paces, but also his artificial airs: in short, every thing where perfection and skill is necessary." It was "the *Ne plus Ultra* of Equestrian execution" and required both the rider's musicality and the horse's expressive movement of it.[150] Only with pure cadence, the rhythm of man and horse working together, could something like the minuet come to fruition. If the cadence of horse and rider were broken, the pair would instantly seem out of tune; their dancing would not match the rhythm of Haydn's music.[151] Only with cadence properly performed, and the strong, healthy, and active body of the horse attuned to the strong, healthy, and active body of the rider, could Astley show an edifying ideal on the Amphitheatre stage.

In the Amphitheatre, men could learn the skills needed for a happy and healthy life and the skills necessary for Astley's image of ideal military heroism, especially important in a time of corrupted horsemanship ability and atrophied military masculinity. A reform of masculinity and of the equestrian institutions that allowed for its creation was necessary. As Astley recalled, "My late general, George Augustus Elliot, (Lord Heathfield) as well as his son, the present gallant Lord, also the present gallant Earl of Pembroke, and the brave General Floyd were with me in the old Equestrian School; and I know well these heroic noblemen most anxiously wish for scientific schools in order to promote a more extensive knowledge of Equestrian Education, and I am convinced they would afford every assistance to professors of this art." The Amphitheatre was such an institution, where instructors who were visibly spectacular in their horsemanship abilities could carry out scientific approaches to equestrian education, but it was also an institution created through private commercial enterprise. Astley's was not like the equestrian academies of Europe or the Royal School in Edinburgh; however, Astley anticipated that it was a step in the right direction, and if, during their hoped for patronage of future royal riding schools, places like Astley's received "every assistance," so much the better. In the meantime, the Amphitheatre continued to do everything in its power to promote horsemanship and military prowess for the benefit of the nation. The minuet by father and son was, after all, "the admiration of every Professor" who saw it, and the Amphitheatre was the riding school of choice, according to Astley's advertising, for men who wished to see young recruits enter into their military careers properly developed for honorable success.[152] With the teaching of Philip and John Astley, pupils could vault and manège a horse as burgeoning heroes in their own right.

These young men, if correctly educated in Astley's mongrel system of high and low equestrian tradition, would also begin to improve the quality and serviceability of the nation's horses. A discourse frequently found in other horsemanship manuals, a discourse that lamented the apparent decline in quality horses for want of worthy riders, makes its appearance in Astley's writing, but with a difference. Astley's theories of public and military equestrianism expressly drew upon his own experiences in military service. There, riders who were capable of producing quality horses were not enough; the horses needed to be serviceable prior to their introduction to the battlefield. They needed to be educated at home.

> The present mode of training and breaking Horses, is highly reprehensible, and injurious to the character of a country, so distinguished as this is for the breed of Horses. There is not a scientific riding school in this kingdom, or any regular professor of *Equestrian Education:* neither are there any authors who have written on the subject, that have as yet noticed in any of their publications, an effectual method of teaching Horses to stand fire! so that one of the most useful and necessary points appertaining to the art of war, seems still at sea, floating on the surface of absurdity, and driven by the tide of prejudice from the shore of amendment!![153]

In typical theatrical fashion, Astley argued that he was the one who could heroically swoop in to save the day. He purposely developed a horse-training methodology expressly intended to rectify the current lamentable situation, which had led to multiple British losses in battle and, by the time his manual was published in 1801, saw Britain in a protracted war with Napoleonic France. According to Astley, there was only one "scientific riding school" in the kingdom that could not only prepare riders for battle but teach horses to withstand all the sensory experiences associated with the battlefield.

In 1782 Astley received a royal letters patent for

> a new and peculiar method of rendering horses tractable and docile, preventing in a great measure that kind of fear which most of them are subject to on the road, and whereby certain agile, manly, and war exercises may be performed upon them without danger, and effectually teaches them to stand the explosion of large ordnance, beating of drums, all kinds of music, and every other violent noise, without emotion, and likewise the recoil of small ordnance fixed upon and fired from the saddle by a single Dragoon, every way equipt as Light Dragoons commonly are (carbine only excepted).[154]

"Mr. ASTLEY's new Method of training Horses for Road, Field, his Majesty's Service, &c," expressed in his patent and his three riding manuals, conflated riding on the road for pleasure with the commonsense use of any man's horse for military service (fig. 21).[155] With the patent, Astley could create those cherished and invaluable horses so much in demand by present and future soldiers. He could create horses who were unflappable in the face of everything that horses not desensitized to such sights and sounds would strenuously object to by "instantly turn[ing] tail"— certainly no more desirable on the road than in battle.[156] By teaching horses to calmly withstand fire and firearms (especially the extreme of instructing horses to stand calm while small ordnance was fired from their backs), and then placing such horses on the Amphitheatre stage, Astley showed his audiences not only the necessity and practicalities of such training but also the possibility of their coming to be worthy of such an animal. Spectators too could become Astley and Elliot figures, secure in their horsemanship, and their horses could become figures like the Gibraltar Charger. Together, Astley's horse and human pupils could learn to become courageous, great, and glorious for both their own improvement and that of the nation. At Astley's "Royal Riding-School," as the Amphitheatre was dubbed in some advertising that highlighted the royal letters patent (see fig. 21), if given enough training, pupils could join the musical heroes in the Amphitheatre ring. They could vault, manège, and dance on horseback with the "first Stage Dancers in *Europe*," and they could come to embody the militarism and measured grace of Astley and John as ideal(ized) masculine men. At the same time, their horses could learn the devilish tricks of the Amphitheatre's Learned Horses alongside

FIGURE 21 Philip Astley, handbill, 1782. The British Library. Photo © The British Library Board, LR.301.h.3-11.

the truly enviable ardor to serve as the "army's friend and guide" performed by the Charger while "entirely covered with fire" in their heroic defense of the nation.

MANLY EXERCISES

Astley's Amphitheatre was an essential part of the eighteenth-century London theater scene, regardless of what theater critics and patent theaters stated to the contrary. As Charles Dibdin the Younger argued, "Minor Theatres possess much more importance than is allowed them by some, and Minor Actors, are equally more significant than is considered by others; and if the genuine voice of Criticism in our superior diurnals, would occasionally point out their merits, and defects, it would be of essential service to them, and (in as much as the Theatres—minor as well as major—produce a strong effect upon the public mind) of great use to the Community."[157] For Philip and John Astley, Astley's Amphitheatre possessed more merit than the many other illegitimate theaters of the time; it was essential to the nation and of the greatest use to the community because of its equestrian focus. The Astleys argued that their performances with horses did more than entertain. "If the Management of the Horses through all its various, useful, and extensive Parts, can boast of publick utility, Master ASTLEY stands unrivalled." The Astleys' continued popularity suggests that they touched deep chords in English audiences. Performing with horses, especially ones like the Gibraltar Charger, remained central not only to the Amphitheatre's idea of "publick utility" but also to fundamental conceptions of nationalistic gendered display. For Astley, the performance of courage and partnership on the battlefield with a mount of uncommon ability, an extension of himself, was properly masculine. For John, bodily control, grace, and physical allure, and his embodiment of national heroism through his horse, were the key to maintaining a prosperous nation. Both father and son performed rememorations of a glorious past "aimed at forgetting the more recent and pressing defeat in America" and at helping the kingdom survive the many crises of the 1788–89 seasons in exchange for a glorious construction of masculinity on horseback.[158]

But not all Amphitheatre reviewers considered these performances useful or beneficial to Britain. Accusations of uselessness formed an undercurrent to the rhetoric of masculinity and horsemanship on the Amphitheatre stage. John's "VARIOUS SURPRISING NEW ATTITUDES of

DANCING on a Single Horse" were, one critic complained, "thought by every horseman in *England, Germany,* and *France* impracticable."[159] No public utility was to be found in a man who took the potentially effeminizing practice of dance and transferred it to the back of a horse, regardless of that horse's own glorious past or the ability of man and horse to perform an image of beneficial politics; there was no morality or advantage in such acts. This was also the case with Philip Astley's pantomimic performances with his horses, which critics sometimes considered corrupting, dangerous, and opposed to everything legitimate theater stood for. For some, Astley's brand of performance, much like illegitimate theater in general, was destructive, dangerous, and sacrilegious to "traditional" visual, performance, and textual arts and their associated ideal virtues.[160] The Amphitheatre offered a hodgepodge of acts, undermining heroic speeches by famous playwrights and delivered by famous actors on the legitimate stage. These uncomfortable elements of the Amphitheatre and its actors opened Astley's and other minor theaters to criticism and ridicule from those distressed by their apparent corrupting influence.[161] Many feared that the attractiveness of such popular commercial entertainment, regardless of the time and effort spent emphasizing the full support for English patriotism and monarchy, would lead to the devastation, violation, and general neglect of beneficial masculine pastimes and morals.

For example, Samuel Collings's 1784 caricature *The Downfall of Taste & Genius, or The World as it goes* shows Astley's motley troupe of circus performers, which included the Learned Pig, General Jackoo (the monkey mounted on a large dog), various clowns (including a harlequin and a Mother Shipton), dogs and other animals masquerading in human dress, the Frenchman Vincent Lunardi with his air balloon (a popular act at the Amphitheatre), Astley (or "Philip the Big") on foot, and John in his characteristic role of equestrian dancer (fig. 22).[162] The motley group of (animalized) humans and (humanized) animals are shown chasing and knocking down taste and genius, in the feminized form of the arts and truth, while trampling underfoot examples of truly tasteful and virtuously English artistic works—those of Pope and Shakespeare. Painting, Music, and Sculpture—the fine arts—are the first to be trampled by the Frenchified mob. All three arts have dropped the respective tools of their trades and look pleadingly at the charging beastly masses. Truth herself has fallen victim to Faction and Discord, in the guise of a hooded woman on the far left who is holding a snake aloft in her left hand and, in her right, Truth's mirror, which she has stolen and cracked, rendering Truth's power useless.

FIGURE 22 Samuel Collings, *The Downfall of Taste & Genius, or The World as it goes*, 1784. Photo © Trustees of the British Museum. All rights reserved.

Collings has depicted Nature as a fertility idol, and has shown her as incapable of escaping the ravages of human vanity and immorality associated with the Amphitheatre. These social vices are represented as a grotesque jester who is busy transforming Nature into a vain, effeminate, frivolous woman by dressing her freshly frizzled hair with the finishing touches of powder. Behind the chaotic scene of desecration are Fame (holding two broken trumpets), Wisdom (holding a broken spear, beheaded and with her owl perched on the remaining stump), Justice (with a broken sword and scales), and Virtue (crippled and begging for charity) in the form of classical sculptures on battered stone columns.[163]

Critics also discussed the horsemanship performances and skill of Astley and sometimes found them wanting. One knowledgeable commentator on the development and patenting of Astley's unique form of training horses to withstand the shock of drums, fire, and other battlefield noise, for example, was particularly scathing in his views. According to him, Astley's methods and methodologies (not to mention success) in horsemanship were nothing more than "exhibitions of folly and manœuvring ribaldry" at "the *Astleyan* stables near Westminster Bridge." "Mr. Astley's *equestrian patent,*" he continued, was "in one point of view, well enough adapted, *i.e.* to himself; he would therefore do well to confine his industry to the exclusive practice it entitles him to——Instead of *Ladies* and *Gen'men,* in the theatre, the words *mares* and *horses,* in a stable, would grace the mouth of this Knight of the *Pad* much better."[164] Astley's patented horsemanship was useful only to Astley, and the ridiculous and irrational frivolity of the Amphitheatre masqueraded as beneficial displays of horsemanship. In the view of this critic, Astley embodied animality rather than the refined gentility he professed to model. He and his performers and patrons were not ladies and gentlemen but veritable horses themselves; they were animals practicing and enjoying a degenerative, unnatural, and irrational form of horsemanship unsuited to any proper horsemanship community. Instead of enjoying status as a master of horsemanship, for this critic Astley was derogatorily described as "Knight of the *Pad*," or master of the lady's horse of choice (a position Mr. Carter may also have found himself occupying); Astley, by extension, was something of a woman himself, this writer implied. His patented horsemanship was effeminate and unsuited to useful theater or horsemanship. Astley's Amphitheatre was not, for everyone, the temple of innovative horsemanship that Philip and John Astley made it out to be, and the most entertaining and powerful attack against it came from the Astleys' equestrian contemporary Henry William Bunbury.

4.

HENRY WILLIAM BUNBURY AND THE MOCK MANUALS OF HORSEMANSHIP

Certain comic effects can be achieved by a
brand-new rider, especially a man who dresses
like a fashion model and rides like a tailor.

—C. J. J. MULLEN

But he in the whirl of dust lay mighty and
mightily fallen, forgetful of his horsemanship.

—HOMER

"This ludicrous work . . . is, in many instances, executed with very great humour, and irresistibly provokes our laughter," gushed the reviewers for the *European Magazine, and London Review* in October 1787. Similarly, the *British Critic* of 1809 found that "the singular, and truly original humour of the writing, and the unrivalled burlesque of the plates, have always made these books prime favourites," while the reviewer for the *New Annual Register* of 1792 simply stated "that those who can read and view it, with unmoved muscles, do not belong to that company with which we wish to associate."[1] Dubbed the "Second Hogarth" and "the Raphael of Caricaturists," Henry William Bunbury's (1750–1811) pseudonymous *Academy for Grown Horsemen* (1787) and *Annals of Horsemanship* (1791) provide a unique perspective on the men of London.[2] Both hilariously satirical, these publications merged textual observation with the increasingly popular genre of caricature to form two books that not only were popular during Bunbury's lifetime but prompted William Cowper to comment that "Bunbury sells humour by the yard, and is, I suppose, the first Vender of it who ever did so."³ Bunbury was one of the eighteenth century's preeminent caricaturists, a "proto-celebrity" whose work went on to influence some of the greatest caricaturists and authors of subsequent ages.⁴

A renowned horseman throughout his life (he became equerry to the Duke of York the same year *An Academy for Grown Horsemen* was published, and he was probably known to both Astley and Angelo), Bunbury was uniquely situated to produce his many illustrations and stories of horsemen in various states of mounted ineptitude.⁵ The second son of Baronet, Reverend Sir William Bunbury, Henry Bunbury was educated at the elite institutions of Westminster and Cambridge, undertook a grand tour to France, Florence, and Rome to improve his artistic abilities, and was friends with many notables from the Angelo circle, including Joshua Reynolds, David Garrick, Oliver Goldsmith, Horace Walpole, and Samuel Johnson. He was also an honorary exhibitor at the Royal Academy at Reynolds's invitation; wrote the mock-gothic collection *Tales of the Devil* and various poems for Matthew Lewis's *Tales of Terror* (1801); illustrated the 1773 edition of Laurence Sterne's *Tristram Shandy;* illustrated an edition of *The Arabian Nights,* and became lieutenant of the West Sussex Militia (though he never saw battle), from which he retired with the rank of lieutenant colonel. As this brief biography indicates, he was a well-known personality within London's elite riding house, theater, and literary circles.⁶

While both his great-grandson and recent scholars have described his caricatures as "social comments" and as essentially apolitical, Bunbury's caricatures and written satires followed in the footsteps of previous works on horsemanship and as such were innately politicized.⁷ Taking a direct interest in changing social conventions of ideal masculinity and political thought, Bunbury's mock manuals were satirical comments on the history of English horsemanship practice, along with the many changes made to the traditionally elite art form during the eighteenth century. Bunbury expressed many of the same ideological goals as his equestrian contemporaries, who were busy wowing their audiences at Astley's Amphitheatre or consuming the teachings of men like Charles Hughes, J. L. Jackson, and Charles Thompson, but he did so from the traditional heart of horsemanship practice. Bunbury was of the social elite, and spent his time associating with the men and women of the legitimate theater and fine arts rather than the itinerant performers who showcased a hybrid (arguably corrupted) form of horsemanship. Like the anonymous critic who considered Astley's patent and Amphitheatre performances better suited to mares and horses than to men and women, Bunbury was at heart a traditionalist. He considered the maintenance of older forms of social stratification, political engagement, and elite behavior sacrosanct, while he thought horsemen like Mr. Carter and the Astleys the living embodiment of complete degeneration. For Bunbury, men like the Astleys were symptomatic of larger social changes and discourses that increasingly turned away from "traditional" forms of political involvement, acceptable social behavior, and gendered display.

The late eighteenth century, as Linda Colley has shown, saw an increased attack on the British elite from below—especially during the French Revolution, when similar anti-elite sentiment spread throughout Europe. There was a definite trend toward seeing the British upper classes, particularly the highest echelons, as parasitic and subversive of the nation's interest rather than as exemplars of patriotic civic virtue. One anonymous author wrote, "Our nobility placed on an eminence among the people, instead of supporting the dignity of their station, are become a shame and disgrace to it." Furthermore, said another critic, "Our young noblemen are jockies, whoremasters, and spendthrifts, while those advanced in years are repairing the waste of their youth, by a shameful plunder of the public."[8] Jockeyship, by the second half of the century, was synonymous with "rogue" or "jock," and was a vulgar term meaning "to coit with a woman." Accusations of jockeyship, by the time Bunbury was writing, also effectively equated the governing elite with grooms who rose above their station.[9] Thus, like the jockey, the elite were accused of untrustworthiness and of performing actions they were not suited to, and of becoming irresponsible servants of the nation who would rather, like Cavendish, spend their time and effort in personal pleasures (to their and the nation's shame and disgrace) instead of doing their duty to the public.

Coupled with these general attacks on the uselessness of the elite was a discourse against luxury, which argued that it was corrupting for the middling sort. This discourse was also leveled against the ruling elite, and it stipulated that the elite's perceived luxurious, effeminate, and degenerate lifestyle resulted in a weak, impotent, and useless sector of society. James Graham commented in 1780 that "the labouring poor, who, in some sense, are forced to be temperate and active, are seldom without numerous and healthy issue, whilst the rich—those persons I mean whose time is spent in frivolous [sic] pursuits, in the gratification of every appetite, and in racketing about, turning day into night, and night into day, have generally a scantily puny offspring, and often none at all."[10] Likewise, Thomas Newenham remarked in 1803, "The greatest enemies to population are the artificial wants, the accumulation of property, and the luxury and vices which are the constant attendants of opulence, and which prevent a regular and early union between the sexes."[11] As a healthy population was widely thought to be a hallmark of a thriving and powerful nation with a strong commercial economy and clear division of labor, those who did not or could not participate in its increase because of their own (perceived) degenerate lifestyle and luxurious indulgences were not assisting in their nation's wealth, upholding the social contract, or fulfilling their civic duties.[12] Unlike the discourse of commerce, which maintained that private benefit resulted in public profit, the discourse of civic humanism—the backlash against such notions of profit—maintained that the state would benefit only from the performance of public duty.[13] Those, like the elite, who dissipated themselves in luxury were accused of turning their backs on the social virtues of civic humanism in order to indulge "*self-affections* which lead to the Good of THE PRIVATE" rather than cultivating "the *natural Affections,* which lead to the Good of THE PUBLICK."[14]

A final aspect of the attack on the gentry, and perhaps for Bunbury the most worrying, was the continual infringement of the newly wealthy and self-made man on elite circles. More lower-class people were practicing horsemanship, even attempting to teach it, and were, for Bunbury, completely monstrous as a result. These new instructors, exemplified by Philip Astley and Mr. Carter, were not masters (or professors) in the conventional sense of those who had personally perfected the art of horsemanship; they adopted the title of master without earning it. They may have been proficient in riding to a degree, and were able to "break" horses for diverse uses, but for Bunbury they were not true horsemen. These new riders were willing to dispense what knowledge they had to older beginners, and to men and women from the middling sorts if they could pay the instruction fee. As a result, they had commodified the sacrosanct pursuit of the hereditary elite while hijacking and corrupting their betters' teachings and values for their own ends.

This infiltration of ruling society by the lower orders, the frequent political attacks against them, and the elite's prolonged associations with effeminacy resulted in a closing of ranks and an increased social homogeneity among Bunbury's peers in the latter half of the century. However, as Colley phrases it, the elite were still left with the problem of "how, crudely, could the distinctive wealth, status and power of the new British ruling class be packaged and presented so as to seem beneficent rather than burdensome, a national asset rather than an alien growth?"[15] For Bunbury and other elite horsemen, the answer was to retreat into the traditionally aristocratic and militaristic practice of the manège, while lampooning the equestrian efforts of men from other horsemanship communities, thus killing two birds with one stone. As Étienne-Jules Marey asked in 1899, "Did we not see that during the past century the equerries made it their ideal to assemble their horses for the purpose of inducing them to execute movements that were considered elegant? They even went so far as to ridicule the rider who seemed to demand nothing more of his horse than the quickest possible arrival at his destination."[16] Bunbury was the preeminent satirist of the eighteenth century who ridiculed the new breed of horseman because they viewed horsemanship as a mechanical pastime rather than an art. Instead of looking to simplify their personal display, as many elite men did in order to distance themselves from the conspicuous consumption of the middling sort, Bunbury looked to ostentatious display. The manège was thought of as not only allowing gentlemen to become versed in military duty and learn the patriotic and civic skills that would allow them successfully to defend the nation; it would also instill the proper masculine virtues central to civic humanism.[17] They would become socially refined men who embodied both the old-school model of public, properly aristocratic civic virtue and a modern sensitivity to social benevolence and fellow feeling.

Bunbury (practicing during the "golden age of graphic satire," and mirroring the rhetoric of civic virtue voiced by members of the Royal Academy) echoed the work of other eighteenth-century horsemen by employing the potential didacticism of visual and textual satire to (re)assert, (re)normalize, and reintroduce the manège as the chief means of instilling socially refined discourse and centauric grammatical exactness in the elite along with proper governing values.[18] He, like the civic humanist John Brown, was working to generate "the *Capacity, Valour,* and *Union,* of those who *lead* the People" through his satire.[19] By lampooning inept horsemen, Bunbury engaged with popular sociopolitical discourses on the role and deportment of the elite in society, on civic humanism, and on ideal masculinity. By perpetuating the discourse of horsemanship found in the writings of William Cavendish, Henry Herbert, and Richard Berenger, he attempted to draw other elite to the manège, like these horsemen before him, in order to solidify a community of horsemen defined by shared languages—a community that would promote the masculine virtues of the sensitive military man while continuing to solidify the weakened ranks of the elite against the seemingly increased embourgeoisement of society. By sketching antitheses to his image of the properly masculine and socially elevated horseman, Bunbury drove home the idea that anyone not socially or naturally worthy of practicing the manège, or anyone who attempted to mask his essential unsuitability for the art, would be betrayed in his efforts through the visible spectacle of horsemanship itself. He argued that horsemanship through the manège (if performed discursively and with sensitive feeling by those deserving of the activity) would promote a passion for the nation and instill the necessary virtues in those in power. As John Brown put it, the "Manners and Principles of those who *lead,* not of those who *are led;* of those who *govern,* not of those who *are governed;* of those, in short, who *make* Laws or *execute* them, will ever determine the Strength or Weakness, and therefore the Continuance or Dissolution, of a State."[20] Horsemen were to lead, govern, and make laws for the betterment of the nation. Anyone not of their hereditary, "self-selective and self-authenticating" ranks who attempted to appropriate horsemanship for themselves, a model exemplified by the Astley family, would be without civic ability and interest, and would ultimately endanger the nation and its inhabitants.

THE CIVIC HUMANISM OF EQUESTRIAN CARICATURE

John Barrell argues that in a time of perceived dissolution of the civic polis, in exchange for a society fragmented along the lines of rampant individualism and the division of labor, the rhetoric of civic humanism was alive and well among artists of the late eighteenth century. These men, primarily members of the Royal Academy, considered their art one of the chief means of creating a sense of public spirit and individual virtue that would in turn ensure a man's citizenship in a healthy body politic.[21] In order to establish this political republic of select citizens, artists used their paintings to establish a "republic of taste" that would determine who possessed the republic's civic virtues and who did not or were incapable of doing so. As Joshua Reynolds argued, "no taste can ever be formed in manufacturers; but if the higher Arts of Design flourish, these inferior ends will be answered of course."[22] For Reynolds, only artists and connoisseurs, those men of independent means and civic virtue who looked to art as art, as something greater than mere nature, as something to be practiced at its highest level, could possess taste. Those who copied others in their work, for example, and those who painted for money or simply recorded what they saw around them in nature, were mere mechanics and were automatically excluded from this republic of taste.[23]

As a close friend of Reynolds's (who was godfather to Bunbury's second son, Henry Edward) and a repeat exhibitor at the Royal Academy, Bunbury was also working to recoalesce a republic of taste made up of elite horsemen who exhibited "public spirit" through their horsemanship.[24] He worked to do "good to all," and to reaffirm, with a properly masculine feeling, a sense of public spirit firmly rooted in "traditional" forms of civic humanism.[25] In doing so, Bunbury followed the writings of the early eighteenth-century authors who argued that only the elite could be civic in virtue and in actual practice, and thus were fit to be citizens of the political republic of taste.[26] These truly public men would have fulfilled the three basic requirements of civic humanism in its most "traditional" form, as expressed by authors like Anthony Ashley-Cooper, Earl of Shaftesbury, and James Thomson, rather than those of the increasingly influential middling and commercial sort. These requirements were, for Thomson, an "independent life; Integrity in office; and, o'er all Supreme, a passion for the commonweal."[27] The first qualification required men who enjoyed landed property or other independent incomes that removed all necessity of "mechanical" employment or speculative endeavors, allowing them enough leisure time to devote themselves to public office or the bearing of arms—activities indispensable to a liberal man's second qualification, "integrity in office." The third, and certainly the most necessary, qualification was that of a true devotion to the nation and its inhabitants. Without this belief in the primary goal of civic humanism, those both best suited by birth to achieve it while possessing the means to do so could not achieve the protection and prosperity of the state.[28]

While this civic desire was a core value for many late eighteenth-century artists, such as Reynolds and William Hazlitt, their ability to generate it was limited primarily to history or epic painting. Artists organized the fine arts within a hierarchy of political power and civic discourse, with history painting situated firmly at the top and more domestic or private genres of painting, such as portraiture, at the bottom.[29] Visual satire, or caricature and comic painting, was often considered one of the preeminent private genres of art and hence not capable of generating a republic of taste or a sense of shared civic virtue. Reynolds was somewhat ambiguous about the genre's function, suggesting that it was either a private medium and hence not suitable for instruction in public virtue, or exempt from the requirement to provide it. Barrell does not question

Reynolds's position here and argues, drawing on Thomson's theory of the nonpublic nature of "rapid Pictures" or comic images, that comic painting was an essentially private medium, where its connoisseurs would enjoy it in a parlor or other "private" part of a home. There, the comic images could be taken out and enjoyed at leisure; they were ephemeral, temporary, transitory in interest and effect. They were images to be consumed rapidly in an environment where men were "not required to act responsibly" as public men. Comic images were unable and unintended to engage with the public man in his civic capacity; in Thomson's words, they "ask no questions, and make no statements, that have to be engaged in a public, in a political space."[30]

However, for practicing caricaturists such as Captain Francis Grose and Bunbury, comic painting could and should work, like public heroic or history painting, to create feelings of civic virtue and the desire to act on those feelings. Eighteenth-century caricature asked questions, made statements, and engaged with a political and public discourse. Caricature could create desires in an audience of men of taste, desires to follow not the satirized subject but its opposite in virtuous behavior. As the foundational Roman caricaturist, Annibale Carracci, reflected: "Is it not the caricaturist's task exactly the same as the classical artist's? Both see the lasting truth beneath the surface of mere outward appearance. Both try to help nature accomplish its plan. The one may strive to visualise the perfect form and to realise it in his work, the other to grasp the perfect deformity, and thus reveal the very essence of a personality. A good caricature, like every work of art, is more true to life than reality itself."[31] It is through this projection of reality that caricature could improve civic morals and "help nature accomplish its plan" by influencing an elite public depleted in virtue, and for Bunbury, whose caricatures were "remarkable for their truthful force," feelings of civic duty.[32] Francis Grose, one of the pioneering British caricaturists and a clear model for Bunbury, discussed the forcefulness of comic painting in his 1788 *Rules for Drawing Caricatures* in language that mirrors the political discourse of artists such as Reynolds and is firmly civic humanist in form. "In order to do justice to the art in question," Grose posited, "it should be considered, that it is one of the elements of satirical painting, which, like poetry of the same denomination, may be most efficaciously employed in the cause of virtue and decorum, by holding up to public notice many offenders against both, who are amenable to any other tribunal; and who, though they contemptuously defy all serious reproof, tremble at the thoughts of seeing their vices of follies attacked by the keen shafts of ridicule."³³ The power of caricature was grounded on fear, and could indeed have a forceful impact on those targeted by the artist's pencil. However, instead of illustrating an ideal like history painting, caricaturists illustrated the monstrous, deformed, and ugly in order to ridicule their subjects and establish a shared republic of taste. According to Vic Gatrell, caricatures operated within a "shame-culture where public demolition of reputation was the most feared of social sanctions." This was a real fear for the Prince of Wales, who was mercilessly satirized by caricaturists like George Cruikshank. Cruikshank's attacks on the prince were his "one fear," according to the Duke of Wellington, and they resulted in his withdrawal from public view from 1812 to 1820. Eventually, after trying to have his caricaturists prosecuted for seditious libel, he resorted to bribing them for their silence.³⁴

Although Bunbury, unlike Cruikshank, Thomas Rowlandson, and James Gillray, did not often comment on specific individuals, his written and figurative work could generate worry over the preservation of public reputation and honor among the British social elite. Frances Burney, for example, recorded in June 1781 that during an evening in Streatham, "Dr. Johnson" (renowned for his unusual height) "*forced* me to sit on a very small sofa with him, which was hardly large enough for himself; and which would have made a subject for a print by Harry Bunbury that would have diverted all London; *ergo,* it rejoiceth me that he was not present."³⁵ Upon meeting Bunbury for the first time on August 14, 1787, Burney complained, "So now we may all be caricatured at his leisure!" "A man with such a turn, and with talents so inimitable in displaying it, was a rather dangerous character to be brought within a Court!" Burney feared that Bunbury might just print a caricature that emphasized qualities, both moral and physical, that his subjects would rather have kept quiet as part of a lesson in proper decorum and civic feeling. Later, on Sunday, August 23, after meeting with Colonel Gwynne, General Bufe, and Bunbury at Windsor, she noted, "All the household has agreed to fear him, except Mrs. Schwellenberg [Queen Charlotte's former nurse], who is happy he cannot caricature her because, she says, she has no *Hump.*"³⁶ In Burney's opinion, Bunbury was troubling and untrustworthy (although he did manage to entertain her on a couple of occasions, and she was on good terms with his wife, Catherine Horneck) while his sociability and "mildness and urbanity" in discourse never did "lead . . . [her] to forget his pencil and the power of his caricature."³⁷ Bunbury was a formidable individual within elite literary, political, and military circles, and was famed (and feared) for his powers of social defamation.

Yet his fame was not restricted to the drawing rooms of the London literary set. Bunbury's name, along with his pseudonym, Geoffrey Gambado, became synonymous with socially and politically inept men on horseback within months of the publication of *An Academy for Grown Horsemen* (September 1, 1787). The newspaper *World* reported in the February 14, 1788, issue that "towards half past two, various Members [of Parliament] were amusing themselves very pleasantly in the [Hyde] Park, practising the Rules of Riding laid down by *Geofry* [sic] *Gambado*—or BUNBURY for him." Also, one commentator in the February 23, 1798, edition of the *Morning Post and Gazetteer* (shortly after Bunbury's two manuals were reissued together in one volume) sneered, "Heavy complaints have been made of the many *dreadful* accidents which have befallen several members of the Glasgow Troop of Cavalry, from a *want* of knowledge in the equestrian art, we recommend to their *serious perusal,* the excellent Hints to bad Horsemen of GEOFFREY GAMBADO, Esq."[38] Over the course of the late eighteenth century, the images and writings of "Geoffrey Gambado" became useful for describing the gambols of Hyde Park equestrians, and essential for the improvement of those whose horsemanship abilities were not up to acceptable standards and were now a drain on the nation. As Tobias Smollett commented in his glowing review of Bunbury's *Annals of Horsemanship,* "Geoffrey illustrates horsemanship, by praising the absurdities to be avoided; the facetious painter points the ridicule so strongly, that every picture becomes a forcible lesson."[39] Supporting Grose's and Carracci's perspective on the purpose of caricature, every picture was a powerfully visual lesson on the necessity for men to embrace and practice horsemanship for their own benefit as masculine men, and, more important, for the overall benefit of the nation.

Many of Bunbury's images, like other caricatures of the time, were available to the public and would have been viewed by men and women of all ages and every social, occupational, and financial status.[40] However, while all men had "the ability to recognise general ideas, and so the general classes into which men are grouped," only some could grasp the true message, the true knowledge—and hence the power—of a caricature.[41] Only some men would be able to see the detail and extrapolate the abstract, the political, from it as liberal and civic men. As Reynolds put it, "A hundred thousand near-sighted men, that see only what is just before them, make no equivalent to one man whose view extends to the whole horizon around him, though we may safely acknowledge at the same time that like the real near-sighted men they see and comprehend as distinctly what is within the focus of their sight as accurately (I will allow sometimes more accurately) than others."[42] A liberal man of taste, freed from mechanical occupation, would not only be able to understand the coding in liberal art; he would also grasp the role of the public and private in generating civic feeling. As Bunbury confidently stated in the language of civic humanism, "I doubt not, but every true judge of the noble art [horsemanship], will acknowledge the excellence of my instructions, and every true lover of it applaud my public spirit, in circulating them abroad for the benefit of mankind at large."[43] A vulgar reader or viewer would understand Bunbury's comic contribution (Bunbury's prints are full of slapstick and scatological humor that did not require specialized knowledge to decode) while being able to distinguish the properly elite elements of the art, but without understanding the subtleties of the many horsemanship-specific puns and jokes (and the many literary references), contained in Bunbury's work.

An Academy for Grown Horsemen and *The Annals of Horsemanship* were intended specifically for an audience that displayed exemplary equestrian knowledge and good taste in horsemanship methodologies. These men were the true judges and lovers of horsemanship. They were public men who, because of their elite, traditional, and properly masculine upbringing, were able to understand and appreciate the civic lessons in Bunbury's work. Because of their social position and independent means, they were able to pursue manège horsemanship for the nation's benefit from a young age and to become accepted horsemen within the horsemanship community. For Bunbury and other artists of the late eighteenth century, only those of "just taste" who possessed practical and theoretical experience in the art of horsemanship could avoid the appellations of bad horseman, unskillful rider, or man without taste.[44] Only those whose independent life and integrity in office possessed a passion for the benefit of mankind as citizens of the commonwealth and community of horsemen, and only true horsemen, born, bred, and properly instructed in the art, could pose a proper community of tasteful horsemen and come to reserve the civic sanctity and security of the nation.

To form his message of civic humanism, Bunbury looked to the popular *Annals of Agriculture* for inspiration. Begun in 1784, this serial periodical covered topics ranging from politics, weather, and methods of agricultural improvement to voyages of exploration and important European events. An influential text, it saw contributions from eminent political leaders like Lord Townshend and Joseph Banks, intellectuals such as Jeremy Bentham and Thomas Malthus, and even George III (writing under the pseudonym Ralph Robinson). Focusing on the "real prosperity and happiness of the human race" and the "improvement of the people in regard to their health, industry, and morals," the *Annals of Agriculture* mirrored the public improvement discourse of civic humanism found in many artists' writings, including Bunbury's.[45]

However, for Gambado, and the "Editor" of Bunbury's *Annals of Horsemanship*, the information contained in the *Annals of Agriculture* was inferior to the teachings of Geoffrey Gambado, Esq.:

> A paltry publication has lately made its appearance, on the same construction as this. It is a periodical thing, entitled The Annals of Agriculture, and will, I dare say, be of much use in the chandlers shops. This too, like Geoffrey's edifying collection of letters, treats on propagation, cultivation, preservation, the good of the nation, &c. &c. But when we once consider for a moment the different objects the authors claim our attention in behalf of— Should even a potatoe enter the lists with a poney, my blood rises— my choler is excited.
>
> Talk of propagation! Would the blockheads have us hesitate between a horse chesnut, and a chesnut horse! Common sense forbids it (particularly as it is to be the fashionable colour in harness this time five years); and as for preservation— Which should humanity first extend her arm to save? A cabbage or a cockney— A captain or a cauliflower? For these reasons I lament seeing, monthly, the names of several respectable friends of mine, affixed to a work of such subordinate consideration. Had they spent as much time in riding upon turnips, as they have in writing upon them, they might ere now have belonged to the first hunts in the country, and most fashionable clubs in town. But I fear the silk purse and the sows ear are but too applicable to most of them.
>
> ... And whilst the frantic farmers that furnish their stuff for the Annals of Agriculture, shall be puzzling their brains to preserve a ragged flock of sheep from the rot, the fair sex shall be more nobly employed in the preservation of beauty, and what is more puzzling, though we daily see it attempted— the preservation of even The Human Face Divine, itself.
>
> Emboldened by these considerations, that the Annals of Horsemanship will speedily drive the Annals of Agriculture out of the

house of every man and woman of taste and feeling, I do not hesitate to foresee.[46]

Bunbury wrote this complicated passage, riddled with double entendres, in typical oppositional and canting language. It conveys his reasons for writing and his hope that his mock manuals will be of use in the improvement of the nation by generating a culture of civically beneficial feeling among the governing elite. For Bunbury, a work like the *Annals of Agriculture* (and his own *Annals of Horsemanship*) could be highly influential (not a paltry publication), and the participating authors (those blockheads) were fulfilling the goals set out in civic-humanist discourses. Those frantic and improving farmers were the saviors of the nation, while the men and women of noncivic "taste and feeling," occupied with modish consumption, to whom the feminizing sow's ear and silken purse applied, were the lovers of luxury, vanity, and useless pastimes, the corrupters of social virtue (trying to improve the unimprovable "Human Face Divine") to the destruction of masculine civic duty. For Bunbury, the kingdom should support both potatoes and ponies for their life-giving and nation-improving potential, and, indeed, humanity should extend its arm to save the cabbage over the commercial, luxury-loving, gouty, and consumption-oriented cockney. The properly civic, militaristic, heroic, and publicly virtuous captain should be preserved over cauliflowers—defined by Grose in his *Classical Dictionary of the Vulgar Tongue* (one of Bunbury's primary sources for inspiration) as "a large white wig, such as is commonly worn by the dignified clergy, and was formerly by physicians. Also the private parts of a woman."[47] These effeminate clergy, quack physicians, and immoral women did not and could not subscribe to the civic teachings of the *Annals of Agriculture*. Only the genteel agricultural improvers and heroic men of the military—along with other civically virtuous men—and those who could understand Bunbury's civic coding as community-sanctioned horsemen in his *Annals of Horsemanship* (and who procured a copy to sit alongside *Agriculture* on their shelves) could cultivate civic feeling in the public, while convincing those with the means to do so to improve the nation. However, those who took Gambado's teachings at face value were unable to distinguish between a horse chestnut and a chestnut horse, and could not see the civic teachings contained in the satirical text and images. They would be the lovers of modish and luxurious display (riding in coaches drawn by a pair of fashionable chestnuts), and they would become whoring (riding upon turnips) figures of irrationality, cowardice, and monstrosity, open to attack from Bunbury's keen shafts of ridicule.

GEOFFREY GAMBADO, ESQ.

Both *The Annals of Horsemanship* and *An Academy for Grown Horsemen* were epistolary texts constructed along the same lines as some of the most famous horsemanship manuals from the past centuries, including Pluvinel's *Maneige royal* and, ironically enough, *Astley's System of Equestrian Education*. However, unlike these earlier works, Bunbury's texts were pseudonymously authored and, thanks to their fragmentary nature, edited. An antithesis to the civically minded and rational horseman of feeling, Bunbury's pseudonym was Jeffrey Gambado (who preferred to go by the more modish spelling "Geoffrey").[48] Described as the son of a Devonshire tailor, Gambado's brief story portrays a sedentary life, dubious intelligence, and an untimely end. As the tale goes, after a lifetime of striving to establish himself as a master of horsemanship with little success, his dreams were finally realized in the form of an invitation from the Doge of Venice to become his "Riding Master, Master of the Horse, and Grand Equerry." Gambado of course accepted, but on the way to this fictitious post (Venice, being a city on water, had little use for horses and no post of "Grand Equerry," as Gambado's friends tried to tell him), his ship sank in rough weather. Gambado attempted to deploy his largest and luxuriously new saddle as a floatation device, but without success. While his life was cut short ("Alas ! POOR GEFF!"), his writings lived on thanks to the surviving sailors, those "modest creatures," who used the manuscript pages for "the same use our first parents did the fig leaves."[49] These strange beings in their stranger clothing were washed ashore and spied by the "Editor" of the *Annals,* who, after some difficulty in communicating his desires, salvaged and published Gambado's now fragmentary manuscript out of "patriotic hopes of being useful to my country."[50]

Luckily, the surviving fragments also contained a portrait of the author. Surrounded by equestrian paraphernalia and sporting art, Gambado clearly was a horseman—of a sort (fig. 23). With his spatterdashers hanging on the wall, his saddle placed incorrectly on the floor, an open bottle on the table, and his left, gout-afflicted foot wrapped in flannel, Gambado was a man as far away from the image of an ideal horseman (regardless of what he professed) as he could possibly get. *Geoffrey Gambado, Esq.,* for Roy Porter and G. S. Rousseau, was an image depicting the "evils of excess" and the result of a life lived wallowing in luxury and sloth, both certainly aspects of Gambado's history. However, Porter and Rousseau also argue that the image signified the uselessness of equestrianism as a cure for gout, or "the

FIGURE 23
Henry William Bunbury,
Geoffrey Gambado, Esq.,
in *An Academy for Grown
Horsemen*.... (London:
W. Dickinson, S. Hooper,
and Mess. Robinsons,
1787). Photo courtesy
of The Lewis Walpole
Library, Yale University.

jolly disease." While exercise on horseback was a commonly prescribed cure for the affliction during the eighteenth century, the association of Gambado with riding for medical purposes, or riding for any reason, was entirely misplaced. Gambado was not a member of any "fraternal tribe" of riders, and riding was never "his pre-eminent remedy for prevention" of gout.[51] Instead, Gambado, the immoral, lazy, and vice-ridden drunkard, was first and foremost intended as a literary and visual embodiment of false horsemen, failed masculinity, and the perceived corruption growing within traditional civic-humanist discourse.

Like other self-professed civic humanists, Bunbury/Gambado intended his manuscript to be of use to the nation. Even though on the surface Gambado was performing an act of public benevolence by writing his manuals, he was following the sentiments of the new commercial discourses of the new school of horsemen and of Scottish Enlightenment philosophers such as Adam Smith and James Steuart. He was writing principally for his own benefit, where the "public good" could be "animated" with "a spirit of avarice" instead of ungovernable public spirit that, in contrast to

Bunbury, "would spoil all."⁵² Bunbury, mirroring common fears voiced by "the old elite but also by writers and professionals," was uneasy about the new social mobility the commercial revolution brought to England. Like Samuel Johnson, Bunbury worried that "a merchant's desire, is not of glory, but of gain; not of publick wealth, but of private emolument."⁵³ Bunbury pointed to the harmful degeneration of elite morals that insisted on hospitality, generosity, and fair dealings in the face of men who only sought personal wealth, perverting the economic norm and redefining the meanings of citizenship and independence. From one based on income from land to one determined by cutthroat mercantilism and the courting of Lady Fortune, this new form of citizenship and civic humanism belonged to men who sought personal wealth and rode for business. Such men did not practice the manège, favoring instead an "amble up and down in *Rotten Row*," a ride on "a *stiff-neck'd* horse," and "a *snaffle* to a *bitt*"—with all of the sociopolitical connotations associated with those decisions.⁵⁴

The Annals of Horsemanship's "Letter the Fifth" speaks directly to this issue, and evidences Bunbury's view regarding the instruction of those not worthy or capable of horsemanship, along with his contempt for the "masters," like Astley, who would teach them. In this letter, a young man proposes to Gambado a manual of horsemanship designed for "the lower classes of life" that would be produced for "the benefit" of others who lack equestrian skill.⁵⁵ However, this manual would differ considerably from others, and Bunbury exaggerates the commonness and vulgarity of subjects covered by previous authors, such as J. L. Jackson and Charles Hughes, in order to make his point exceedingly clear. The idea that "London Riders, or Bagsters," could be "gentlemen" or "genteel," that a man should ride in front of a "lady" "*à la gormagon*" instead of on his own steed, or that advice for less genteel members of the public had any place in a manual of horsemanship was too ridiculous to contemplate, let alone put into practice.⁵⁶ The instruction of the common merchant, the effeminate and monstrous, or the civically backward and unfeeling was not worth pursuing. Horsemanship instruction could not and should not be provided to such individuals, and those who offered it were utterly contemptible. The author of this letter was "James la Croupe," a name associated with Frenchified effeminacy and notions of republicanism; more tellingly, however, the word *croup* is the term applied to the equine hindquarters—its "arse"—a word synonymous with stupidity, ignorance, and foolishness.

Instead of love for the nation, the core of "traditional" civic humanism, we see in the new commercial rider a positive view of commerce and luxury based on the belief, as James Steuart put it, that "every man is to act for his own interest in what regards the public; and, politically speaking, every one ought to do so."[57] Gambado insisted that he was writing for his "fellow creatures; that they are to profit by it, and not myself," but they would profit through his personal financial gain, a continual preoccupation. It "is the combination of every private interest which forms the public good," Gambado and Steuart agreed, just as Adam Smith believed that "publick happiness" resulted from a society whose members act "merely from a view to their own interest" in "turning a penny wherever a penny was to be got," a sentiment expressed by Gambado in the extreme.[58] Gambado even asked one of his letter-writing clients to send more money, explaining that, he was "sorry to add, my Maid tells me, that two shillings out of your five were very bad ones."[59]

Further emphasizing Gambado's connection with commerce, while introducing the feared destruction of ideal masculinity that accompanied this turning away from traditional civic-humanist discourse, was his occupation prior to his ill-fated stint as master of horse for the Doge of Venice. Gambado was a tailor, which as a breed was accused of lacking "valour," "courage," "wit," and "consequence"; consequently, tailors were frequently "cast off, and despised, like an old garment" by civic humanists for their focus on foppish dress and consumable luxury.[60] Tailors enabled their customers to partake of the latest fashion; meanwhile, they engaged in unsavory business practices that placed their monetary interests above the needs of those customers. As a result, tailors were effeminate, emasculated figures of comedy. However, they were also dangerous. These men were inherently unable to display martial, civic, and sensitively polite masculine virtues for the betterment of themselves, their families, or the commonwealth, and as a result were one of the leading causes of social corruption.

Their profession unsurprisingly and automatically made tailors ineligible for inclusion within any community of horsemen, regardless of the form of horsemanship practiced, and instead made them into popular figures for demonstrating the feared connections between luxury and wasted masculinity. Philip Astley was aware of this, having served in a regiment that was primarily composed of tailors, and he used their stereotyped image to further enforce his Amphitheatre's agenda of chivalrous masculinity. His rendition of "The Taylor Riding to Brentford, or The Unaccountable Sagacity of the Taylor's Horse" (later expanded as "The Tailor's Disaster" and "The Hunted Tailor") was one of the Amphitheatre's longest-running acts.[61] First introduced to the stage in July 1768, this act became the subject

Two horses display a wonderful sagacity, one moment wild and ungovernable, tearing the taylor's coat, and repelling by force his correction; after which obedience and vice occasionally take place in the one horse, and reflection and extraordinary sagacity in the other.

FIGURE 24 *A Taylor Riding to Brentford*, n.d. The British Library. Photo © The British Library Board, C.103.k.11.

of William Cowper's popular 1785 poem "The Entertaining and Facetious History of John Gilpin" (itself subsequently adapted to the circus stage and illustrated in multiple nineteenth-century caricatures).[62] Describing the adventures of a "Linen-draper bold" from London on his way to vote in the Wilkesite elections, the Astleyan act involved a horse called "Formidable Jack" who had "been trained so as to withstand every horseman dressed in the garb of a tailor (those gentlemen being equally singular in their dress and bad horsemanship)," but who "is nevertheless gentle and governable to every other horseman." In the performance (fig. 24), if a man dressed in the garb of a tailor approached him, Jack "kicks, rears up, and by every means he can, fights the taylor, runs at him, tears his coat, lays hold of his whip with his teeth, and effectually masters his adversary, the taylor."[63] A firm audience favorite until the Amphitheatre's closure in the nineteenth century, "The Taylor Riding to Brentford" was one of the Amphitheatre's flagship productions, illustrating not only the notion of the tailor as a "bad horseman" (to emphasize this element of the role, the part was sometimes played by a monkey instead of by Astley) but also the gendered ramifications inherent in that state of ignorance.[64] In this performance, Formidable Jack, much like the Little Military Horse discussed in the previous chapter, embodied ideal male virtues. By witnessing, throwing, and ultimately humiliating an actor in the guise of failed masculinity, Jack bodily worked to uphold the virtues of courage in opposition to the tailor's cowardice. As Jack illustrated, riding an animal epitomized ideal masculine virtue, but association with luxury and conspicuous consumption was enough to irrevocably destroy equestrian skill and the associated civic abilities that went along with the title of horseman. This was a somewhat ironic message from an institution that prided itself on its commercial endeavors and fantastical spectacle.

In *A Taylor riding to Brentford*, also from 1768, John Collet introduced a further element of criticism commonly leveled against tailors in the eighteenth century, while, as Bunbury would, making clear the dubious connections between tailors and the new commercial riding houses discussed in chapter 2 (fig. 25). In this image, the tailor is dressed in ostentatious clothing and an unsuitable hat, in contrast to the two sportsmen or jockeys behind him, who display the new emphasis on sartorial restraint ideal for masculine performance. Coupled with this evident inability to conform to ideal standards, the tailor has also proved himself incapable of establishing any communication or centaur status with his mount. Here, the horse has mastered the man, and the tailor's ineffective attempts at

FIGURE 25 John Collet, *A Taylor riding to Brentford*, 1768. Photo courtesy of The Lewis Walpole Library, Yale University.

learning to ride are signaled by his possession of inferior manuals of horsemanship such as Thompson's *Rules for Bad Horsemen*—there is a copy of the manual in the tailor's coat pocket alongside his measuring tape. To make matters worse, this tailor is an Amphitheatre rider. On the wall behind him is a poster that reads, "Various feats of horsemanship performed this evening by the fainous [sic] Sampson." This poster symbolically and spatially links the tailor to the trick riding of Astley's first employers—Mr. and Mrs. Sampson—and to their and Astley's innovations in horsemanship, which were grounded in fairgrounds notorious for associations with vagrants and blackguards. For Collet, Amphitheatre horsemanship was associated with a specific tradition that was emasculating, effeminate, and useless (regardless of what Amphitheatre puffs stated to the contrary). For Collet, who seemingly was on some level seduced by the Amphitheatre's continual rememoration and recollection of the self while performing another persona, the performances of the tailor onstage blurred the already unstable lines between Astley as a sergeant in a regiment primarily composed of tailors, an actor playing a part, and the part he so successfully played. Furthermore, Collet also emasculates and animalizes his subject through reference to the dropped riding stick and the donkey in the foreground.

By offering the tailor a piece of cabbage, the vegetable that the donkey is eating, the sniggering drover questions both the tailor's masculinity and his status as a human. Cabbage was canting language that signified dishonesty in business practice, and was for Grose a direct indicator of the tailor's asinine qualities.[65] Therefore, in this image the tailor is useless, emasculated, brutish, and inhuman because of his inability to ride or to participate in society as a masculine citizen dedicated to the benefit of the nation.

Gambado shared many similarities with Collet's tailor. He was actively passing (attempting to, anyway) as a "master" of horsemanship and incorrectly instructing others in the art. As the "Editor" of the *Academy for Grown Horseman* (the occasional voice of reason in the mock manuals) observes, "That such an author," a tailor professing to be a horseman, "should be no rider may appear marvellous at first, but, on reflection, we must acknowledge that we daily find people speaking and writing on what they know nothing at all about. Herein Geoffrey exceeds all I ever heard of: for such a book of knowledge as his Academy for Grown Horsemen, never yet made an appearance in the world."[66] Not only was Gambado not a horseman by any stretch of the imagination; he also provided erroneous information on the practicalities of horsemanship and the proper virtuous behavior of its practitioners.

What made these renditions of the tailor so influential, however, was their engagement with contemporary political events. Astley, Collet, and Bunbury connected the figure of the tailor to John Wilkes, the leader, in effect, of radical Whiggism, and the associated views of liberty and government, at the opposite end of the political spectrum from reigning party politics and civic humanism as practiced by Bunbury. Wilkes espoused the independence of all men, regardless of their social status, from the direct control and interference of an oligarchical government, and the independence of the individual in matters of personal conduct and self-display.[67] The Wilkesite movement promoted popular politics and a new discourse of civic humanism that considered commercial endeavor a defining feature of masculine citizenship. For Wilkes and his supporters, government was systematically driven by the destruction of civil liberties through tyrannical legislation and nonjudicial actions that together pointed to only one conclusion: that the government as it stood was thoroughly corrupt. What the nation needed was "the interposition of the body of the people itself."[68] For Bunbury, in contrast, Wilkesite discourse and the overt invitation of men from traditionally excluded sectors of society to political citizenship was a key indicator of the absolute necessity for civic humanism in its oldest form to take center stage. Men like Wilkes and his followers should never be allowed to participate in political debates, as they were by definition not men who could subscribe to civic-humanist thought. They were not independent and evidently did not share a love of the nation, only a love of radical politics.

Bunbury was not alone in this view. A famous rake and beau about town, Wilkes enjoyed a contradictory public image; on the one hand, he was praised as the father of liberty and fashionable dress, while on the other, he was thought to be dangerous, treasonous, and a veritable devil in disguise.[69] Mercilessly lampooned by William Hogarth, who was a firm supporter of the court, the Earl of Bute, and Tory views of government, Wilkes's less than attractive features were ripe for caricature. In Hogarth's famous and much-copied image (fig. 26), Wilkes's squinting features and gap-toothed, leering smile (he had possessed a severe squint from birth and, according to Henry Angelo, was also missing most of his teeth) are caricatured in a way that points not only to his libertinism but also to his apparent monstrosity.[70] Depicting Wilkes with devil horns, or wig, and wildly rolling eyes, the caricature intimates that Wilkes is not to be trusted in government or polite society (a sentiment echoed by Henry Angelo, who pointed out Wilkes's aptness for "trespassing upon decorum" unless reined in) and was evidently not the ideal of polite masculinity or civil conversation.[71]

This critique of Wilkes was central to Bunbury's depiction of Gambado (fig. 23) as a tailor. In Gambado's portrait, we see his wild hair, rolling eyes ("a likeness that tinctures of the prejudice of friendship," as "Jeffrey was not so slim, nor was his eye so poignant"), and symbols of liberty, in this case the sporting prints on the wall and the crutch on which he leans to offset the pain of his consumption-caused gout. Bunbury portrayed Gambado in *Geoffrey Gambado, Esq.* as a false champion of commerce, liberty, and the English hunting seat.[72] Gambado was one of Wilkes's middling-sort supporters, who took the ride to Brentford in order to vote, and he was the embodiment of everything that was false, dishonest, treasonous, ungoverned, dangerous, and animalized about the men of commerce and social liberty under Wilkes.

In contrast to the character/caricature of Gambado, to be considered a gentleman suitable for membership in the community of taste, a man had to be elite, independent, a supporter of the king, and against popular Wilkesite liberty. While doing so, however, he had to display appropriate

FIGURE 26
William Hogarth, *John Wilkes, Esq.ʳ*, ca. 1763. Yale Center for British Art; Yale University Art Gallery Collection; Gift of Allen Evarts Foster, B.A. Photo: Yale Center for British Art.

masculine behavior—not libertinism or a love of wealth but the normative models of masculinity generated through attendance at institutions such as Angelo's Academy.

For Bunbury, such behavior was only part of the story. Connecting the discourse of civic humanism with the conversationalist proficiency inherent in politeness, a truly masculine horseman was also required to "speak" the "languages" of horsemanship with perfection and grace. During the seventeenth and eighteenth centuries, the possession of verbal speech was one of the primary distinguishing characteristics of humanity denied to most animals.[73] However, the possession of intelligible speech could further distinguish not only human from animal but also those considered "civilized" from those who were evidently not. Lack of speech indicated the barbarous and racialized Other, an Other that, even if possessing verbal discursive skills, would not be intelligible to the "civilized" Briton because of its very barbarity and beastliness.[74] With this understanding of speech in mind, then, for the nation's governing elite the possession of speech was not enough to be considered human; to be able to speak, to maintain visible, aural, and social boundaries between themselves and the governed—especially the middling sorts—further communicative abilities were required.

THE LANGUAGE OF HORSEMANSHIP

The demonstration of proper horsemanship language, the jargon of the practice, was one of the distinguishing characteristics of a horseman and something he could not do without. While Bunbury prided himself on correct horsemanship language, Astley and his sort were a different matter. As Charles Dibdin complained, Astley regularly had trouble with the use of correct horsemanship language, and never more so than in his widespread use of his favorite word—*cadence*. The concept of cadence was fundamental to Philip and John Astley's notion of grace and horsemanship ability. Without it, neither man nor horse could dance, and neither man nor horse could embrace militaristic and chivalrous masculinity. However, as Dibdin's scorn indicates, the word was designed, at least in the horsemanship community, to be used only in equestrian situations. Astley, in contrast, applied the word to everything in life, equestrian and otherwise: "'You don't act in cadence, Sir' one day said he [Astley] to a performer, who was I believe practising a scene in a pantomime,—'Cadence, Sir, everything should be done in cadence; my horses perform in cadence, as well as singers sing, Cadence is the *staminer* of everything, Sir, Cadence, Sir'—taking apiece of Chalk which lay by him, and writing upon the Chimney piece of the practising room—speaking while he wrote—'C.A. Ca—D.U.N.C.E.— dunce—Cadence—Sir, remember that another time.'"[75] Astley "had got hold of the word *Cadence*" and proceeded to apply it to each and every situation; the term lost its equestrian specificity when he used it. Because of his nonequestrian upbringing, cockney origins, and incomplete horsemanship education, Astley's incorrect use of language betrayed his nonhorseman status. Likewise, Gambado frequently used terms unsuitable to his professed horsemanship proficiency and knowledge; however, while Astley was unsure how to use a term, Gambado was ignorant of even the most basic of horsemanship words. The word "Wohey" made his lack of knowledge of equestrian language especially pronounced. Upon hearing the word, Gambado was at a loss to explain its meaning, and complained, "I have searched Chambers and Johnson for this Wohey! but cannot find him. I do not recollect such a word in all Shakespeare, and he dealt at large in the language. Neither is it to be met with in Master Bailey's delicate Collection of Provincialisms. What is Wohey?"[76] "Wohey," or "whoa" today, was a word that indeed could not be found in Shakespeare's plays, Samuel Johnson's immensely popular dictionary, Ephraim Chambers's *Cyclopædia,* or Nathan Bailey's many dictionaries and English grammar guides. It was a term of command, meaning to halt or slow a horse, passed down by horsemen through oral tradition, and apparently was not at this point, it seems, part of the popular lexicon.[77] It was the same for the term "restive." For Cavendish, a restive horse was one disinclined to move off when asked and one considered extremely difficult to retrain. Gambado, again, did not understand the word's use and substituted for it the incorrect word "rusty" in an attempt to make sense of it. "A strange epithet this, and I wonder who coined it," he muses; "tell me of a rusty horse, and I shall know what it means, for I know what rusty locks are and rusty weathercocks."[78] These were terms learned through practical exposure to horses and horsemen, through homosocial education, and were some of the many terms that identified, affirmed, and helped to create evidence of belonging to the elite community of horsemen.

A man's unsuitability to the community and its language was also frequently signaled through the association of the sea and seafaring—occupations and language that were the exact opposite of adept equestrianism. Gambado often used seafaring language (not to mention that he died at sea while on his way to the water-locked city of Venice) instead of discourse that was properly masculine and an essential aspect of horsemanship. For example, he used "tackle" to describe tacking up a horse, "steerage" for directing the horse where to go, and "broadside" as an action used by a Frenchman to stop a runaway horse.[79]

Bunbury's fellow caricaturist Piercy Roberts, along with Thomas Rowlandson, also frequently satirized sailors on horseback, and Roberts clearly illustrated the inevitable hopelessness of sailors when associated with horses and equestrian pursuits in his 1807 *Proof Positive or no Deceiving a Sailor* (fig. 27). Here we have the untrustworthy dealer physiognomically visualized and monstrously racialized (a common construct in the Enlightenment), taking advantage of the ignorant "master" and his attempt to return defective goods.[80] The sailor, in trying to articulate his case, says to

BECOMING CENTAUR

FIGURE 27 Piercy Roberts, *Proof Positive or no Deceiving a Sailor*, 1807. Photo courtesy of The Lewis Walpole Library, Yale University.

the dealer: "you tell me you Lubber: do you think I don't know better than that I tell you I examined the works, and my Vessel was not half so much bent in the bows and the Cabin lights were clearer—but what Grapples the whole is this. My Vessel leaked towards the Midships—and this d'ye see leaks abaft." The language is stereotypically that of a sailor and the visual symbolism is feminine. The horse, scatologically represented, is a mare. A mare, as we saw in the earlier discussion of Mrs. Coltman's horse, was the preferred mount for women, and for a man to be caught riding one was a sure method of symbolically equating his ignorance and ineptitude with a loss of manhood. Although riding a mare by this point in the eighteenth century was not considered, in principle, emasculating (and while Richard Berenger did comment that "in other respects there is no reason to think them inferior to horses, and, *cæteris paribus,* always superior, as being perfect in nature, to *Geldings*"), satirists continued to consider mares instantaneously symbolic of the rider's manliness (or lack thereof).[81]

Roberts further satirized this symbolically emasculated "horse-marine," so incomprehensible in his human and animal communication, through subtle indicators only understandable to horsemen.[82] The markings of the horse drove home for Roberts, as if it was not clear enough, the reprehensible nature of the dealer who sold the animal and the sailor who naively purchased it. The mare has a half-white, or bald, face, white feet and socked (hosed) legs, and, most important and most easily missed, a blue eye or walleye. An animal with "a bald face, wall eyes, and white legs (if your horse is not a grey one) is to be preferr'd," Gambado argued, "as, in the night, although you may ride against what you please, yourself; no one will ride against you." However, in a throwback to seventeenth-century humoral theory, these physical characteristics signified a horse—and by extension a rider—who was vicious, unreasonable, and extremely dangerous.[83] As Thomas de Grey noted, "All good Horsemen doe attest, that the Horse with much white upon his face, raw nosed, sheath, yard, tuell, & hooves white, skin white, and legs hosed, & wal-eyed; is generally weake, faint, of a cowardly condition, tender, and washy of flesh, subject to rebellion, restisenes [sic], to starting, stumbling, evill-sighted, subject to tire, dangerous to his Keeper, for biting and striking; and in a word, of a most base, and evill condition."[84]

What Roberts was working from, and what Bunbury used to brilliant effect (while connecting it to yet another Amphitheatre reference), was one side of a dual and contradictory image applied to sailors during the eighteenth century. On the one hand, sailors were "a source of national pride both as the life-line of the nation's commerce, the carrier of its imperial wealth, and as the chief bulwark of the nation's defence" (an ideal that was a perennial favorite at Astley's Amphitheatre, and that was staged on horseback as "The Blunt Tar, or True Love Rewarded" in 1791 and as "Jack Junk" in the nineteenth century).[85] On the other hand, commentators frequently considered sailors less than human, uncivilized, and savage. Jean-Jacques Rousseau and Philibert Commerson both questioned whether they had souls, and Henry Fielding wondered why seamen would "think themselves entirely discharged from the common bands of humanity, and should seem to glory in the language and behaviour of savages."[86] It was their reputation for savagery and inhumanity from which Bunbury took his inspiration. In his story of finding Gambado's fragmentary writings, Bunbury mirrored Fielding's derogatory remarks: the editor, on seeing the surviving "ultramarine beings" after the sinking of Gambado's ship, was forced to communicate "by signs," coupled with "much reason," to gain some understanding of how Gambado had died. He was also able to understand how the "monstrous Craws" came to be decorated with Gambado's manuscript; however, he was at a loss as to why such inhuman beings would have preserved the sheets. He questioned whether their motives were "owing to an innate modesty of the creatures, or to their natural admiration for learning, and a wish to preserve sheets, although adorned with characters totally unknown, and unintelligible to them." All of these conclusions were mere "conjecture," and understanding the sailors was a job best left for "the deeper searchers into the wonders of nature."[87]

In addition to the many seafaring connections, the monstrous Craws, or "the most extraordinary bipeds that perhaps ever visited this country," were also famously performing at Astley's when Bunbury published his *Academy for Grown Horsemen* in 1787. Eventually found to originate from a town in the Italian Alps known for iodine deficiency (the Craws suffered from goiters), the three Craws were originally billed in the London newspapers as "two Females and a Male, of a very small stature, and most extraordinary shape and form, with large Craws under their throat, full of moving balls, or glands, which play all ways as directed, and stimulated by either their eating, speaking, or laughing. Their speech, country, and language are unknown to all."[88] All three performed at the Royal Circus with Charles Hughes as trick riders, were exhibited as wonders of nature (led around on horseback by Astley at his newly named Royal Grove while carrying illuminating candles so the audience could better see their goiters), were used as examples of gluttony and ungoverned appetites by social commentators like James Gillray, and performed imitations of nonhuman beings (including animals) before adoring audiences.[89] The Monstrous Craws were wildly popular figures of spectacle and curiosity. The *Morning Herald* called them "extraordinary and curious savage beings, of our nature"; the *Morning Post* described them as "the most astonishing prodigies of our nature ever beheld by all the known world"; and they were equated not only with "Wild Born Human Beings" but, for a female Craw, with the "OURANG OUTANG" for her animalistic mimicry abilities.[90]

Bunbury combined sailors and the Monstrous Craws to form a new breed of Craw. He portrayed them as wondrous and freakish beings, less than human, almost animal, savage and unreasoning brutes. As a result, the editor, taken aback by their incomprehensible nature, much like the Craws' surprised audiences, cannot communicate with them vocally or through writing because of their impenetrable language and illiteracy. Forced to attempt discourse by signs, the editor never does fully understand the ultramarine beings that possessed less reasoning ability than reasoned beasts, and he leaves their study to the natural scientists.[91] Signing, being unable understandably and verbally to discourse, was representative of "entities who were humanoid but not fully *human* ('savages,' 'barbarians')," and was often racialized through association with "nonwhite races" during the century. As Lord Monboddo remarked, "in the woods of Angola, and other parts of Africa ... races of wild men, without use of speech, are still to be found."[92] They could not speak, were required to sign their intentions, and were "monsters" who existed "precisely on the boundary of what is humanoid to define the limits of the human."[93] The power of speech defined a (civilized) human, but to define a horseman, a gentleman needed to be intelligible to fellow horsemen of the community. Bunbury's other characters' association with the sea, wild-born humans, sailors, and the admiralty would have been proof positive of the absolute necessity of not only avoiding muteness in horsemanship's languages but of perfecting them as a means to obtain the virtues of civic humanism. Thus, for John Locke, the "want of Propriety, and Grammatical Exactness, is thought very misbecoming one of that rank, and usually draws on one guilty of such faults the censure of having had a lower breeding, and worse company, than suits with his quality."[94] Moreover, the want of such exactness in horsemanship could associate the "master" with cowardice, savagery, bestiality, devilishness, and monstrosity, while emasculating the target of the satirist's wit. "*Not to know the terms or principles*" of horsemanship, wrote Thomas de Grey, was "*to be ignorant of the Art itselfe*," and was to prohibit the civic virtues and feelings so indispensable to Bunbury's form of elite masculinity.[95] Indeed, to be human-animal was to be able to speak; to be a gentleman was to speak with politeness; and to be a masculine horseman was to "speak" the languages of horsemanship with perfection and grace.

INTERSPECIES EMBODIED DIALECTIC

In chapter 1, I introduced William Cavendish and his notion of the centaur. Within this discourse, a man was required to display himself as a dual-species being that shared one hierarchical body and one will in order to be considered a proper horseman. Such performances were conspicuous by their absence within the new horsemanship practices developing at the turn of the century. There was no notion of superior governance leading to a fluency in language, a meeting of worlds, the creation of one mind in one body within the new schools of horsemanship. However, this absence does not speak to a disappearance of the centauric ideal from wider horsemanship practice. Instead, it illustrates the many differences in horsemanship communities and methodologies that emerged during the eighteenth century. The notion of the horse-man as centaur was alive and well among the heirs of Cavendish's community, such as Richard Berenger, Sir Sidney Meadows, and the Earl of Pembroke. These men of the old school argued that horsemanship was by necessity to be centaur. As Berenger explained:

> For the getting upon the back of an horse, to be conveyed from one place to another, without knowing what the animal is enabled by nature, art, and practice to perform, is not *Riding:* the knowledge and utility of which consists in being able to discern, and dextrous to employ the means by which the horse may be brought to execute what the rider requires of him, with propriety, readiness, and safety; and this knowledge in the man, and obedience in the horse, like soul and body, should be so intimately connected, as to form *One Perfect Whole*; this union being so indispensably necessary, that were it not, there is no meaning between the man and horse, they talk different languages, and all is confusion.—While many and fatal mischiefs may ensue; the man may be wedged in the timber which he strives to rend, and fall the victim of his own ignorance and rashness.[96]

Exhibiting a similar discourse of becoming, one evident in Cavendish's writing and Astley's performances of chivalrous masculinity, Berenger's views of horsemanship also expressed some of the developments within the art that moved centaurism away from an absolutist discourse to one grounded upon discursive practice. According to Berenger, the horsemen of the new school of horsemanship were incapable of intelligent communication with their mounts because they did not understand or execute the potential of their equine partners; they did not learn, or have the desire to learn, the necessary language of horsemanship that allowed for the creation of two in one. In contrast, for Berenger and his old-school peers, intelligible somatic communication with an animal was *the* feature that distinguished the civic governor from the effeminate noncitizen.

This communication in turn was grounded upon a learned common language between rider and horse. This horse-man interspecies language was evident in earlier equestrian traditions, but it was only in the late eighteenth century that horsemen came to place ever increasing importance on its practice as a central tenet of horsemanship. Termed "correspondence" by Adams, "discourse" by A. S., and *"appui"* (defined as a continuous

"Reciprocal Sentiment or Feeling, betwixt the Rider's hand, and the Horse's mouth") by Henry Herbert, William Hope, and John Adams, equestrian practice was increasingly about conversation rather than dictation.[97]

The language of equestrian relationships gave voice, opinion, and agency to the horse through alternative definitions of what constituted speech. In the Cartesian tradition, animals are seen as naturally devoid of speech of any kind because they cannot reason, understand, or respond in the way that humans do. However, in the language of horsemanship, animals were often understood to be able to reason and communicate, as Cavendish pointed out in contravention of Hobbes's theories, but in a way that differed from human forms of communication. Horses communicated through their bodies, while humans communicate primarily by oral speech. It was the learning of the other's foreign language, learning "the proper mode of communicating" between man and horse, as Sidney's pupil Strickland Freeman put it, that created the reciprocal and dual-natured relationship so necessary for Cavendish and other masters of horsemanship.[98] Therefore, as Berenger asserted, "the Centaur is the symbol of horsemanship, and explains its meaning as soon as it is beheld: for there is such an intelligence and harmony between the rider and the horse, that they may, almost in a literal sense, be said to be but one creature; the horse understanding the *Aids* of his rider as if he was a part of himself, and the rider equally consulting the genius, powers, and temper of the horse, justifies the allegory; and may almost be said, in the expressive words of Shakespear [Hamlet] 'incorpsed and deminatured with the brave beast.'"[99] Within this republican horsemanship practice, where the rider directly consulted the opinions of his horse, both horse and man learned to feel, understand, and promote a harmony of speech between them; one looked to the other for information and opinion in order to become something more than a purely human or purely animal self.

Man and horse performed horsemanship as a somatic language through bodily actions that required extensive instruction before it was effective or understandable. A man could sit on a horse and possibly get him to do what he wanted through trial, error, and force, but to communicate truly, to "correspond," both man and horse had to learn a sensitivity of feeling governed by reasoned self-control.[100] Scholars such as G. J. Barker-Benfield and James Kim have studied the eighteenth-century male culture of feeling and sentiment, and have traced the impacts, acceptances, and contestations of these aspects of masculine ideals, specifically in relation to bodily expressions of emotion—sighing, tears, trembling, etc.—found in many sentimental texts of the time.[101] However, feeling, in their view, remains a part of the human emotions (sentiment) rather than a closely related intersubjective somatic sense (sensibility), and is associated with many sentimentally polite virtues such as gentility, grace, social morality, and refinement. It remains a late eighteenth-century phenomenon, and while sensitivity in feeling does increase in importance during that time, feeling had a much longer history for horsemen.[102] Horsemanship, at least in its ideal form as described in the manuals, was a language of sensitive refinement for both man and animal. As Herbert argued, "'tis necessary that the greatest attention, and the same gentleness, that is used in teaching the horses, be observed likewise in teaching the men, especially at the beginning. Every method and art must be practised to create and preserve, both in man and horse, all possible feeling and sensibility, contrary to the usage of most riding masters [like Gambado], who seem industriously to labour at abolishing these principles both in one and the other."[103] Later, John Adams also gave voice to the traditional idea that it was primarily through the rider's hands and horse's mouth that sensitive correspondence occurred, that the horse learned "perfect obedience to the rider, the Hand directing him with the greatest ease, so that the horse seems to work by the will of the rider, rather than the compulsion of the Hand."[104] Feeling and sensitivity, then, would further "guarantee and preserve . . . refined sociability" for the nation's benefit.[105]

However, such reasoned feeling, like horsemanship itself, was not perfectible for everyone. While horsemen of taste were to be men "of judgment, temper, sagacity, and courage" and could perfect the art of horsemanship through "reason" (which "is, indeed, the inherent property of every man"), the physical tools that allowed for this improvement were not universally bestowed.[106] According to Berenger, an individual proficient in horsemanship must first and foremost have a "goodness and quickness of feeling; and . . . [a] delicacy which nature alone can give, and which she does not always bestow." For him, voicing the new scientific breakthroughs in human anatomy so essential to the development of sensibility, and its Lockean emphasis on the primacy of external stimuli in forming internal ideas and behavior, everyone was given an equal share of nerves, but not everyone's nerves functioned in the same way.[107] Only some people had nerves that conducted the "subtle and quick" feeling necessary for horsemen; even if highly functional and sensitive, these nerves would not allow perfection if they were not trained or improved. Herbert argued that sensitivity and feeling, as determined by delicacy in the use of the hands and legs, may be given by the teacher to a certain degree; but "'tis nature alone that can bestow that great sensibility, without which neither one nor the other can be formed to any great perfection."[108] This "sensibility" or sensitivity in somatic feeling could "produce gentleness in behaviour," according to Hugh Blair, and sensibility was the "refinement which polishes the mind" and provided "that gentleness of manners which sweetens the intercourse of human society," according to John Logan.[109] Some men could be socially and civically beneficial horsemen, but only if they possessed innate sensitive abilities and were properly guided and nourished by a master of horsemanship—opportunities, alas, that poor Gambado did not enjoy.

RIDING "MASTERS" AND "PROFESSORS" OF HORSEMANSHIP

Bunbury considered the views of these illustrious horsemen the hallmark of ideal horsemanship practice, and he illustrated the need for correspondence and the requirement of natural talent most clearly in his story of different riders being able to produce different ways of going on a single horse (figs. 28 and 29). In "Letter the Fourth" in *The Annals of Horsemanship*, the fictitious correspondent Tobias Higgins writes to Gambado requesting advice about a horse he has recently purchased. When trying out the animal, he has the horse dealer, who "knew how to make the most of" his mounts, ride him first, under whom "a very fine figure the gelding cut." But once Tobias brings the horse home and tries him out for himself, he discovers a vastly different horse, one that "goes in a different manner with me, for instead of his capering like a Trooper, he hangs down his head and tail, and neither whip nor spur can get him out of a snail's gallop."[110]

Both of these characters were in need of natural ability, proper equestrian knowledge, and, specifically for Tobias, the experience and practice to improve the other two qualities; these characters represent the completely ignorant Londoner, or "cit," and the professed "master" of horsemanship, and graphically illustrate Bunbury's views toward both types of rider. The dealer, the seventeenth- and eighteenth-century equivalent of today's stereotype of the dishonest used-car salesman, is shown with an ideal seat and position on the horse, for the most part, and the horse is indeed "capering like a Trooper" (fig. 28). However, his actions are all part of his recognizably dishonest commercial interactions with his clients, and by extension his inability to be a polite, sensitive, or civic member of society.

FIGURE 28
Henry William Bunbury, *How to make the most of a Horse*, in *The Annals of Horsemanship* (London: W. Dickinson, S. Hooper, J. Archer, and R. White, 1791). Photo courtesy of The Lewis Walpole Library, Yale University.

FIGURE 29
Henry William Bunbury, *How to make the least of a Horse*, in *The Annals of Horsemanship* (London: W. Dickinson, S. Hooper, J. Archer, and R. White, 1791). Photo courtesy of The Lewis Walpole Library, Yale University.

Dealers were frequent symbols of the social corruption blamed on rampant commercialism and the incessant drive for consumption. Known for their underhanded methods of making a horse fiery and spirited by whatever means necessary, whether it was in the stable or on a horse's back, they repeatedly and without any qualms broke one of the cardinal rules of horsemanship—gentle and sensitive hands.[111] As it was through the hands that horsemen carried out meaningful, measured correspondence, language, speech, or *appui*, any discord in their function would negate even the possibility of a dialogue that would result in obedient perfection. According to Charles Thompson, dealers and unschooled hobby riders were "always pulling at their horses; that they have the spur constantly in their sides, and are at the same time continually checking the rein." While our dealer is not shown in the act of doing any of these things and appears to sit quite nicely, the physical language of the horse states otherwise. The contradictory aids of asking for forward movement while continually checking it were intended to "make them [horses] bound, and champ the bit, while their rage has the appearance of spirit." It was a false and wrathful correspondence between man and horse, and one associated with emasculating characteristics harmful to the individual and to the wider commercial civil society, such as dishonesty, violence, corruption, and the loss of reason. A mouth open in "fury," "transport," "derision," and "contempt" for the rider's methods and inability to discourse or govern, as we see here, was "one of the most horrible and shocking sights, in fine the most unpleasant and unbecoming action, that a Horse can possibly perform under a man."[112] Because of his overriding drive to produce horses quickly with plenty of flash that could then be sold for maximum profit, the dealer was only capable of producing a fantasy, or false and violent behavior in a horse, rather than true spectacles of interspecies communication. Through his violence, heavy-handedness, and inability to govern himself, along with his inability to avoid offense in conversation owing to a lack of sensitivity to the other's feeling (a requirement of genteel conversation described in eighteenth-century conduct literature), the dealer has created contempt not only in the spectators but also in the horse, who appears to possess more reason than his rider.[113]

Like Cavendish before him, and using language in common with the increasingly influential animal rights discourse, Herbert described a rider who used violent and false methods of communication as a "madman" devoid of reason, who, "by false and violent motions and corrections, drives the horse, through despair, into every bad and vicious trick, that rage can suggest."[114] For much of the seventeenth and eighteenth centuries, madmen were considered beastly and subhuman, in the sense that, "if possession of reason be the proud attribute of humanity, its diseases must be ranked among our greatest afflictions, since they sink us from our pre-eminence to a level with animal creatures," as Joseph Mason Cox put it in his *Practical Observations on Insanity* of 1804.[115] While some theorists, by the end of the eighteenth century, believed that madmen retained their humanity in the face of irrationality, the equation of irrationality with beastliness continued to hold sway over the popular imagination. Madmen like the dealer in Bunbury's drawing were "unhappy objects afflicted with this disorder," and were "in a peculiar manner distressful, since besides their own sufferings, they were rendered a nuisance and a terror to others; and were not only themselves lost to society, but took up the time and attention of others," as John Aiken observed in his *Thoughts on Hospitals* (1771).[116] They were contemptible, unreasonable, and unfeeling men who took up the valuable labor and time of those who were better employed elsewhere.

Bunbury's dealer was, finally and most damningly, devoid of all manliness. By describing his mount, a gelding, as cutting a fine figure, Bunbury, again exploiting the vulgar definition of the term, effectively castrated his rider. Berenger, who considered a mare better than a gelding at any time, also thought that a gelding, while useful for riders unable or uninspired to work with a stallion, was deprived "of a considerable part of his strength, spirit, and courage." "*Castration* . . . robs him, in fact, of his very *Soul*, and leaves him a mutilated, dastardly, and unnatural creature."[117] For Francis Grose, in his *Classical Dictionary of the Vulgar Tongue*, the term *gelding* was synonymous with *eunuch*, the "most monstrous manifestation" of "enfeebled masculinity—enervated, luxurious, and sodomite," and thus particularly threatening to imperial and militaristic Britain.[118] By associating his monstrous dealer with an eunuch, Bunbury cut away not only the horse's and his rider's manhood; he also depicted his dealer as a man-made and soulless monster who provided a clear, and possibly uncomfortable, gesture toward his readers regarding the necessity of gentle, reasoned, tasteful, and true horsemanship for elite governance, political success, and intact manliness.

In contrast to the dealer's dubious success in directing the horse's actions, Tobias cannot manage to bring him to do anything beyond moving at "a snail's gallop." Tobias was possibly inspired by Cavendish's 1667 publication, or by William Hope's 1696 reworking of it. "I conclude," wrote Cavendish, "that a *Knowing Horse-man* is not so Happy for Horses, as a *Citizen* of *London*, that knows Nothing, more Than to Buy a Horse in *Smithfield*, for Eight Pound Ten Shillings, or there-abouts, to Carry him to *Nottingham*, or to *Salisbury;* and let him have never so many Faults, his Ignorance finds none: Wherein he is very Happy."[119] Tobias, from the London slum of Shoreditch, does indeed appear to be "very Happy," a happiness that usually would be all out of proportion to the difficulty he experiences with a presumably inexpensive horse purchased for travel from a dealer in "Moorfields." His ignorance of horses results in an inability to discourse, although with a very different outcome from that of the equally illiterate dealer.

Even though he is depicted here in the act of using his switch and kicking with his heels (following Gambado's advice, no doubt), generally indicators of rage and disrespect toward the horse, the lack of concern on the horse's face—note the dropped and passive head, the forward-pointing ears, and relaxed mouth—indicates Tobias's complete equestrian and civic ineffectuality (fig. 29). The horse does not respect the rider and has taken control of the relationship, in a reversal of the desired horse-rider partnership. This reversal, in turn, places Tobias under the care and protection of his mount in a manner similar to that advocated for the new horsemen of the community and for eighteenth-century female equestrians. His horse is docile, steady, and safe, but Tobias's inability to master this gelding—a mount that even women should be able to ride after a few lessons with instructors like Mr. Carter—shows that he is a "coward" who has been demoted on the chain of being, through his inability to discourse, to a status below that of beasts. Like the dealer, Tobias has also been gelded, and has become an unnatural figure of emasculated femininity and civic uselessness as a result. He has allowed his "animal to have his own way," which "not only confirms him in his bad habits, but creates new ones in him."[120] Individuals like Tobias lacked valor, courage, wit, and consequence; they displayed cowardice, which, as Philip Carter argues, was a characteristic closely associated with feminine timorousness, on one hand, and the lack of compassion and affection for their fellow man, on the other. In other words, as Hugh Blair states, "Manliness and sensibility are so far from being incompatible, that the truly brave are, for the most part, generous and humane; while the soft and effeminate are hardly capable of any vigorous exertion of affection."[121] Thus neither Tobias nor the dealer exhibits the complimentary and necessary social qualities that would ensure their politeness, bravery, gentleness, and usefulness. As a result, they "will very much hurt, if not endanger the total loss of the most excellent qualities in his noble beast."[122]

This familiar discourse of masculinity was essentially the same as performed by Philip and John Astley at Astley's Amphitheatre. For them, men were to be militaristic, great equestrians, honorable, and polite, and it was no different for Bunbury. However, what distinguished the various views were the acceptable class and sensitive behavior of the horsemen involved. For the Astleys, coming from the lower orders of society and performing horsemanship in a hybridized form before an audience for money was beneficial to society. For Bunbury, using a gendered and political rhetoric remarkably similar to that found in the Amphitheatre, such men as the money- and fame-hungry Astleys were completely reprehensible. While all three men were working to improve the nation through their horsemanship abilities and instructions to the public, how they went about that teaching was at issue. Bunbury brought together his views of ideal civic humanism and commerce and his antagonism toward the Amphitheatre in the last two letters of his *Annals of Horsemanship*.

"Letter the Seventeenth," "truly comic," according to the *Monthly Review,* was written as a mock trial testimony with a liberal dash of common gossip thrown in for good measure.[123] It details the appearance of a "phænomenon" that was for a long time the talk of Highgate Hill, where the events of the sixth, "precisely at the hour of eight, A.M.," are related to Gambado by one Mr. Gorget, barber and self-styled surgeon. He relates that on this cold and icy morning various residents of the area (Mary Jenkins, servant at the Fox and Crown public house; Mamselle Bellefesse, teacher at the local boarding school; a blind beggar; a chimney sweep; and a "saloup" woman named Alice Turner)[124] saw "a man, drest much after the manner of the English, but of a fierce and terrifying aspect . . . mounted on something like a horse," although it was an animal that Mary could not identify, as she had never seen such a creature before. The phenomenon had "the head, neck, and fore-legs of" a horse, "saving that the legs were stretch'd out and void of motion." It "was furnish'd with a pair of wings, and his hind parts descended from his head obliquely to the ground"; it also "had a forked tail, but that hind-legs he had none." The rider "sat very stiff and upright, and continued his shouts" for the duration, which "much resembled the war-hoops of the Indians." Mamselle Bellefesse further described the fantastic creature: "Il me 'sembloit avoir le visage de Cupidon avec les ailes de Psyche.' . . . (Which I learn means—He seem'd to have the face of Cupid and Psyche's wings)." This figure, during its loud and disturbing, although whirlwind, tour of Highgate Hill, created much "controversy," and even "knock'd down and went over Alice Turner." While a rumor circulated that this figure was a "sea-horse" from "Lapland or theraways" (which was entirely possible, as the event took place on the road leading from the Lords of the Admiralty, and as they are "exhibiting two in the front of their House of Office at Whitehall," there must be "horses of this kind in nature"), some thought it must have been Mr. James Jumps, and many concluded that it was a figure of a "Conjurer or Cupid, Psyche or the Devil himself" (fig. 30).[125]

As it turns out, this "Phænomenon of Highgate Hill" was, unsurprisingly, Mr. James Jumps, tailor. After hearing about the commotion his performance caused, he wrote to Gambado to explain:

> I have an extraordinary story to tell you, that happened to me t'other day as I was a bringing two pair of stays to Miss Philpot's, at Kentishtown. I lives, Sir, at Finchley; and a-top of Highgate Hill my horse makes a kind of slip with his hind feet, do you see, for it

FIGURE 30
Henry William Bunbury, *How to travel upon two Legs in a Frost*, in *The Annals of Horsemanship* (London: W. Dickinson, S. Hooper, J. Archer, and R. White, 1791). Photo courtesy of The Lewis Walpole Library, Yale University.

was for all the world like a bit of ice the whole road. I'd nothing for't but to hold fast round his neck, and to squeeze me elbows in to keep the stays safe; and, egod, off we set, and never stopt till I got to the bottom. He never moved a leg didn't my horse, but slided promiscuously, as I may say, till he oversate somebody on the road; I was too flurrisome to see who; and the first body I see'd it was a poor man axing [*sic*] charity in a hat. My horse must have had a rare bit of bone in his back, and I sit him as stiff as buckram.[126]

The character of James Jumps functions, as tailor figures do for Astley and others, as Bunbury's antithetical horseman, the opposite in every way of ideal masculinity. This pièce de résistance was an illustration that embodied all elements of truly atrocious horsemanship: effeminacy, emasculation, cowardice, inaction, artifice and affected social superiority, incomprehension, deadness of feeling, and missing civic virtue.

FIGURE 31
Statue over the entrance gate of the Old Admiralty Building, 26 Whitehall, London. Photo © the author.

James Jumps, as his name indicates, was the embodiment of artifice and social climbing. His effeminate and foppish profession as a tailor, including his zealous protection of his wares during such a harrowing experience, categorically excluded him and those like him from masculine horsemanship and civic citizenship. His lack of equestrian skill and ability to communicate with his mount (note that he clings to his horse's neck instead of using his body to productively ride the horse, or help him balance) not only caused the situation and prevented him from aiding his horse out of it; it also created a figure of deformity and monstrosity associated with the devil and uncivilized Indian savagery. He had ceased to be a "bad horseman" and instead became, at least in the eyes of the unskilled, inhuman, satanic, and fantastically and dangerously foreign. This imagery and similar language is also found in Cavendish's *New Method, and Extraordinary Invention*. "An Ill Horse-man," according to Cavendish, "never thinks how to make his Horse go Well; for he Knows not how to Do it, But Holds by the Main, and the Pomel, and his Head at the Horses Head, ready to Beat out his Teeth, and his Leggs holding by the Flank." For William Hope, this individual appeared, remarkably like Mr. Jumps, "so Deformed on Horse Back, as if he were a Strange African Monster." The horse is "so Disordered" from the man's position and inability to be understood and understand (feel) "that to see him Sit in that Manner, is the most Nauseous Sight that can be, and the most Displeasing to the Beholders."[127]

While Philip Astley was accused of devilry for his ability to train his animals in human behavior and for his vaulting, in this instance, the brutishness, vulgarity, savagery, and deformity associated with the Other were intimately connected to individuals—such as Astley himself—who were incapable of horsemanship. Bunbury could see Astley's training with the eyes of a horseman, and he concluded that it was his unschooled and hybrid riding, not his training, that was monstrous; riders like Astley and Jumps were foreign in interest (French and Italian), monstrous in appearance, savage in behavior (Indian), and imminently dangerous not only to the British nationalistic agenda, especially in the last decade of the century, with the imminent threat of French invasion, but to society in general.[128]

Furthermore, seafaring connections with the monstrous, devilish, and dangerous were also present in James Jumps. As the denizens of Highgate Hill hypothesized, Jumps's promiscuously sliding horse resembled the seahorse outside the admiralty's office, or one from Lapland, rather than a recognizable creature (fig. 31). As Felicity Nussbaum argues, Laplanders were generally considered "diminutive and degenerate people"; similarly, Oliver Goldsmith argued in *An History of the Earth* that "their persons are thus naturally deformed, at least to our imaginations, [and] their minds are equally incapable of strong exertions." "The climate" of Lapland, Goldsmith thought, "seems to relax their mental powers still more than those of the body; they are, therefore, in general, found to be stupid, indolent, and mischievous."[129] Like the savage subhuman sailors, Jumps was incapable, like the Laplander and in typically effeminate tailor style, of beneficial civic virtue. This can be seen if we look at his horse, which has not moved a muscle during his slide down the hill, or at Jumps himself, who has also not lifted a finger to halt or remedy the situation (sitting "stiff as buckram"). As the pathognomy of the horse informs the viewing of the man and vice versa, their inability to prevent injuring a woman reveals their lack of communication, and Jumps's improper education or even mental incapacity to avoid contravening all expectations of "traditional" civic humanism. Like Tobias, James Jumps is too cowardly, effeminate, and ineffectual (he has flung himself around the neck of his horse to preserve his own skin) to halt his course before harm is done.

This predisposition to harm was further illustrated by Bunbury's fellow caricaturist Thomas Rowlandson (fig. 32). Rowlandson, a friend of Henry Angelo's, reworked the prints from both of Bunbury's mock manuals for the 1798 edition of the *Academy* and *Annals* (printed together in one volume), often preserving the original image while embellishing the background with other Bunbury-type figures.[130] His illustration for the seventeenth and eighteenth letters in Bunbury's *Annals of Horsemanship* was

FIGURE 32 Thomas Rowlandson, *How to Travel upon Two Legs in a Frost*, in Henry William Bunbury, *An Academy for Grown Horsemen*.... (London: Printed for Vernor, Hood, and Sharpe et al., 1808). Photo: Rare Books and Special Collections, McGill University Library.

no exception. While maintaining the general figure of Mr. Jumps sliding down the hill, he added another figure to the caricature, and although most of his reworkings involved the addition of horsemen practicing their gambades, this image deviated from that trend. Instead of illustrating others who have fallen victim to the icy roads, or even the spectators who witness the phenomenon, as one might expect, Rowlandson chose to depict a figure being "oversate" by Jumps. In Bunbury's story, the person who suffered this fate was Alice Turner, the saloup woman, but instead of showing her being tumbled head over heels, Rowlandson, in direct contrast to Bunbury's story, drew in her place the blind beggar "axing charity in a hat."

The depiction of the blind beggar was a telling decision by Rowlandson that spoke to Bunbury's civic agenda and the image's power. As Paul Youngquist has argued, physical deformity in the shape of war wounds (wounded veterans were often portrayed as similar to Rowlandson's one-legged beggar) was not a sign of personality or physical monstrosity, unlike bodily unconformity possessed since birth, but was to be admired as a badge of courage and a sign of national duty fulfilled.[131] In other words, "deformities of war are of a different sort than deformities of birth.... They incarnate martial ideals that readily reinforce a national norm of embodiment," a militaristic national norm similar to the one Bunbury was likewise attempting to (re)normalize.[132] Furthermore, asking for charity appealed to the rider's sense of polite generosity toward strangers and civic duty.[133] Indeed, "*that common Benevolence* and *Charity* which every Christian is oblig'd to shew towards all Men" was, as Shaftesbury noted, one of the "heroick Virtues" necessary for a healthy nation.[134] It was also a virtue for which Bunbury himself was praised. As Bunbury's obituary in the *Gentleman's Magazine* observed, "All who had the slightest acquaintance with him will bear witness to the extraordinary tenderness of his disposition, to his kind and active friendship, to his universal benevolence."[135]

In contrast to the elite who claimed to practice benevolence, charity, and other heroic virtues, we have James Jumps and the Astleys. Jumps was one of the new men of fashion known for their disregard for their fellow man. Jumps was the perfect illustration of jumped-up artifice, Frenchified effeminacy, and linguistic and kinesthetic incomprehension—and we see all of these qualities literally overriding English patriotism and militaristic masculinity in a contravention of all that the civically virtuous held dear. According to Bunbury, then, and similarly Rowlandson, eighteenth-century men were required to practice all aspects of patriotic Britishness to preserve the nation in light of threatened French invasion and revolution. Horsemanship, as the epitome of masculinity and military duty—Berenger defined a manège horse simply as one who underwent military training—was the quintessentially indispensable activity for the preservation and unity of Britain and the British people.[136] However, when its teachings were neglected or practiced incorrectly, everyone would suffer, especially the most vulnerable and those most in need of protection, such as women, the disabled, and the poor. The social fabric would be torn and British freedom (along with the associated social norms and stratification) would fall.

MASTERS AND HORSEMEN

In contrast to the inept, civically useless, and ultimately dangerous "masters" of the new school of horsemanship, Bunbury's ideal horseman was to be the embodiment of elite discursive and interspecies masculinity. Bunbury did not often visualize his concept of a centaur (where nature, knowledge, and practice were perfectly present), and he only did so in two images, neither of them to be found in his mock manuals. The first appeared in a large visual narrative detailing the outrageous social and equestrian

FIGURE 33 Henry William Bunbury, *Hyde Park,* 1781. Photo courtesy of The Lewis Walpole Library, Yale University.

spectacles common to eighteenth-century Hyde Park (fig. 33).[137] This early comic strip incorporated many of the stock equestrian characters found in Bunbury's written work while introducing new, ideal subjects, such as the woman elegantly cantering (center panel) and the calm cavalry figure (left background, last panel). This soldier is in military uniform and is the only figure who is not presented as a caricature. As Karen Marie Roche argues, this figure symbolized "martial and equestrian perfection." He is "Bunbury's representation of the ideal equestrian," in direct contrast to the other riders around him.[138] This figure is indeed a symbol of perfection, and is displaying admirably refined communication abilities while embodying the "traditional" ideal of masculine courage, strength, and military valor. He is the ideal of "manly ... ancient nobility and gentry ... rough, bold, and handy to pursue the sports in the field, or wield the spear and battle ax against the enemies of their country," as the March 1771 issue of *Town and Country Magazine* put it, but he is also a master of feeling and graceful refinement in civic-equestrian dialogue.[139]

He is physically a part of the crowd, but is depicted as morally and epistemologically superior to it. While everyone else is shown committing various acts of equestrian folly (using poor hands, losing control, leaning back, about to be tossed, etc.), the soldier is the only horseman who is elegant, relaxed, and uncontested on horseback; he is the only one who has cultivated the proper seat and graceful position that would maximize the clarity of his discourse. As Herbert argued, mirroring Cavendish, "A firm and well balanced position of the body on horseback is . . . of the utmost consequence; as it affects the horse in every motion, and is the best of helps: whereas on the contrary the want of it is the greatest detriment to him, and an impediment in all his actions."[140] This military figure possesses a firm and well-balanced position, but he has also developed a "gentle" and discursive "*appui*" with his mount. The reins are taut, but the horse shows no visible discomfort (his mouth is closed and his ears are forward); the rider's hands must move with the action of the horse to avoid discomfort (readily apparent in many of the other riders) and to maintain masterly and masterful communication. As Thompson summarized, "One may, at a distance, distinguish a genteel horseman, from an awkward one; the first sits still, and appears of a piece with his horse; the latter seems flying off at all points."[141] Unlike the fashionable Londoner under attack by a pack of dogs—Bunbury's caricature resembles Collet's *Soft Tumble after a Hard Ride,* portraying the questionable morals of the man interested in conspicuous consumption and the perpetuation of luxury—the mounted soldier situated in wonderful contrast is a citizen of the old school. He has become "Well-fashion'd" by displaying "inward civility" through the behavior of his horse.[142] His "gentleness," "forbearance," "experience," and "sagacity" are all exhibited in the intersubjective discourse.[143] As it was deemed impossible to train a horse to any degree of finesse by nonvirtuous or ungentle methods, a horse that had been treated in such a manner was soon reduced to a state of broken spirit, abject rage, or contempt for his rider; the common argument that the late eighteenth-century concept of identity defined it as internal or hidden from public view, or the idea "that outer conduct might be separated from inner feeling," was not a possibility for a man whose horse immediately made visible his internal qualities.[144] The officer, a member of the knowledgeable elite, is illustrated as a man who sits his horse as if born to riding and sensitive discourse, while his horse calmly surveys the scenery, completely ignoring the chaos around him in an admirable show of superior training dutifully performed.

The officer was not an "Everyman" figure. He was not there "to offer those within the picture, as well as the viewers outside it whose foibles he portrays, an unthreatening and attainable ideal," as Roche argues and as Astley attempted to put into practice. Instead, this figure is that of an ideal attainable by only a select portion of the population—the elite military and sensitive gentlemen who participated in the manège.[145] This figure possesses the requisite nerved body for sensitive feeling and has received proper instruction by masters of the art to cultivate it correctly. According to the *Academy for Grown Horsemen,* "*Every Man his own Horseman,* an ingenious professor in Dublin assured me [Gambado], it was a bull";[146] in other words, for a rider to provide his own instruction without the aid of a master, or to go to one who was commercializing the simplified and new horsemanship for a popular audience, was a completely contradictory concept, or an Irish bull.[147] Only those who could gain instruction from a master of horsemanship, such as Sidney Meadows or Domenico Angelo, from an early age as part of their elite education could self-identify and be identified as horsemen. Those who believed in the benefit of an academy for grown horsemen, like Mr. Carter's, or who began riding only once they were adults, like Philip Astley, were figures of comedy, derision, and absolute ludicrousness.

For example, another of Bunbury's fictitious correspondents, this one named "Samuel Fillagree," writes to Gambado for advice on how best to keep a horse and how to go about the basics of riding, questions that Gambado, unsurprisingly, is unable to answer. Fillagree writes sheepishly that a horse is an "animal [to which] I confess I am rather an alien, although I have happily attained (yesterday it was) my thirty-fifth year."[148] He has spent his youth and early adulthood in the counting house rather than in a proper education that would instill in him the heroic and civic virtues of strength, valor, and horsemanship. He has not participated in the late eighteenth century's developing "cult of heroism," the same cult of which John Astley took advantage in his performances of celebrity and equestrian extravaganzas. The all-pervasive militarization of the period gave the elite, in Linda Colley's words, "a job and, more important, a purpose, an opportunity to carry out what they had been trained to do since childhood: ride horses, fire guns, exercise their undoubted physical courage and tell other people what to do."[149] However, horsemanship was for Bunbury the most necessary and the least followed aspect of patriotic militarism that allowed the elite to be visibly beneficial to the nation and its people. Without it, and without its being taught to children at an early age, the Astleys, Fillagrees, Gambados, and Gilpins of the world would predominate, and social upheaval, including widespread transgression of class hierarchy, would result.

The second of Bunbury's depictions of the ideal horseman appears in his large illustration *A Riding-House* of 1780 (fig. 34). Here, Bunbury symbolically represented the nation's civically virtuous rulers, shown in one of the many eighteenth-century London riding houses, and he has caricaturized the frequent and multiple mistakes that these pupils or the affected social climbers would have made during any one lesson. The drawing also comments on the unsuitability of the nouveau-riche Londoners to enter the historically elite equestrian, or civically virtuous, governing environment. The cowardly Londoner in this image is literally being run out of the circle of riders by the worst offender against the social stratification and genteel morals, and the most effete individual, of the bunch. This figure on the bucking horse has dropped his stick (symbolically emasculating him, like the tailor in Collet's earlier caricature) and is clothed in an ostentatiously foppish and frilly shirt and a coat with a ridiculously large collar.

FIGURE 34 Henry William Bunbury, *A Riding-House*, 1780. Photo courtesy of The Lewis Walpole Library, Yale University.

In contrast to the ungenteel characters enjoying their gambades around the manège, Bunbury illustrated his ideal civic horseman as a centaur. His white horse, seen from behind at left center, sports the manège tail—long and full like Cavendish's, Angelo's, and Sidney's horses, and like the horse favored by the *Lucky Mistake*'s macaroni (fig. 8)—which Gambado, in keeping with his social-climbing tendencies, erroneously considered beneficial for a "master." Long tails were "to be had for love or money" as a means of social mobility, but were also immediate indicators—if the equestrian ability displayed did not keep pace with pretensions—of effeminacy and foppishness; a rider's right to the status of horseman was pure "wind" if the tail did not keep pace with the seat.[150] The master in *A Riding-House*, however, is worthy of the long tail, like the elite horsemen before him. Like the officer in *Hyde Park*, he is part of the action yet spatially and kinesthetically separate from it. He has become the reasonable governor of his own body and has learned to deploy his own natural talents in meaningful communication with his mount while refusing to enter into the circle of jumped-up riders. Even motionless, this horseman exudes his mastery of horsemanship language. He is sitting in the advocated position required for intelligible discourse (straight and elegantly tall, with his heels stretching down and legs positioned under the body). Most tellingly for Bunbury, who generally depicted horses in motion, this rider's mount is standing still. That in itself does not seem like a great feat of horsemanship, but for a horse to stand still, to stand square and upright at attention, waiting for his next command, not fussing when others around him are excited, enraged, or doing their utmost to throw their riders, does require obedience to the rider's mastery in the sense of forming one perfect whole. As Strickland Freeman argued, "the greatest art of horsemanship consists in being able to bring forth the utmost powers of the horse, without its being vexed by it; in which case it will stand quite still the moment it is called upon to do so."[151] This rider could not simply rely on the innate sedateness of his horse's training or temperament, like Mrs. Coltman's mare; even when visibly doing nothing, the invisible somatic communication of the horse-man continued.

The need to keep a horse calm, collected, and attentive to its rider in the midst of chaos was one of the chief challenges faced by inept riders on improperly trained horses. The horsemanship manuals, beginning in the early seventeenth century, continually complained about these individuals, and the new manuals of the eighteenth century devoted many pages to the subject of how to train a horse not to shy or spook when confronted by frightening distractions. Bunbury lampooned the proliferation of such inept riders, their improperly trained mounts, and the advice literature meant to remedy the situation in the *Academy for Grown Horsemen*: "On the road, what dangers do we incur from the weakness of our horses! The pitiful spider-legged things of this age fly into a ditch with you, at the sight of a pocket handkerchief, or the blowing of your nose."[152] Those who did suffer their horses to act in this way were "*common*," "bad horsem[e]n," "unskilful," and unable to communicate with their mounts. According to J. L. Jackson—one of the "masters" Bunbury ridiculed—"most of the errors and mistakes in horsemanship, proceed from a misunderstanding between the horse and his rider." For Jackson and his ilk, a "horse that has been taught the true and just rules of his duty, is easily guided by the hand that observes those rules. But when a person rides him, who is ignorant of his temper and natural disposition, and at the same time is a stranger to the proper methods of directing his motions; no wonder he finds himself in an uneasy situation, and his horse disobedient and refractory."[153] This ignorance and inability to discourse in horsemanship language are missing in Bunbury's ideal horsemen, but they are present in spades in his other satires.

What is also odd about the horseman in *A Riding-House* is his nontraditional positioning within the image frame. Curiously, Bunbury has not chosen to position him in a way that would overtly connect him with traditional elite and royal equestrian portraiture: he is not shown *en levade, en piaffe*, or *en passage*. Instead, Bunbury has chosen to sketch his centaur with his back to the viewer. Roche argues that this deliberate positioning, also found in unmounted figures in Bunbury's other large visual satires, *Hyde Park* and *Richmond Hill*, was a nod to Hogarth's 1753 *Analysis of Beauty*, plate II, and was meant to "heighten the overall comic effect" of *A Riding-House*. She also argues that such positioning, belonging to a tradition of similar (also unmounted) figures in older landscape and country house paintings, suggested ownership of the scene; and she sees Bunbury as the owner, whereby "the act of viewing involves the making of choices and Bunbury acknowledges his own dichotomous nature in being both detached from and involved in the life that he composes."[154] Bunbury was probably familiar with Hogarth's satires and his publication on human beauty, and seems to utilize his figures of "infinite variety" to help "*fix . . . the fluctuating ideas of taste*" in the horsemanship community, just as Hogarth was attempting to do in his earlier treatise.[155] It is also likely that Bunbury deliberately depicted this centaur from behind in order to tie his ideally discursive horseman to the elite as civically propertied and enabled citizens of the nation. That said, Bunbury designed his centaur's position above all to connect, symbolically and ideologically, his governing ideal to the much longer practice of horsemanship in the Cavendish vein, while subtly calling for a return to the properly elite, manly, civic, militaristic, and perfect manège and haute école of the seventeenth-century riding house and the elite riding houses of the eighteenth-century old-school masters.

Bunbury took this centaur directly from Charles Parrocel's illustration *A Riding Academy* (fig. 35), which appeared in William Cavendish's *General System of Horsemanship* and again in Parrocel's collaboration with Guérinière for the latter's *Ecole de Cavalerie*. Both manuals focused on the haute école, and Parrocel's work reflected the homosociality and stringent government inherent in the practice. Like Philips Wouwerman, Parrocel was an artist who, for Gambado, depicted horses that "never existed," and that, "when we do meet with a horse, that in the least resembles their designs, he is bad and dangerous in the extreme."[156] Using Gambado's oppositional language, Bunbury argued that these continental (French and Dutch) equestrian portraitists depicted horses and, by extension, riders and riding practices that were worthy of emulation for the horsemanship community's benefit and that would be of "service and use" to the nation, in Herbert's words.[157] In Parrocel's *Riding Academy* we see horsemen practicing their art in its most elevated form under the tutelage of a qualified master. In Bunbury's caricature, with its depiction of the master with his back to the viewer, Bunbury was making a direct symbolic and ideological connection to Parrocel's image specifically (the positioning of a horseman in such a manner cannot be found elsewhere), and by extension to the manège as it should be practiced. Bunbury associated his long-tailed horseman with the academies of the Angelo brothers and Sir Sidney Meadows, who followed Cavendish's principles while instructing their pupils in gentlemanly virtues in the manège. Bunbury, ironically enough, argued for the same alteration to English horsemanship practice as the very men he was caricaturing, but he was also insisting that such instruction could only come from a true, community-sanctioned, socially virtuous master of horsemanship. This distinction is similar to the one Berenger made when passing judgment on Astley's trick riding.

> [Astley's] extraordinary feats of agility; which, though wonderful and unusual, are not equal to what the *Rope-dancers* constantly exhibit in their public shews, and which can by no means be allowed to pass for horsemanship; which depends upon the exactness, readiness, and fidelity with which the horse obeys the

FIGURE 35
Charles Parrocel, *A Riding Academy* (detail), in William Cavendish, *A General System of Horsemanship* (London: J. Brindley, 1743), 15. Photo: Yale Center for British Art, Paul Mellon Collection.

directions of his rider, who is required to give them according to the known rules of the *Art,* and the capacity of the horse to execute them. While these feats, are only a display of the activity and suppleness of the man, without any attention to the horse, beyond the ordinary method of riding.¹⁵⁸

Therefore, a man was required, as far as Berenger and Bunbury were concerned, not only to start his equestrian education at an early age but to practice it as Cavendish did, as an art to be perfected.

As an art, then, horsemanship was composed of proper linguistic abilities, both inside and outside the riding house, and of proper kinesthetic language, as practiced and advocated by Cavendish. Dialectical conversation with the horse while in company with other horsemen was a chief way to "temper Mankind" "and sooth them [horses] into Tenderness and Compassion." Through the training of a horse, not only would the potential effeminacy of feminine conversation be alleviated, but the necessity of sensitivity of feeling, rationality, and gentleness would generate tenderness and compassion in a horseman, and in the process horsemanship would achieve the goal of genteel conversation. It would "polish" and "refine" "out those Manners which are most natural to" men, Joseph Addison argued, such as selfishness and pride.¹⁵⁹ Indeed, without properly refining horsemanship language, there would be "no meaning between the man and horse, they talk different languages, and all is confusion." This gentleman, as Berenger made clear, would "fall the victim of his own ignorance and rashness."¹⁶⁰ The man would not only endanger his own safety through his inability to control a flighty and large animal, but he would also be unpolished, uncivilized, unrefined, effeminate, selfish, and unable to value the public over the private.

It was through the academies that properly masculine and elite horsemen could be produced, men who would be a part of a public of civic feeling and have the means and method of preserving the safety and prosperity of the nation. "This art has so long been neglected [as] to conclude that a fatality had constantly attended it in this country; favoured as it is with every advantage for breeding, nourishing, and procuring the finest horses of all sorts," complained Berenger, again voicing the long-standing discourse of the manège in decline. The nation was also furnished, he continued, "with a nobility and gentry, whose love of exercise, activity, courage, personal endowments, and commanding fortunes, would qualify them to take the lead, and *witch the World with noble Horsemanship;* yet, with all these high privileges, they have suffered it to languish, and almost perish in their hands: for a length of time it has been able to boast but a very few persons who have stood forth as its avowed friends and protectors."¹⁶¹ In the academy, for Berenger in 1771 as for Bunbury later, the elite would learn true horsemanship and become the promoters and protectors of the art in their own right.

THE HORSEMAN'S RIPOSTE

"We should certainly have paid our respects to the pleasant and ingenious Master Gambado, long ere this, had not some *experimental accidents,* similar to those which he so well describes, *unhorsed* us, and dislocated our intentions," wrote Ralph and G. E. Griffiths in the *Monthly Review* in 1793. "Arts have been truly said to have made a more surprizing progress in this country during the last twenty or thirty years, than at any other period of our civilization," they continued. "Not only the art of riding without the trouble of going to the *manage,* has been greatly improved among fox-hunters, and jockies, but even the arts of falling, of laming a horse, and of breaking a neck, are here reduced to a science!" Indeed, for the Griffiths, "the present period has been frequently called the age of *invention;* and what production can better illustrate the fact, than the work before us? and what a colloquial philologer is our author! and what a master of the *technica* of the turf, the field, and the road!"[162] The Griffiths, in their sarcastic praise for Gambado's questionable equestrian advice, neatly summarized the state of horsemanship and the manège in late eighteenth-century England. Every "*technica* of the turf, the field, and the road" considered himself a master of commercially civic virtue; such men were usurpers of elite horsemanship who did more harm than good to the nation and its human and animal inhabitants. As a result, for Bunbury, they were monstrous, satanic, illiterate, unreasoned, and completely incomprehensible individuals who, unlike the elite who were attacked for being a drain on the public, were themselves "jockies, whoremasters, and spendthrifts" more interested in personal profit and fame, "that universal passion," than in providing for the nation. Bunbury, through his caricatures of horsemen, took anti-elite rhetoric and turned its attacks back on its perpetrators. For him it was the plundering, social-climbing, "gauche," "common," private "master" of the increasingly wealthy and influential middling sorts whose private interests only benefited himself, while negating any benefit to (and often actively harming) the polis. Bunbury wanted the categories of horsemanship, expressed by the very "masters" he so despised, to remain sacrosanct against common co-optation. Riding the great horse was to remain the exclusive right of the military and governing elite, regardless of the virulent anti-elite rhetoric and satire that argued otherwise.

Bunbury's views were not that far removed from those of many of his equestrian predecessors. Most horsemen also argued for the maintenance of a strong and exclusive equestrian community that excluded those who did not conform to the community-sanctioned understanding of proper horsemanship practice. Intimately connected to political power and period performances of masculinity, horsemanship throughout the seventeenth and eighteenth centuries was a central means of creating identity and status. For Cavendish, membership in the horsemanship community required expert interspecies performances of honor and power. To be sovereign was to be masculine, and to be masculine was to be a centauric horseman. By the mid-eighteenth century, the emphasis on honor as a defining element of masculine behavior was on the wane, and was giving way to politeness, chivalry, and sentiment as central features of male performance. Often entangled in hybrid understandings of masculinity, politeness was important as a means of communication and social stability; however, it was also physical, and as such was connected to chivalry and sensibility through an interspecies language system that relied upon bodily control, proficiency, and community sanction. Horses and horsemanship were pivotal to the lives of the men who intra-acted and practiced it; the animals defined social status, gender displays, and political beliefs while allowing the continuation of a close community of fellow practitioners who shared similar beliefs and understandings of the world.

These men's lives revolved around interspecies relationships with animals—relationships that frequently blurred the boundaries between what was known as human and what was known as animal. The perfection of horsemanship, to use Nicholas Morgan of Crolane's phrase, was for many men of the seventeenth and eighteenth centuries a process of becoming Other, of becoming wonderful, delightful, and spectacular. While there were exceptions that placed necessity over art, centaurism, whether polite, honorable, chivalrous, or sensitive, was the normative masculinity within the horsemanship communities. For community members such as Cavendish, Carter, Angelo, Astley, and Bunbury, to become a horse-man, a centaur, or to eschew the inhumanity of that status, was to perform a gendered identity that intimately knew the animal.

NOTES

INTRODUCTION

1. Boyle, "Monumental Inscriptions on an Urn"; Montluzin, "'Oh! He Was All Perfection.'"
2. Tague, "Dead Pets."
3. "Horse, an, epitaph upon," *Annual Register* 14 (1771): 237.
4. Morgan of Crolane, "Author to the Gentlemen of Great Britain," in *Perfection of Horse-manship*; Bewick, *General History of Quadrupeds*, 1; Guillet de Saint-Georges, *Gentleman's Dictionary*, s.v. "horse."
5. Edwards and Graham, "Introduction," in Edwards, Enenkel, and Graham, *Horse as Cultural Icon*, 1.
6. See, for example, Raber and Tucker, *Culture of the Horse*; Edwards, Enenkel, and Graham, *Horse as Cultural Icon*; McShane and Tarr, *Horse in the City*; Thompson, *Horses in European Economic History*; Thirsk, *Horses in Early Modern England*; Edwards, *Horse Trade of Tudor and Stuart England*; Worsley, "Courtly Art"; Moore-Colyer, "Horse Supply and the British Cavalry"; Swart, *Riding High*.
7. Cole et al., "Speciesism, Identity Politics, and Ecocriticism," 97.
8. Horlacher, "Charting the Field."
9. Harvey, "History of Masculinity," 311.
10. Shepard, "From Anxious Patriarchs," 282.
11. Harvey, "History of Masculinity," 298.
12. Shepard, "From Anxious Patriarchs," 284. See also Elias, *Civilizing Process*.
13. Fletcher, *Gender, Sex, and Subordination*, 322; Shepard, "From Anxious Patriarchs," 284.
14. Shepard, "From Anxious Patriarchs," 289.
15. Harvey, "History of Masculinity," 303; Andrew, "Code of Honour"; Shoemaker, "Male Honour and the Decline."
16. See McGirr, *Eighteenth-Century Characters*, 14–16.
17. Klein, "Politeness and the Interpretation," 874–75; Cohen, "'Manners' Make the Man," 313.
18. See Carter, *Emergence of Polite Society*; Cohen, *Fashioning Masculinity*.
19. Harvey, "History of Masculinity," 303, 311, 306.

20. Shepard, "From Anxious Patriarchs," 287; Harvey, "History of Masculinity," 307.
21. Bryson, *From Courtesy to Civility*, 25.
22. LeGuin, "Man and Horse in Harmony," 181; Walker, *Horse*, 13.
23. Berenger, *History and Art of Horsemanship*, 1:214.
24. See Derrida, *Animal That Therefore I Am*; Benston, "Experimenting at the Threshold," 550. Thank you to Donna Haraway for her suggestion of "models" as a way of framing this exploration of gender and horsemanship. Models are indeed good to think with.
25. Haraway, *Companion Species Manifesto*, 32.
26. See Landry, *Noble Brutes*, as an example of scholarly work that takes the agency of horses as central to British history.
27. Cole, "Introduction," 1.
28. Fudge, "Left-Handed Blow," 14; Barad, "Posthumanist Performativity."
29. Barad, "Posthumanist Performativity," 812–17; see also Barad, *Meeting the Universe Halfway*.
30. Butler, *Gender Trouble*, 33; Birke, Bryld, and Lykke, "Animal Performances," 173.
31. Birke, Bryld, and Lykke, "Animal Performances," 169.
32. Brandt, "Language of Their Own," 299. Donna Haraway also argues for a recognition and understanding of this mutual "*dance of relating*" in "Encounters with Companion Species," 110.
33. Wolfe, *What Is Posthumanism*, 141.
34. Birke, Bryld, and Lykke, "Animal Performances," 177.
35. Brindley, "Dictionary Explaining the Technical Terms."
36. Walker, "'To Amaze the People,'" 21.
37. MacDonald, "Horsemanship as a Courtly Art," 4; Walker, *Horse*.
38. "Xenophon's Treatise on Horsemanship," 1:228, 239; Podhajsky, *Complete Training of Horse*, 17–20.
39. MacDonald, "Horsemanship as a Courtly Art," 15–20.
40. Nelson, "Introduction: Antoine de Pluvinel," viii.
41. MacDonald, "Horsemanship as a Courtly Art," 1.
42. Landry, *Noble Brutes*, 21–22.
43. Worsley, *British Stable*, 54.
44. Nelson, "Introduction: Antoine de Pluvinel," vii; Worsley, *British Stable*, 57.
45. Walker, "'To Amaze the People,'" 16.
46. Worsley, *British Stable*, 58.
47. Quoted in ibid., 54.
48. Ibid., 57.
49. Ibid., 56–58.
50. Quoted in MacGregor, "Household Out of Doors," 110.
51. Worsley, *British Stable*, 58.
52. Baret, *Hipponomie*, bk. 1, dedication.
53. De Grey, *Compleat Horseman and Expert Ferrier*, dedication to James, Marquesse Hamilton.
54. Raber, "'Reasonable Creatures,'" 46; Dent, *Horses in Shakespeare's England*, 92.
55. Cavendish, *New Method, and Extraordinary Invention*, 14.

CHAPTER 1

Sections of this chapter appear in an earlier form in Monica Mattfeld,

"Embodying 'Bonne homme a cheval': Newcastle and Centauric Masculinity," in *Authority, Authorship, and Aristocratic Identity in Seventeenth-Century England: William Cavendish, 1st Duke of Newcastle, and His Political, Social, and Cultural Connections,* edited by Peter Edwards and Elspeth Graham (Leiden: Brill, 2017). They are reproduced here with the gracious permission of Koninklijke Brill NV.

1. Cavendish, *New Method, and Extraordinary Invention,* 13. The epigraphs to this chapter are from Shakespeare, *First Part of Henry IV,* 4.1.109–10; Durell quoted in Angelo, *Reminiscences,* 1:438.
2. For the most detailed works on this subject, see Raber, "'Reasonable Creatures'"; Tucker, "Early Modern French Noble Identity"; and Liedtke, *Royal Horse and Rider.*
3. Raber, "'Reasonable Creatures,'" 50–51. See also Pocock, *Machiavellian Moment.*
4. Cavendish, *Newcastle's Advice to Charles II,* 46.
5. Dryden, "Evening's Love," 275.
6. Edward Hyde, quoted in Walker, "'To Amaze the People,'" 29.
7. Ibid., 24; Worsley, *Cavalier;* Hulse, "'King's Entertainment.'"
8. See Graham, "Duke of Newcastle's 'Love,'" for connections between his horsemanship and his personal sense of self-worth.
9. Hope, "Supplement of Riding," 3. For further information on Cavendish's education and experiences while on the tour, see Walker, "'To Amaze the People,'" 34–37.
10. Edward Hyde, quoted in Walker, "'To Amaze the People,'" 29.
11. See Slaughter's introduction to Cavendish, *Newcastle's Advice to Charles II,* xxv–xxvi.
12. Walker, "'To Amaze the People,'" 25–27; *A true Relation of my Lord Ogle's Engagement before the Battle of Edgehill and after; written by Himself, about the year 1645,* BL, Add. MS 27402, fol. 83r; anonymous pamphleteer quoted in Van Beneden and de Poorter's introduction to *Royalist Refugees,* 13. Even though he was not widely recognized for his military prowess, he was intimately acquainted with the horrors of warfare. See his poem "The Battle" for an example of this, in BL, Add. MS 32497, fol. 80. For his horsemanship, see, for example, Raber and Tucker, *Culture of the Horse;* Worsley and Addyman, "Riding Houses and Horses"; and Edwards, *Horse and Man.* On his patronage, see the articles in Maber, "The Cavendish Circle," special issue, *Seventeenth Century* 9, no. 2 (1994).
13. Guérinière, *School of Horsemanship,* 78.
14. Cavendish, *New Method, and Extraordinary Invention,* "To the Readers."
15. See William Steinkraus's foreword to Cavendish, *General System of Horsemanship.*
16. Guérinière, *School of Horsemanship,* 78.
17. Walker, "'To Amaze the People,'" 12; Herbert, *Method of Breaking*

Horses, 86; Berenger, *History and Art of Horsemanship*, 1:213.
18. Raber, "Cavendish's Horsemanship Treatises."
19. Ibid.
20. Skinner, *Hobbes and Republican Liberty*, 14.
21. BL, Add. MS 70499, fols. 184r–185v (see fols. 210r–213v in the same manuscript for examples of his philosophical and scientific [on optics] correspondence with Cavendish); Skinner, *Hobbes and Civil Science*, 3–6. For both halves of *The Truth of the Sorde*, see BL, Harley MSS 5219 and 4206.
22. Rogow, *Thomas Hobbes*, 110–11, 117.
23. Hobbes, *Leviathan*, 161.
24. Ibid., 223, 81.
25. Derrida, *Beast and the Sovereign*, 1:27–28.
26. Ibid., 1:26; Hobbes, *Leviathan*, 28.
27. Derrida, *Beast and the Sovereign*, 1:26–27.
28. Ibid.
29. Hobbes, *De Cive*, 42–43.
30. Derrida, *Beast and the Sovereign*, 1:55.
31. Barad, "Posthumanist Performativity," 821.
32. Walker, "'To Amaze the People,'" 139.
33. Hobbes, *Leviathan*, 93–94.
34. Ibid., 93, 127–28.
35. Hobbes, *Leviathan*, 197; Skinner, *Hobbes and Republican Liberty*, 46.
36. Hobbes, *Leviathan*, 100.
37. See Slaughter's introduction to Cavendish, *Newcastle's Advice to Charles II*.
38. Descartes, *Discourse on Method*, 74–76.
39. Cavendish, *General System of Horsemanship*, 12.
40. Fudge, *Brutal Reasoning*, 164.
41. Oswald, *Cry of Nature*, 120–21.
42. Cavendish, *General System of Horsemanship*, 12.
43. Haraway, *Companion Species Manifesto*, 32.
44. Game, "Riding: Embodying the Centaur," 5.
45. Cavendish, *General System of Horsemanship*, 82; see also Gailhard, *Compleat Gentleman*, bk. 2, 50.
46. Cavendish, *New Method, and Extraordinary Invention*, 16.
47. Cavendish, *General System of Horsemanship*, 44.
48. Karen Raber has shown that this language of love and friendship had a long history and was common in manuals by the time Cavendish was writing. What was new was the connection of this discourse to Hobbesian political theory. Raber, "From Sheep to Meat," 76. For a detailed look at the history of cherishing and fear as they relate to Cavendish's horsemanship, see LeGuin, "Man and Horse in Harmony."
49. Cavendish, *General System of Horsemanship*, 105; Cavendish, *New Method, and Extraordinary Invention*, 13.
50. Cavendish, *New Method, and Extraordinary Invention*, 198.
51. For information on Hobbes, love, and fear, see Kahn, *Wayward Contracts*, 165.
52. Cavendish, *New Method, and Extraordinary Invention*, 196; see also Cavendish, *General System of Horsemanship*, 138–39; Hope, "Supplement of Riding," 30; Hobbes, *Leviathan*, 188.

Cavendish also advised Charles II to "Governe by both Love and feare mixte together as ocation serves." Quoted in Walker, "'To Amaze the People,'" 129.
53. LeGuin, "Man and Horse in Harmony," 181; see also Walker, "'To Amaze the People,'" 123–24.
54. Cavendish, "On the best of kings," unpublished poem, quoted in Walker, "'To Amaze the People,'" 200. See also Hobbes, *De Cive*, 24.
55. Derrida, *Beast and the Sovereign*, 1:26–27; see also Tribe, *Land, Labour, and Economic Discourse*, 38.
56. Kahn, *Wayward Contracts*, 67.
57. Derrida, *Beast and the Sovereign*, 1:40–41; Cavendish, "On the best of kings," quoted in Walker, "'To Amaze the People,'" 200.
58. Sidney, *Countess of Pembroke's Arcadia*, 248.
59. Blagrave, *Whole Art of Husbandry*, 227; S., *Gentleman's Compleat Jockey*, 37.
60. See Skinner, *Hobbes and Republican Liberty*, 211.
61. Hobbes, *Leviathan*, 261. For more on Hobbes's letter to Cavendish, see Skinner, *Hobbes and Republican Liberty*, 10. See Sarasohn, "Hobbes and the Duke of Newcastle" for details on Cavendish's patronage of Hobbes and their shared political and philosophical ideas.
62. Hobbes, *Elements of Law*, 228, 118.
63. Cavendish, *General System of Horsemanship*, 107.
64. Ibid., 13, 105.
65. Cavendish, *New Method, and Extraordinary Invention*, 190; Cavendish, *General System of Horsemanship*, 105.
66. Cavendish, *Newcastle's Advice to Charles II*, 58.
67. Cavendish, *General System of Horsemanship*, 105; see also Walker, "'To Amaze the People,'" 121.
68. Cavendish, *New Method, and Extraordinary Invention*, 185.
69. Cavendish, *General System of Horsemanship*, 105.
70. Cavendish, *New Method, and Extraordinary Invention*, 200.
71. Ibid., 185.
72. Cavendish, *General System of Horsemanship*, 131.
73. Cavendish, *New Method, and Extraordinary Invention*, 39.
74. Raber, "'Reasonable Creatures,'" 63.
75. Cavendish, *General System of Horsemanship*, 14.
76. For more information on Bellerophon and the myth of Pegasus in horsemanship tradition, see MacDonald, "Horsemanship as a Courtly Art," 13–14.
77. Vice-Chancellor and the Whole Senate, "Letter to the Most Eminent Prince," 51–52.
78. Walker, "'To Amaze the People,'" 123–24; see also Tribe, *Land, Labour, and Economic Discourse*, 96.
79. Cavendish, *General System of Horsemanship*, plate 4. His advice to Charles II remarkably resembles the iconography in this image: "therefore your Majestie will bee pleased to keepe itt [ceremony] upp strickly, in your owne, person, & Courte, to bee a presedent to the reste

of your Nobles, & not to make your selfe to Cheape, by to much Familiarety, which as the proverb sayes, breedes Contempte. But when you appeare, to shew your Selfe Gloriously, to your People; Like a God, . . . & when the people sees you thus, they will Downe of their knees, which is worshipp, & pray for you with trembling Feare, & Love." Cavendish, *Newcastle's Advice to Charles II*, 45.
80. Hobbes, *Leviathan*, 161, 155, 238, 272.
81. Cavendish, *Truth of the Sorde*, BL, Harley MS 4206, fol. 2v.
82. Fletcher, *Gender, Sex, and Subordination*, 126; Foyster, *Manhood in Early Modern England*, 5, 7–8; Dabhoiwala, "Constructions of Honour," 204.
83. James, *English Politics*, 74, 78.
84. Shepard, *Meanings of Manhood*, 174, 46; Foyster, *Manhood in Early Modern England*, 29–31; Shepard, "Manhood, Credit and Patriarchy," 83, 85.
85. Segar, *Honor Military, and Ciuil*, 208.
86. Gailhard, *Compleat Gentleman*, bk. 1, 29.
87. Morgan of Crolane, *Perfection of Horse-manship*, dedication.
88. James, *English Politics*.
89. Thomas Milles, *Catalogue of Honor*, quoted in ibid., 65.
90. S. [Segar], *Schoole of Vertue*, unpaginated (7 of 29).
91. Cavendish, *General System of Horsemanship*, 14.
92. King, *Gendering of Men*, 4–5.
93. Berenger, *History and Art of Horsemanship*, 2:214.
94. Lawrence, *Philosophical and Practical Treatise*, 1:18.
95. Cavendish, *New Method, and Extraordinary Invention*, 41.
96. See Pembroke and Montgomery to Cavendish, May 20, 1631, BL, Add. MS 70499, fols. 143r–144v.
97. James, *English Politics*, 22; see also Foyster, *Manhood in Early Modern England*, 58.
98. Raber and Tucker, "Introduction," *Culture of the Horse*, 22–23.
99. Baret, *Hipponomie*, bk. 1, 21–22.
100. Shepard, *Meanings of Manhood*, 46.
101. James, *English Politics*, 18–19.
102. Walker, "'To Amaze the People,'" 221.
103. Cavendish, *General System of Horsemanship*, plate 3.
104. Sidney, *Defence of Poesie*, unpaginated (first page).
105. Boehrer, "Shakespeare and the Devaluation," 95.
106. Derrida, *Beast and the Sovereign*, 1:87–88.
107. Peacham, *Compleat Gentleman*, 185–86.
108. Alexandra Shepard argues that only once a man arrived at an age at which he was able to control rampant youthful desires and actions (generally age twenty-five, though possibly as late as thirty-five and ending around fifty, when old age began) could he properly be considered a man. Shepard, *Meanings of Manhood*, 54–56.
109. Baret, *Hipponomie*, bk. 1, 21–22, 47.
110. Pembroke and Montgomery to Cavendish, May 20, 1631, BL, Add. MS 70499, fols. 143r–144v.

111. Baret, *Hipponomie,* bk. 1, 21–22.
112. Hobbes, *Leviathan,* 161. William Cecil, in his advice to his son, also pointed to a sliding scale of honor partially defined by visible behavior and the performance of defined normative virtues. As Shepard argues, Cecil's first point of advice was to gain social advancement, the second to secure a good reputation, and the third to achieve "popularity." Cecil quoted in Shepard, *Meanings of Manhood,* 35.
113. Benedict, "Reading Faces," 314.
114. Giambattista della Porta, quoted in Lavater, *Essays on Physiognomy,* 2:107. In the eighteenth century, della Porta's work on physiognomy was interpreted as a commentary on Aristotle's *History of Animals* and *Treatise on Physiognomy,* and was widely followed and copied by other physiognomists, artists, theorists, and caricaturists, including Charles Le Brun, Francis Grose, Henry William Bunbury, and Thomas Rowlandson. See Mayer, "Man's Animal Nature," 128–29; Sørensen, "Portraits of Animals," 166–69.
115. Lavater, *Essays on Physiognomy,* 2:180.
116. Baret, *Hipponomie,* bk. 1, 41.
117. De Grey, *Compleat Horseman and Expert Ferrier,* 23.
118. Brathwaite, *English Gentleman,* 5.
119. Cust, "Honour and Politics," 81; Shepherd, *Meanings of Manhood.*
120. Cust, "Honour and Politics," 61.
121. Worsley and Addyman, "Riding Houses and Horses," 216; Booth and Clayton quoted in ibid.
122. Shepard, *Meanings of Manhood,* 75.
123. Dent, *Horses in Shakespeare's England,* 89.
124. Baret, *Hipponomie,* bk. 1, 28.
125. Ibid., 22–27.
126. Markham, *Cauelarice,* bk. 2, 74, 100.
127. Baret, *Hipponomie,* bk. 1, 24, 21–22.
128. Worsley and Addyman, "Riding Houses and Horses," 217.
129. Cavendish, *New Method, and Extraordinary Invention,* "To the Readers." For further information on Cavendish's visitors to his manège at Antwerp, see Van Beneden and de Poorter, *Royalist Refugees,* 50.
130. Charles Parrocel (1688–1751) was also the illustrator for François Robichon de La Guérinière's 1733 *Ecole de Cavalerie* (*School of Horsemanship*), and was in high demand and greatly respected for his representations of horsemen. See Schuman's introduction in Guérinière, *School of Horsemanship,* xii–xiii.
131. Cavendish, *General System of Horsemanship,* plates 23–28.
132. Cavendish, *Newcastle's Advice to Charles II,* 61.
133. Raylor, "Manuscript Poem," 175.
134. Cavendish, *Newcastle's Advice to Charles II,* 61.
135. Westwood, "Royal Journey Ode," 193.
136. See Slaughter's introduction to Cavendish, *Newcastle's Advice to Charles II,* xviii.
137. Westwood, "Royal Journey Ode," 190–91.
138. Edwards, *Horse and Man,* 130.

139. Condren, "Casuistry to Newcastle," 175.
140. Cavendish, *Newcastle's Advice to Charles II*, 44–45.
141. Hulse, "'King's Entertainment,'" 378.
142. Cavendish, *General System of Horsemanship*, 14.
143. Kahn, *Wayward Contracts*, 7.
144. Quoted in Edwards, *Horse and Man*, 27.
145. Cavendish, "Letter to Charles II," quoted in Slaughter's introduction to *Newcastle's Advice to Charles II*, xxvi.
146. Cavendish, *General System of Horsemanship*, 13. Cavendish seems to follow the period's insistence on male education as a means to gentlemanly status, as his involvement in scientific circles indicates, but he also insists that horsemanship was an essential element of that education, unlike other authors of the time. For further information on gentlemen and education, see Solinger, *Becoming the Gentleman*, 19–20.
147. Markham, *Cavelarice*, bk. 2, 74, 100.
148. Hobbes, *Leviathan*, 236; see also Skinner, *Hobbes and Republican Liberty*, 105–6. Cavendish argued that "Monarchy is the Govermente in Cheeff off the whole Bodye Poletick, In all Itts partes, & Capaseties by one Person only." Quoted in Walker, "'To Amaze the People,'" 128–29.
149. Cavendish, *Newcastle's Advice to Charles II*, 12, 35, 56, 57; see also Condren, "Casuistry to Newcastle," 169, 180.
150. Robert Ashley, *Of Honour* (ca. 1596–1603), quoted in Foyster, *Manhood in Early Modern England*, 33.
151. Cavendish, "Au Roy de la Grande-Bretagne," quoted in Walker, "'To Amaze the People,'" 186.
152. Hobbes, *Leviathan*, 187.
153. Cavendish, *Newcastle's Advice to Charles II*, 45.
154. Quoted in Edwards, *Horse and Man*, 82.
155. Cavendish, *New Method, and Extraordinary Invention*, 6–10.
156. Worsley, "Courtly Art," 29.
157. For details on Cromwell as a stock improver, see Edwards, *Horse Trade of Tudor and Stuart England*, 42.
158. Worsley, "Courtly Art," 42–45; Worsley, *British Stable*, 71, 69.
159. Sympson, *Twenty Five Actions*, 1.

CHAPTER 2

1. Langford, *Polite and Commercial People*, 1–7 (quotation on 2); Hoppit, *Land of Liberty*, 313–16; Porter, *Creation of the Modern World*, 26–47. The epigraph to this chapter comes from the *Gazetteer and New Daily Advertiser* (London), September 6, 1777.
2. Landry, *Noble Brutes*, 3, 40.
3. Kuchta, *Three-Piece Suit*, 1–2; Hoppit, *Land of Liberty*, 223–24; Jirousek, "Ottoman Influences in Western Dress," 241–42.
4. Kuchta, *Three-Piece Suit*, 4, 64, 79, 86–89, 97, 171–72.

5. De Grey, *Compleat Horseman and Expert Ferrier*, "Epistle Dedicatory II."
6. Thompson, *Rules for Bad Horsemen*, 3–4.
7. Jackson, *Art of Riding*, 3; Hughes, *Compleat Horseman*, 7–8.
8. Porter, *Creation of the Modern World*, 40.
9. See Pocock, *Machiavellian Moment*; Harris, *Politics and the Nation*, 68–69.
10. Quoted in Van Beneden and de Poorter, *Royalist Refugees*, 13.
11. Porter, *Creation of the Modern World*, 175.
12. Pope, "First Epistle of the Second Book," 640–41.
13. See Erskine-Hill, "Pope and the Poetry," 134, for details on Pope's politics; and Leonard and Tronto, "Genders of Citizenship," 34, for information on Charles I's court.
14. Porter, *Creation of the Modern World*, 175.
15. Pope, "First Epistle of the Second Book," 640–41.
16. See Pocock, *Machiavellian Moment*, esp. chap. 14.
17. The statue of Charles I was part of a popular seventeenth- and eighteenth-century rhyme. Halliwell, *Popular Rhymes and Nursery Tales*, 10. The statue was also the focus of anti–George III rhetoric that argued that the Hanoverian succession had made the English commonwealth—Charles's manége horse, his "battle beast," which was calm and well governed in "a double rein" under Charles—"mad" with fury over his absenteeism, corruption, and interest in foreign wars, as symbolized by the mocking and ungoverned white horse of Hanover. *Hue and Cry*, 2.
18. See "Paddy Bull's Expedition."
19. Canny, "Irish Resistance to Empire?"
20. Carré, "Introduction," 6.
21. Markham, *Markhams maisterpeece*, preface. For information on Markham, see Poynter, *Bibliography of Gervase Markham*; for Markham's manuals, see Graham, "Reading, Writing, and Riding Horses"; Nash, "Joy and Pity," 49–51.
22. Vernon, *Young Horse-man*, "To the courteous Reader and Desirous Practitioner, of Martiall Discipline."
23. Thompson, *Rules for Bad Horsemen*, 5–6. De Ornellas has also pointed out the shift toward simplicity and practicality in these manuals in "Troping the Horse," 266–67.
24. Thompson, *Rules for Bad Horsemen*, 2–3. See also Jackson, *Art of Riding*, 2–3.
25. Thompson, *Rules for Bad Horsemen*, 3, 5–6.
26. Langford, *Polite and Commercial People*, 391.
27. Thompson, *Rules for Bad Horsemen*, 7–8.
28. Jackson, *Art of Riding*, 3.
29. Myrone, *Bodybuilding*, 112–13; Rauser, "Hair, Authenticity," 102.
30. Quoted in George, *Hogarth to Cruikshank*, 59.
31. Wahrman, *Making of the Modern Self*, 60–64.
32. Langford, *Polite and Commercial People*, 576.

33. W. H., *The True Picture and Relation of Prince Henry* (1636), quoted in Worsley, "Courtly Art," 38; see also Landry, *Noble Brutes*, esp. chap. 2 on Eastern breeds. For information on the domestic horse trade, see Edwards, *Horse Trade of Tudor and Stuart England*.
34. Raber, "Horse of a Different Color"; Landry, "Learning to Ride in Early Modern Britain."
35. Rauser, "Hair, Authenticity," 105. See Nash, "'Honest English Breed,'" for a history of the Thoroughbred.
36. See Nash, "'Honest English Breed'"; and Landry, "Bloody Shouldered Arabian."
37. See Smythe, *Horse Structure and Movement*, for an introduction to the relationship between skeletal formation and horse movement.
38. Landry, *Noble Brutes*, 43.
39. Sympson, *Twenty Five Actions*, 4.
40. Jackson, *Art of Riding*, 3.
41. Cox, "John Milton's Politics," 1568.
42. Hobbes, *Leviathan*, 261.
43. Cox, "John Milton's Politics," 1569.
44. Locke, *Essay Concerning Human Understanding*, 237–38.
45. Porter, *Creation of the Modern World*, 184.
46. Ibid., 191; Pocock, *Machiavellian Moment*.
47. Wilson, *Sense of the People*, 213.
48. Langford, *Polite and Commercial People*, 352–60.
49. Wilson, *Sense of the People*, 215.
50. Ibid., 214.
51. Cavendish, *General System of Horsemanship*, 82.
52. Anthony Dent argues that snaffle use was common for men when riding ambling or racking palfreys or other horses in training "except [for] the highly specialised one of training the Great Horse." *Horses in Shakespeare's England*, 13–14, 90, 93, 97.
53. Freeman, *Art of Horsemanship*, 12–15.
54. Landry, *Noble Brutes*, 68; Freeman, *Art of Horsemanship*, v–x.
55. Landry, *Noble Brutes*, 66.
56. Sympson, *Twenty Five Actions*, 4.
57. Surtees, *Ask Mamma*, 83, 91.
58. Cavendish, *New Method, and Extraordinary Invention*, 14.
59. Blome, *Gentleman's Recreation: In Two Parts*, pt. 2, 67.
60. Angelo, *Reminiscences*, 1:161–62.
61. Smollett, *Adventures of Peregrine Pickle*, 37–41.
62. Angelo, *Reminiscences*, 1:161–62.
63. Ibid., 162.
64. H. [Howlett], *School of Recreation*, 3; Beckford, *Thoughts on Hunting*, 205.
65. Somervile, *Chace*, 2–3.
66. Stringer, *Experienced Huntsman*, 292.
67. Blome, *Gentleman's Recreation: In Two Parts*, pt. 1, ii.
68. Maurer, *Proposing Men*, 77.
69. Leonard and Tronto, "Genders of Citizenship," 34.
70. Langford, *Polite and Commercial People*, 464.
71. Stringer, *Experienced Huntsman*; Blome, *Gentleman's Recreation: In Two Parts*; Blome, *Gentleman's Recreation: In Three Parts*, list of subscribers.
72. Beckford, *Thoughts on Hunting*, 5.

73. Somervile, *Chace*, 97–99. The hunt field was never as egalitarian as many authors made it out to be. Many of society's less wealthy members, and those of the lower orders, were excluded. See Thompson, *Whigs and Hunters*, and Landry, *Invention of the Countryside*, for details on the class strife associated with hunting in the eighteenth century.
74. See Ellis, *Coffee-house*; Lillywhite, *London Coffee Houses*; Klein, "Coffeehouse Civility"; Pincus, "'Coffee Politicians Does Create.'"
75. Deuchar, *Sporting Art in Eighteenth-Century England*, 100.
76. Wahrman, *Making of the Modern Self*, 157–65.
77. Hawkes, *Meynellian Science*, 48. For information about the social leveling trends in the sport of foxhunting, see Henricks, "Democratization of Sport," 5.
78. See, for example, Carter's advertisement in the *Morning Post and Daily Advertiser* (London), October 30, 1778 (issue 1883).
79. Raber, "Cavendish's Horsemanship Treatises."
80. *Morning Post and Daily Advertiser* (London), October 30, 1778 (issue 1883).
81. An earlier manual for men, Hughes's *Compleat Horseman*, included a brief section titled "Directions for Ladies to Ride Gracefully." Gilroy, "Habit and the Horse," 47–48.
82. Cohen, "Manliness, Effeminacy, and the French," 46–47.
83. Landry, *Invention of the Countryside*, 145–67.
84. Cavendish, *New Method, and Extraordinary Invention*, 47.
85. Gilroy, "Habit and the Horse," 46.
86. Landry, *Invention of the Countryside*, 146.
87. See Reese, *Master of the Horse*, for information about Berenger and the office of grand equerry or master of the horse.
88. See Berenger's correspondence for details on his relationship with Garrick (including horsemanship advice given to Garrick and Garrick's requests for advice on his theater performances), BL, Add. MS 59438. For information on the subscriptions to his manual, see George Grenville to Berenger, from Wotton, May 28, 1769, ibid., fol. 117r–v; and Lord Chatham to Berenger upon the receipt of his book, from Pallmall, May 4, 1771, ibid., fols. 120r–121v.
89. Ibid., fols. 120r–121v.
90. Ibid., fols. 123r–124v. Elizabeth Montagu was referring to three Arthurian tales: Spencer's *Prince Arthur: An Allegorical Romance* ("Sʳ Guyen the red cross Knight"), the anonymous fourteenth-century *Amadis de Gaule* and its spin-offs of Cervantes's *Don Quixote*, and Francisco de Moraes's *Palmerin of England*. See Moore, "Introduction," ix–xxiii, for information on the text and the larger literary tradition from which it sprang. See also Lennox, *Female Quixote*, 46.
91. Cohen, "'Manners' Make the Man."

92. Montagu to Mrs. Donnellan, Tunbridge Wells, September 26, 1749, in *Letters of Elizabeth Montagu,* 3:93, 95.
93. Burke, *Reflections on the Revolution in France,* 240.
94. Donald, *Picturing Animals in Britain,* 18; Schiebinger, *Nature's Body,* 55–56.
95. Wollstonecraft, *Vindication of the Rights of Men,* 24.
96. For a detailed examination of eighteenth-century constructions of femininity, see Jones, *Women in the Eighteenth Century;* Kittredge, *Lewd and Notorious.*
97. Ruston, "Natural Rights and Natural History," 68; Spencer, "'Link Which Unites Man.'"
98. Carter, *Instructions for Ladies in Riding,* preface, iv–v, viii.
99. On the use of riding for exercise, and the refutation of the "languid" and "pathologic" femininity that Mary Wollstonecraft spoke out against as unnatural, see Landry, "Learning to Ride at Mansfield Park," 60–61; Gilroy, "Habit and the Horse," 46–47.
100. Carter, *Instructions for Ladies in Riding,* 21–23. These criteria for a lady's horse had not changed much by the nineteenth century and were echoed by John Allen in his *Principles of Modern Riding for Ladies,* 3.
101. Carter, *Instructions for Ladies in Riding,* 21. Carter's conception of a blood horse clearly shows the influence of Eastern horse types that were essential to the formation of the English Thoroughbred breed during the eighteenth and nineteenth centuries. Landry, *Noble Brutes.*
102. See Crown, "Sporting with Clothes"; Wahrman, *Making of the Modern Self,* 58–69.
103. See Liedtke, *Royal Horse and Rider,* for details on standard equestrian portraiture.
104. Gilroy, "Habit and the Horse," 46.
105. Landry, *Invention of the Countryside,* 161–62.
106. Carter, *Instructions for Ladies in Riding,* 26, 11.
107. *Morning Post* quoted in Rizzo, "Equivocations of Gender and Rank," 87.
108. Gilroy, "Habit and the Horse," 54.
109. Landry, *Invention of the Countryside,* 165–66.
110. Berenger's preface to Bourgelat, *New System of Horsemanship,* iii–iv.
111. Hackforth-Jones, "Mai/Omai in London"; Wahrman, *Making of the Modern Self,* 122–26.
112. Angelo, *Reminiscences,* 2:55–56.
113. The paradoxical language used to discuss Omai bears many similarities to Edward Said's formulation of Orientalist discourse, hegemonic power relations, and imagery of the "Other." Said, *Orientalism.*
114. Burney to Samuel Crisp, December 1, 1774, in *Diary and Letters,* 2:63.
115. Allan Ramsay, portrait painter, quoted in Gray, "Eighteenth-Century Riding School," 112.
116. Berenger, *History and Art of Horsemanship,* 1:214, quoting Nicholas Morgan of Crolane's 1609 *Perfection of Horse-manship.*

117. See Solkin, *Painting for Money,* 27–45, for details on the social ranking of homosocial environments in the eighteenth century.
118. Angelo, *Reminiscences,* 1:35, 2. Hereafter cited parenthetically in the text.
119. Landry, *Noble Brutes,* 45–49.
120. Rauser, "Hair, Authenticity," 114–15.
121. Rauser argues that it was not until the 1770s that the meaning of "macaroni" changed from connoting extravagant clothing, wigs, and the display of refinement gained on the grand tour and began to apply to anyone who exceeded the boundaries of fashion, regardless of social rank. Ibid., 101.
122. Clark, *British Clubs and Societies,* 198–204; Brewer, *Pleasures of the Imagination,* 36.
123. Cohen, "Manliness, Effeminacy, and the French," 46–47.
124. Carter, *Emergence of Polite Society,* 68–69.
125. Cohen, "Manliness, Effeminacy, and the French," 50, 52.
126. Clark, *British Clubs and Societies,* 198–204.
127. Topham, *Life of the Late John Elwes,* 3; Gray, "Eighteenth-Century Riding School," 117.
128. Quoted in Cohen, "Manliness, Effeminacy, and the French," 61.
129. Nussbaum, *Limits of the Human,* 1–15.

CHAPTER 3

Sections of this chapter appear in an earlier form in Monica Mattfeld, "'Undaunted All He Views': The Gibraltar Charger, Astley's Amphitheatre, and Masculine Performance," *Journal of Eighteenth-Century Studies* 37, no. 1 (2014): 19–36, and are reproduced here with the gracious permission of John Wiley and Sons.

1. *Morning Chronicle and London Advertiser,* June 4, 1788 (issue 5950).
2. BL, "Astley's Cuttings," vol. 1, items 3 and 4 (April 4, 1768), and item 13 (the item is a manuscript note for a piece dated May 20, 1768, for publication on June 31).
3. Dickens, *Old Curiosity Shop,* 127.
4. BL, "Astley's Cuttings," vol. 1, item 936 (April 20, 1787). For a history of Astley's Amphitheatre, see Kwint, "Legitimization of the Circus."
5. *Public Advertiser* (London), June 25, 1788 (issue 16828).
6. *Morning Chronicle and London Advertiser,* June 4, 1788 (issue 5950).
7. *Morning Post and Daily Advertiser* (London), June 5, 1788 (issue 4748); *World (1787)* (London), June 21, 1788 (issue 462).
8. *Morning Chronicle and London Advertiser,* June 4, 1788 (issue 5950).
9. *World (1787)* (London), June 5, 1788 (issue 448).
10. *World (1787)* (London), June 25, 1788 (issue 465); *Morning Chronicle and London Advertiser,* June 16, 1788 (issue 5960).
11. For the broader political and military context, see Conway, *War of American Independence;* O'Quinn, *Entertaining Crisis,* 308; Wahrman, *Making of the Modern Self.*

12. Hilton, *Mad, Bad, and Dangerous People*, 56–57.
13. Worrall, *Theatric Revolution*, 92.
14. O'Quinn, *Entertaining Crisis*, 313. O'Quinn uses the term "rememoration," a practice I have followed in this chapter.
15. Mangan, *Staging Masculinities*, 22.
16. Handbill (n.d.), in Stott, *Circus and Allied Arts*, vol. 2, unpaginated.
17. Kwint, "Legitimization of the Circus," 109.
18. Disher, *Fairs, Circuses, and Music Halls*, 28; Moody, *Illegitimate Theatre in London*, 150;
19. Moody, *Illegitimate Theatre in London*, 4–6.
20. Mattfeld, "'I See Them Galloping!'"; Saxon, *Enter Foot and Horse*; Saxon, *Life and Art of Andrew Ducrow*.
21. Moody, *Illegitimate Theatre in London*, 4.
22. Angelo, *Reminiscences*, 1:99.
23. *Memoirs of J. Decastro*, 28; Kwint, "Astley's Amphitheatre," 15; *Astley's System of Equestrian Education*, 28–29.
24. Kwint, "Astley's Amphitheatre," 107.
25. BL, "Astley's Cuttings," vol. 1, item 11 (May 17, 1768).
26. *Astley's System of Equestrian Education* ran to eight editions within a year of its first publication, and in Europe "it became nearly as influential an ambassador for the 'rational' English school of riding" as Cavendish's *General System of Horsemanship*. Kwint, "Astley's Amphitheatre," 58.
27. Davenant, "Long Vacation in London," 434.
28. *Memoirs of J. Decastro*, 29.
29. Kwint, "Legitimization of the Circus," 77.
30. *Memoirs of J. Decastro*, 30.
31. Moody, *Illegitimate Theatre in London*, 10, 82.
32. The quotation appears in *Astley's System of Equestrian Education*, 8.
33. Berenger, *History and Art of Horsemanship*, 1:30, 48, 124.
34. Stokes, *Vaulting-Master*. For a brief introduction to Stokes's manual, and to the wider circus environment, see Frost, *Circus Life and Circus Celebrities*; Dent, *Horses in Shakespeare's England*, 90.
35. Stokes, *Vaulting-Master*, preface.
36. Ibid.
37. N. H., "To the Reader: On this new and excellent Book, called the *Vaulting-Master*," in ibid., unpaginated.
38. BL, "Astley's Cuttings," vol. 1, item 359 (March 2, 1782).
39. Wahrman, *Making of the Modern Self*, 127–45; Fudge, *Brutal Reasoning*.
40. Quoted in Wahrman, *Making of the Modern Self*, 138, 141.
41. See Bunbury, *Academy for Grown Horsemen*, for example.
42. For examples of this metaconceptualization of animal performers, see the essays in Read, "On Animals."
43. Williams, "Right Horse," 35.
44. Laurie Anderson, quoted in ibid.
45. Ibid., 35–36.
46. Ridout, *Stage Fright*, 97, 114.
47. *Morning Post* (London), April 7, 1785, BL, Lysons, *Collectanea*, vol. 2, pt. 1, fol. 68.

48. BL, "Collection of programmes," vol. 2, item 37.
49. BL, "Astley's Cuttings," vol. 3, item 1522 (December 16, 1855).
50. Fudge, *Brutal Reasoning*, 124. Morocco and Bankes were still well known in the late eighteenth century—see the *Morning Herald and Daily Advertiser* (London), July 30, 1785 (issue 1485).
51. Thomas Bastard, quoted in Griffith, "Inside and Outside," 111.
52. Fudge, *Brutal Reasoning*, 128.
53. Markham, *Cauelarice*, bk. 8, 26; Dando and Runt, *Maroccus Extaticus*, 17; a saloup woman who saw Bankes and Morocco perform, quoted in Fudge, *Brutal Reasoning*, 128.
54. Griffith, "Inside and Outside," 111.
55. De Ornellas, "Troping the Horse," 134.
56. Fudge, *Brutal Reasoning*, 140.
57. Markham, *Cauelarice*, bk. 8, 27–28.
58. Cavendish, *New Method, and Extraordinary Invention*, 157.
59. Benedict, "Spirit of Things," 19.
60. Guichet, "Animality and Anthropology," 148–49; see also Wolloch, "Rousseau and the Love of Animals," 293.
61. Benedict, "Spirit of Things," 19–20.
62. Garrett, "Francis Hutcheson and the Origin," 244; Derrida, *Animal That Therefore I Am*, 32.
63. Astley, *His Management of the Horse*, xiv, 11.
64. BL, Astley, "Miscellanea Collection," fol. 25; BL, "Astley's Cuttings," vol. 1, item 46 (April 25, 1772).
65. BL, "Astley's Cuttings," vol. 3, items 743 (November 15, 1819), 875 (March 1823), and 1354 (April 14, 1833).
66. Quoted in Stoddart, *Rings of Desire*, 66.
67. BL, "Astley's Cuttings," vol. 1, item 927 (March 23, 1787).
68. Stoddart, *Rings of Desire*, 66–67.
69. Ibid.
70. Astley, *Natural Magic*, 9.
71. Astley gave lectures after his horses had performed, and even invited interested parties to his riding house for personal instruction in the training of their own horses. Ibid., 9; BL, "Astley's Cuttings," vol. 1, item 54 (1772).
72. BL, "Astley's Cuttings," vol. 1, item 918 (1786).
73. O'Brien, *Harlequin Britain*, 59; Weaver, *History of Dancing*, 156.
74. O'Brien, *Harlequin Britain*, 86, quoting Weaver, *History of Dancing*, 156.
75. Weaver, *History of Dancing*, 156; see also O'Brien, *Harlequin Britain*, 76, 87–88.
76. Ridout, *Stage Fright*, 127.
77. Wahrman, *Making of the Modern Self*, 47–48; Wilson, *Island Race*, 125; Woodworth, *Eighteenth-Century Women Writers*, 57.
78. See *Morning Chronicle and London Advertiser*, June 16, 1788 (issue 5960), for details on Astley's broadsword displays.
79. See *Morning Post* (London), July 14, 1787, and May 12, 1789, BL, Lysons, *Collectanea*, vol. 4, item 45.
80. O'Quinn, *Entertaining Crisis*, 313.
81. Angelo, *Reminiscences*, 1:99.

82. *London Chronicle for the Year 1800*, 302; McGuffie, *Siege of Gibraltar*, 24.
83. Copy of Astley's certificate of service and letter of discharge from the Fifteenth Light Dragoons, BL, "Astley's Cuttings," vol. 1, item 1028, n.d.
84. *Memoirs of Charles Dibdin*, 26.
85. *Memoirs of J. Decastro*, 30.
86. Roach, "Public Intimacy," 17–19, 24–25.
87. BL, "Astley's Cuttings," vol. 3, item 1345 (1843).
88. Cohen, "'Manners' Make the Man"; Myrone, *Bodybuilding*, 112–13; *General Advertiser* (London), April 15, 1773, BL, Lysons, *Collectanea*, vol. 4, fol. 22.
89. BL, "Miscellanea Collection," fol. 25.
90. Astley, *Profession and Duty of a Soldier*, 11–12.
91. Cohen, "'Manners' Make the Man," 321.
92. *Memoirs of Charles Dibdin*, 26.
93. I am indebted to Donna Landry for pointing out the song's sporting rhythms.
94. BL, "Astley's Cuttings," vol. 2, item 81B (1793).
95. Ibid., item 85B (November 9, 1793).
96. Hayley, "Ode to Mr. Wright of Derby," 6; Drinkwater, *Late Siege of Gibraltar*; Russell, *Gibraltar Besieged*.
97. *Morning Chronicle and London Advertiser*, June 21, 1788 (issue 5965).
98. Game, "Riding: Embodying the Centaur," 5, 1.
99. *Astley's System of Equestrian Education*, 9–10, 21.
100. "An Ode on the Gibraltar Charger," *Morning Herald* (London), June 16, 1788, BL, Lysons, *Collectanea*, vol. 4, fol. 31.
101. Quoted in Kwint, "Legitimization of the Circus," 90.
102. "*Noctes Ambrosianae*."
103. Raber, "'Reasonable Creatures,'" 46–47; Liedtke, *Royal Horse and Rider*; Landry, "Bloody Shouldered Arabian," 49.
104. Blake, "Different Form of Art."
105. *Recollections of Colonel Landmann*, 38.
106. *Morning Herald* (London), June 5, 1788 (issue 2377).
107. BL, "Astley's Cuttings," vol. 1, item 195 (November 24, 1782).
108. Ibid., items 460 (April 3, 1783), 466 (April 25, 1783), 1102 (June 25, 1789), and 182 (December 22, 1780).
109. Weaver, *History of Dancing*, 18, 21–23, 25, 27–28; see also Lewis, "Hester Santlow's *Harlequine*," 80–90.
110. BL, "Astley's Cuttings," vol. 1, item 750 (October 25, 1785).
111. Angelo, *Reminiscences*, 1:2–3; see also Brewer, *Common People and Politics*, 22.
112. Carter, *Emergence of Polite Society*, 68–69; Cohen, "'Manners' Make the Man," 317.
113. Brewer, *Common People and Politics*, 22.
114. Kwint, "Astley's Amphitheatre," 108; BL, "Astley's Cuttings," vol. 2, item 3E (April 26, 1790).
115. Saxon, "Circus as Theatre."
116. Angelo, *Reminiscences*, 2:322–23; Jordan, "'Is He No Man?'"
117. "Small Talk, or Chat on the Turf," *Universal Register* (London),

August 8, 1786, BL, Lysons, *Collectanea*, vol. 4, fol. 43.
118. See Tuttle, "History of the Royal Circus," for details of the acts performed at the Royal Circus.
119. Myrone, *Bodybuilding*, 242.
120. Richard Godfrey, "To Mr. Stokes: Vpon his new and admirable Booke of the Art of Vaulting," in Stokes, *Vaulting-Master*, unpaginated.
121. *General Advertiser* (London), April 15, 1773, BL, Lysons, *Collectanea*, vol. 4, fol. 22.
122. BL, "Astley's Cuttings," vol. 1, items 673 and 469, both undated.
123. Ibid., item 843 (June 20, 1786).
124. Ibid., item 837 (June 17, 1786).
125. *Morning Post* (London), June 18, 1786, BL, Lysons, *Collectanea*, vol. 4, fol. 27.
126. Hunt, *Middling Sort*, 115; Conaway, "'Thou'rt the Man,'" 35.
127. BL, "Astley's Cuttings," vol. 1, item 469, n.d.
128. Roach, *It*, 7, 128.
129. BL, "Astley's Cuttings," vol. 1, item 234 (December 31, 1781).
130. Ibid., item 767 (1785).
131. See Nussbaum, *Rival Queens*, for information on actresses of the period.
132. BL, "Astley's Cuttings," vol. 2, item 69C (June 10, 1793), vol. 1, item 1151 (April 6, 1789), and vol. 2, item 23A (1791).
133. Ibid., vol. 2, unfoliated item, n.d.
134. "*Noctes Ambrosianae*."
135. Moody, *Illegitimate Theatre in London*, 86.
136. *World (1787)* (London), July 5, 1788 (issue 474).
137. Weaver, *History of Dancing*, 141.
138. Ibid., 140.
139. Woodworth, *Eighteenth-Century Women Writers*, 37.
140. Wilson, "Empire of Virtue," 150; BL, "Astley's Cuttings," vol. 2, item 3E (April 26, 1790).
141. BL, "Astley's Cuttings," vol. 1, item 39 (June 16, 1771).
142. John Pringle, quoted in Carter, *Emergence of Polite Society*, 111.
143. BL, "Astley's Cuttings," vol. 1, item 560 (June 19, 1784).
144. Ibid., vol. 2, item 23A (1791).
145. Ibid., item 123B (February 24, 1795), and vol. 1, item 871 (1786). See also *Astley's System of Equestrian Education*, 13.
146. BL, "Astley's Cuttings," vol. 1, item 525 (December 8, 1783).
147. *Astley's System of Equestrian Education*, 74–76.
148. Gray, "Eighteenth-Century Riding School," 125; Orden, "From *Gens d'armes* to *Gentilshommes*." For information on the long history of musicality in horsemanship, see LeGuin, "Man and Horse in Harmony."
149. Handwritten note for an advertisement in the *Morning Post* (London), March 20, 1779, BL, "Astley's Cuttings," vol. 1, item 149.
150. *Astley's System of Equestrian Education*, 3.
151. See Beghin and Goldberg, *Haydn and the Performance of Rhetoric*, for information on Haydn and nationalism.
152. *Astley's System of Equestrian Education*, 28–29.
153. Ibid., 5–6.
154. Surrey Reference and Information Library, patent no. GB1335; see also BL, "Astley's Cuttings," vol. 1, items 359, 386 (August 20,

1782), item 399 (August 29, 1782), and item 412 (April 1, 1782).
155. [Philip Astley], handbill, ca. August 1782, in Stott, *Circus and Allied Arts,* vol. 3, unpaginated.
156. *Astley's System of Equestrian Education,* 184.
157. *Memoirs of Charles Dibdin,* 160.
158. O'Quinn, *Entertaining Crisis,* 313.
159. BL, "Astley's Cuttings," vol. 1, item 222 (October 24, 1781).
160. See Moody, *Illegitimate Theatre in London,* for details on the inherent dangers.
161. See Langford, *Polite and Commercial People,* 609; Moody, *Illegitimate Theatre in London;* and Worrall, *Theatric Revolution.*
162. Quoted in Kwint, "Astley's Amphitheatre," 106. Ursula Southeil (ca. 1488–1561), better known as Mother Shipton, was a reputed English soothsayer, prophetess, and prostitute. Vincenzo (or Vincent) Lunardi (1754–1806) was a pioneering Italian aeronaut known as "the Daredevil Aeronaut"; he demonstrated a hydrogen balloon flight in London on September 15, 1784.
163. George, *Catalogue of Political and Personal Satires,* unpaginated; Wilson, "Empire of Virtue," 137; Conway, *War of American Independence,* 336.
164. BL, "Astley's Cuttings," vol. 1, item 399 (August 29, 1782).

CHAPTER 4

1. Philological Society of London, "Academy for Grown Horsemen—Review," *European Magazine,* *and London Review* 12 (London: printed for J. Sewell, October 1787), 286; "British Catalogue: Miscellanies," *British Critic: A New Review* 32 (London: printed for F. C. and J. Rivington, 1809), 649; "Domestic Literature," *New Annual Register, or General Repository of History, Politics, and Literature* (London: printed for G. G. J. and J. Robinson 1792), 274. The Mullen epigraph at the beginning of the chapter is quoted in Thomas Meagher, ed., *The Gigantic Book of Horse Wisdom* (New York: Skyhorse Publishing, 2007), 190. The Homer is from *The Iliad,* 16.775.
2. Horace Walpole, quoted in Riely, "Walpole and the 'Second Hogarth'"; Willigen, *Aanteekeningen op een togtje door een gedeelte van Engeland, in het jaar 1823 (Notes Made During a Trip Through a Part of England in the Year 1823),* in Voogd, *Henry William Bunbury,* 47.
3. Quoted in Roche, "Picturing an Englishman," 221.
4. Thomas Rowlandson and James Gillray, for example, are heavily indebted to Bunbury's texts (see, e.g., Gillray's equestrian caricatures such as his 1801 *How to Break-in My Own Horse*). In the nineteenth century, R. S. Surtees's many comic novels also used language and imagery from Bunbury's works. Ibid., 46.
5. Garrick, "Old Painter's Soliloquy," 377.
6. For Bunbury's biography, see Roche, "Picturing an

Englishman"; Riely, "Walpole and 'the Second Hogarth.'"
7. Roche, "Picturing an Englishman," 229.
8. Quoted in Colley, *Britons*, 154, 164; see also Wahrman, *Making of the Modern Self*, 151–53.
9. Deuchar, *Sporting Art in Eighteenth-Century England*, 101–2.
10. Quoted in Ganev, "Milkmaids, Ploughmen, and Sex," 48.
11. Quoted in ibid., 48–49.
12. Ibid., 47.
13. Porter, *Creation of the Modern World*, 188–98.
14. Anthony Shaftesbury, quoted in Barrell, *Political Theory of Painting*, 5; see also Wilson, "Empire of Virtue," 146.
15. Colley, *Britons*, 164.
16. Quoted in Mayer, "Physiological Circus," 88.
17. In *Emergence of Polite Society*, Philip Carter has identified a merging of these previously distinct discourses of masculinity, and has tied the resulting redefinition of male refinement to sometime in midcentury.
18. Gatrell, *City of Laughter*, 9.
19. Brown, *Manners and Principles of the Times*, 72. For further information on Brown, see Barrell, *Political Theory of Painting*, 8.
20. Brown, *Manners and Principles of the Times*, 25.
21. Barrell, *Political Theory of Painting*, 1.
22. "Discourse 1," in *Works of Sir Joshua Reynolds*, 1:90.
23. Barrell, *Political Theory of Painting*, 7.
24. Bunbury, *Academy for Grown Horsemen*, vi.
25. Cobbold, *Geoffrey Gambado*, 5.
26. Barrell, "'Dangerous Goddess,'" 102.
27. Thomson, "Liberty," 102.
28. Barrell, *Political Theory of Painting*, 4, 7.
29. Ibid., 83.
30. Barrell, *Birth of Pandora*, 1–24 (Thomson quoted on 15). See also Barrell, *Political Theory of Painting*, 118–19.
31. Quoted in Rauser, *Caricature Unmasked*, 17.
32. Cobbold, *Geoffrey Gambado*, 4.
33. Grose, *Rules for Drawing Caricatures*, 4.
34. Gatrell, *City of Laughter*, 220–21.
35. Burney, *Diary and Letters*, 2:30.
36. Ibid., 3:341, 352; see also Langford, *Polite and Commercial People*, 581.
37. Burney, *Diary and Letters*, 3:352.
38. "Outside the Hall," *World (1787)* (London), February 14, 1788 (issue 352); *Morning Post and Gazetteer* (London), February 23, 1798 (issue 9088).
39. Smollett, "Academy for Grown-Horsemen," 348.
40. Dickinson, *English Satirical Print*, 15.
41. James Barry, quoted in Barrell, *Political Theory of Painting*, 215.
42. Quoted in Barrell, *Birth of Pandora*, 80.
43. Bunbury, *Academy for Grown Horsemen*, vi.
44. Thompson, *Rules for Bad Horsemen*, 1–2.
45. Drayton, *Nature's Government*, 88, 100, 104.
46. Bunbury, *Annals of Horsemanship*, iv–vi.

47. Henry Angelo records that he played a formative role in seeing to the completion of Grose's dictionary. Angelo, *Reminiscences*, 1:171.
48. The OED defines *gambado* or *spatterdasher* as a kind of large boot or gaiter, attached to a saddle, to protect the rider's legs and feet from the wet or cold. The term, interchangeable here with *gambade*, was also applied by 1820 to the bound or spring (of a horse). *Gambade* was also defined in the sixteenth century as a synonym for the movements of the haute école, while by 1821 it was understood as a prank, freak, or frolic. Dent, *Horses in Shakespeare's England*, 65. I would argue that both definitions of *gambade/gambado* may also have been in use in Bunbury's time, or developed out of his writings. His support of the manège and haute école, his mock manuals, their frolicking and mocking nature, and the use of "Gambado" all point to a combination of these two definitions of the word.
49. Bunbury, *Academy for Grown Horsemen*, xvi.
50. Ibid., dedication.
51. Porter and Rousseau, *Gout: The Patrician Malady*, 103, 277, 228. Bunbury seems to utilize the new arguments about the origin and treatment of gout, as opposed to the old view of it as a hereditary, honorable, and purely genteel disease. See Mrs. Piozzi, "Parental Distress," in *The Gentleman's and London magazine: or monthly chronologer, 1741–1794* (London: Published by J. Exshaw, January 1789), 476–78, for an example of how Gambado's teachings became anecdotes about moral reform.
52. James Steuart and Adam Smith, quoted in Barrell, *Political Theory of Painting*, 49.
53. Hudson, "It-Narratives," 293.
54. *Elegy in a Riding House*, 8–9, 11.
55. Bunbury, *Annals of Horsemanship*, 22.
56. The OED defines a *bagster* as a commercial traveler, and Grose defines a *gormagon* as "a monster with six eyes, three mouths, four arms, eight legs, five on one side and three on the other, three arses, two tarses and a **** upon its back; a man on horseback with a woman behind him." *Classical Dictionary of the Vulgar Tongue*, L2.
57. Quoted in Barrell, *Political Theory of Painting*, 49.
58. Bunbury, *Academy for Grown Horsemen*, viii; Smith quoted in Barrell, *Political Theory of Painting*, 49.
59. Bunbury, *Annals of Horsemanship*, 21.
60. Harrison, "Taylor's Soliloquy."
61. BL, "Astley's Cuttings," vol. 1, item 138 (1777), vol. 3, items 165 (May 11, 1808) and 170 (May 16, 1808).
62. In 1786 this poem was performed as a dance at the Royal Circus, and was the subject of the anonymous *Mrs. Gilpin's Return, Being the Sequel to Jonny Gilpin of Cheapside*. See BL, "Astley's Cuttings," vol. 1, item 801 (May 11, 1786).

63. Ibid., vol. 1, item 525 (December 8, 1783); see also Speaight, "Some Comic Circus Entrées."
64. Kwint, "Astley's Amphitheatre," 19. See also the *Gazetteer* (London), December 27, 1768, BL, Lysons, *Collectanea,* vol. 4, fol. 21. By the mid-nineteenth century, "tailor" could stand on its own as shorthand for poor horsemanship and questionable masculinity. Surtees, *Ask Mamma,* 260.
65. Francis Grose's dictionary defined cabbage as "cloth, stuff, or silk purloined by taylors from their employers, which they deposit in a place called *hell,* or their *eye:* from the first, when taxed with their knavery, they equivocally swear, that if they have taken any, they wish they may find it in *hell;* or alluding to the second protest, that what they have over and above is not more than they could put in their *eye.*"
66. Bunbury, *Academy for Grown Horsemen,* vi.
67. Wilson, *Sense of the People,* 213–14.
68. Brewer, *Party Ideology and Popular Politics,* 253.
69. West, "Wilkes's Squint," 71; Clark, "Chevalier d'Eon and Wilkes," 19.
70. West, "Wilkes's Squint," 72; Angelo, *Reminiscences,* 1:55; Cash, *John Wilkes,* 124–26.
71. Angelo, *Reminiscences,* 1:60.
72. Bunbury, *Annals of Horsemanship,* xviii–xix. Thanks to Jennie Batchelor for pointing out the connections between these two images.
73. Nussbaum, *Limits of the Human,* 43; Fudge, *Perceiving Animals,* 56.
74. Nussbaum, *Limits of the Human,* 43.
75. *Memoirs of Charles Dibdin,* 26.
76. Bunbury, *Academy for Grown Horsemen,* 8.
77. The OED is no exception. It only traces the equestrian usage of the term *whoa* (to slow or halt a horse) to 1849, and does not provide a definition for *wohey.*
78. Bunbury, *Academy for Grown Horsemen,* 24.
79. Ibid., ix, 21, 29.
80. Nussbaum, *Limits of the Human,* 42.
81. Berenger, *History and Art of Horsemanship,* 1:169.
82. Surtees, *Jorrocks's Jaunts and Jollities,* 184.
83. Nash, "Of Sorrels, Bays, and Dapple Greys."
84. Bunbury, *Academy for Grown Horsemen,* 6; de Grey, *Compleat Horseman,* 23.
85. Brewer, *Common People and Politics,* 41; BL, "Astley's Cuttings," vol. 2, item 53C (June 29, 1791); see M[R] *Ducrow as Jack Junk,* V&A, Astley's File, 1770–1779, and M[R] *Ducrow in the Vicissitude of a Tar,* V&A, Astley's File, 1780–1828, for illustrations of the equestrian act.
86. Quoted in Lamb, *Preserving the Self,* 114.
87. Bunbury, *Academy for Grown Horsemen,* xi–xvii.
88. BL, Lysons, *Collectanea,* vol. 1, fol. 90, n.d.
89. For Astley's engagement of the Craws, see Kwint, "Astley's Amphitheatre," 321–23; *Morning Post* (London), August 18 and

October 11, 1787, BL, Lysons, *Collectanea*, vol. 1, fol. 93r–v, and *Morning Herald* (London), October 15, 1787, fol. 94.
90. *Morning Herald* (London), January 16, 1787; *Morning Post* (London), April 16, 1787; *Morning Herald* (London), September 21, 1787; *Morning Post* (London), November 6, 1878, all in BL, Lysons, *Collectanea*, vol. 1, fols. 90, 91, 93, and 96, respectively.
91. *Morning Post* (London), April 16, 1787, ibid., fol. 91v.
92. Quoted in Nussbaum, *Limits of the Human*, 43.
93. Ibid., 44.
94. Locke, *Essay Concerning Human Understanding*, 160; Cohen, *Fashioning Masculinity*, 28.
95. De Grey, *Compleat Horseman and Expert Ferrier*, 27.
96. Berenger, *History and Art of Horsemanship*, 1:201.
97. Adams, *Analysis of Horsemanship*, xviii; S., *Gentleman's Compleat Jockey*, 31; Herbert, *Method of Breaking Horses*, 61; Hope, "Supplement of Riding," "Author's Epistle to the Reader."
98. Freeman, *Art of Horsemanship*, ii.
99. Berenger, *History and Art of Horsemanship*, 1:36–37.
100. Adams, *Analysis of Horsemanship*, 41.
101. See Kim, "'Good Cursed, Bouncing Losses'"; Barker-Benfield, *Culture of Sensibility*.
102. Carter, *Emergence of Polite Society*, 89, 94.
103. Herbert, *Method of Breaking Horses*, 3.
104. Adams, *Analysis of Horsemanship*, 39–40.
105. Carter, *Emergence of Polite Society*, 30–31.
106. Jackson, *Art of Riding*, 1.
107. Berenger, *History and Art of Horsemanship*, 2:10; Locke, *Essay Concerning Human Understanding*, 104–6; Carter, *Emergence of Polite Society*, 30; Wahrman, *Making of the Modern Self*, 185–89; Barker-Benfield, *Culture of Sensibility*, 1–36.
108. Herbert, *Method of Breaking Horses*, 8, 22.
109. Blair and Logan quoted in Carter, *Emergence of Polite Society*, 93.
110. Bunbury, *Annals of Horsemanship*, 19–20.
111. The untrustworthiness of dealers had a long tradition. Thomas Dekker, writing in 1608, described the dealer as "in quality a coozener, by profession a knave, by his cunning a Varlet, in fayres a Hagling Chapman, in the City a cogging dissembler, and in Smithfield a common forsworne Villaine." Quoted in Edwards, "Horse Trade in Tudor and Stuart England," 114. Similar sentiments can be found in William Burdon's *Capt. Burdon's Gentleman's Pocket-Farrier* (1742) and Henry Bracken's *Ten Minutes Advice to Every Gentleman Going to Purchase a Horse* (1775).
112. Solleysel, *Compleat Horseman*, 15.
113. Carter, *Emergence of Polite Society*, 64–65.
114. Herbert, *Method of Breaking Horses*, 25–26. Men who resorted to violence were without "Discretion," "mad men," and "presumptuous beast[s]," who acted in "Ignorance" and

"folly." S., *Gentleman's Compleat Jockey*, 38; Blagrave, *Whole Art of Husbandry*, 284; Clifford, *Schoole of Horsemanship*, 22; Markham, *Cauelarice*, bk. 2, 99–100.
115. Quoted in Scull, *Most Solitary of Afflictions*, 92.
116. Quoted in ibid., 39.
117. Berenger, *History and Art of Horsemanship*, 1:138.
118. Nussbaum, *Limits of the Human*, 34.
119. Cavendish, *New Method, and Extraordinary Invention*, 81.
120. Herbert, *Method of Breaking Horses*, 25–26.
121. Carter, *Emergence of Polite Society*, 101 (Blair quoted on 108).
122. Jackson, *Art of Riding*, 2.
123. Griffiths and Griffiths, *Monthly Review*, 178.
124. The OED defines *saloup* as a Turkish hot drink consisting of an infusion of powdered salep (orchid root) or (later) sassafras, with milk and sugar, sold in the streets of London in the night and early morning. A saloup woman would have been a merchant selling the drink to passersby.
125. Bunbury, *Annals of Horsemanship*, 73–79.
126. Ibid., 80–81.
127. Cavendish, *New Method, and Extraordinary Invention*, 16; Hope, "Supplement of Riding," 5.
128. Hilton, *Mad, Bad, and Dangerous People*, 57–65.
129. Nussbaum, *Limits of the Human*, 44 (Goldsmith quoted on 44–45).
130. Angelo, *Reminiscences*, 1:233.
131. Youngquist, *Monstrosities*, 165; see also George, *Hogarth to Cruikshank*, 41.
132. Youngquist, *Monstrosities*, 177; see also Todd, *Imagining Monsters*.
133. Carter, *Emergence of Polite Society*, 75.
134. Quoted in Barrell, *Political Theory of Painting*, 6.
135. Quoted in Riely, "Walpole and 'the Second Hogarth,'" 42.
136. Berenger, *History and Art of Horsemanship*, 1:168.
137. For example: "The SUNDAY EQUESTRIANS sported their *Bits* of *Blood* [the title of an image from Bunbury's *Annals of Horsemanship*] in a most capital style; though our veneration for truth compels us to acknowledge that we now and then observed a *twisted Stirrup Leather, Spurs wrong put on, 'cum multis aliis,'* recorded by the renowned Gambado." *Oracle and Daily Advertiser* (London), April 7, 1800 (issue 22 254).
138. Roche, "Picturing an Englishman," 202–3.
139. Quoted in Cohen, "Manliness, Effeminacy, and the French," 61.
140. Herbert, *Method of Breaking Horses*, 19.
141. Thompson, *Rules for Bad Horsemen*, 21.
142. John Locke, quoted in Carter, *Emergence of Polite Society*, 54.
143. Such language can be found throughout Herbert, *Method of Breaking Horses;* see also Berenger, *History and Art of Horsemanship*, 2:65.
144. Carter, *Emergence of Polite Society*, 57; Wahrman, *Making of the Modern Self*.
145. Roche, "Picturing an Englishman," 202–3.

146. Bunbury, *Academy for Grown Horsemen*, vi–vii.
147. The OED defines *bull* used in this sense as a self-contradictory proposition; in modern usage, an expression containing a manifest contradiction in terms or involving a ludicrous inconsistency unperceived by the speaker. Now often used with the epithet *Irish*.
148. Bunbury, *Annals of Horsemanship*, 5.
149. Colley, *Britons*, 167–70, 178 (quotation).
150. Bunbury, *Academy for Grown Horsemen*, 10, 34–35.
151. Freeman, *Art of Horsemanship*, 142.
152. Bunbury, *Academy for Grown Horsemen*, 4.
153. Jackson, *Art of Riding*, iii–iv.
154. Roche, "Picturing an Englishman," 31, 213.
155. Hogarth, *Analysis of Beauty*, xvi.
156. Bunbury, *Academy for Grown Horsemen*, 2.
157. Herbert, *Method of Breaking Horses*, 6.
158. Berenger, *History and Art of Horsemanship*, 1:124–25.
159. Quoted in Carter, *Emergence of Polite Society*, 68.
160. Berenger, *History and Art of Horsemanship*, 1:201.
161. Ibid., 212–13.
162. Griffiths and Griffiths, *Monthly Review*, 175–76.

BIBLIOGRAPHY

MANUSCRIPTS AND COLLECTIONS

British Library (BL)
Additional MSS 27402, 32497, 59438, 70499
Astley, Philip. "Miscellanea Collection." Scrapbook, 1879. c.13.(25.).
"Astley's Cuttings from Newspapers," 1768–1833. Scrapbook, 3 vols. Th.Cts.35–37.
"A collection of programmes, cuttings from newspapers relating to performances in various circuses from 1772–1885." Scrapbook, 2 vols. Th.Cts.50.
Egerton MS 2005
Harley MSS 4206, 5219
Lysons, Daniel. *Collectanea, or A Collection of Advertisements and Paragraphs from the Newspapers Relating to Various Subjects.* Printed at Strawberry-Hill by Thomas Kirgate for the Collector, Daniel Lysons, n.d. Scrapbook, 4 vols. C.103.k11. [Mic. C.20452–C.20455].

Surrey Reference and Information Library
Patent number GB1335

Victoria and Albert Museum, Theatre and Performance Collection (V&A)
Astley's File, 1770–1779 and Early Years—general. Box 1 of 18.
Astley's File, 1780–1828. Box 2 of 18.

PUBLISHED PRIMARY SOURCES

Adams, John. *An Analysis of Horsemanship: Teaching the Whole Art of Riding in the Manege, Military, Hunting, Racing, and Travelling System.* . . . London: James Cundee, 1805.
Allen, John. *Principles of Modern Riding for Ladies: In Which All Late Improvements Are Applied to Practice on the Promenade and the Road.* London: Thomas Tegg, R. Griffin, and J. Cumming, 1825.
Angelo, Henry. *Reminiscences of Henry Angelo, with Memoirs of His Late Father and Friends.* . . . 2 vols. London: Henry Colburn and Richard Bentley, 1830.
Astley, John. *The Art of Riding Set Foorth in a Breefe Treatise, With a Due

Interpretation of Certeine Places Alledged Out of Xenophon, and Gryson. . . . London: Henrie Denham, 1584.

Astley, Philip. *Astley's Projects in His Management of the Horse.* . . . London: T. Burton, 1804.

———. *Astley's System of Equestrian Education, Exhibiting the Beauties and Defects of the Horse.* . . . 3rd ed. London: T. Burton, 1801.

———. *The Modern Riding-Master, or A Key to the Knowledge of the Horse, and Horsemanship.* Philadelphia: Robert Aitken, 1776.

———. *Natural Magic, or Physical Amusements Revealed.* . . . London, 1785.

———. *Remarks on the Profession and Duty of a Soldier.* . . . London, 1794.

Baret, Michael. *An Hipponomie, or The Vineyard of Horsemanship.* . . . London: George Eld, 1618.

Beckford, Peter. *Thoughts on Hunting: In a Series of Familiar Letters to a Friend.* Sarum: E. Easton, 1781. Reprint, New York: J. A. Allen, 2000.

Berenger, Richard. *The History and Art of Horsemanship.* 2 vols. London: T. Davies and T. Cadell, 1771.

Bewick, Thomas. *A General History of Quadrupeds: The Figures Engraved on Wood by Thomas Bewick.* 5th ed. Newcastle upon Tyne: Edward Walker for T. Bewick and S. Hodgson, 1807. Reprint, London: Ward Lock Reprints, 1970.

Blagrave, Joseph. *The Epitome of the Whole Art of Husbandry: Comprising All Necessary Directions for the Improvement of It.* . . . London: Ben. Billingsley and Obadiah Blagrave, 1669.

Blome, Richard. *Gentleman's Recreations: In Three Parts.* 3 vols. London: R. Bonwicke et al., 1709–10.

———. *Gentleman's Recreation: In Two Parts.* London: Samuel Roycroft, 1686.

Bourgelat, Claude. *A New System of Horsemanship: From the French of Monsieur Bourgelat.* . . . Translated by Richard Berenger. London: Henry Woodfall, 1754.

Boyle, John. "Monumental Inscriptions on an Urn in the Gardens at Marston." *Gentleman's Magazine,* May 1780, 242.

Bracken, Henry. *Ten Minutes Advice to Every Gentleman Going to Purchase a Horse Out of a Dealer, Jockey, or Groom's Stable.* London, 1775.

Brathwaite, Richard. *The English Gentleman.* . . . London: Felix Kyngston [and R. Badger], 1633.

Brindley, John. "A Dictionary Explaining the Technical Terms that Belong to the Stud, Stable, Manage, and Farriery, or Whatever Else Relates to Horses." In *A General System of Horsemanship in All Its Branches . . . ,* by William Cavendish, Duke of Newcastle. London: J. Brindley, 1743. Facsimile reproduction, with a foreword by William C. Steinkraus, North Pomfret, Vt.: J. A. Allen, 2000.

Brown, John. *An Estimate of the Manners and Principles of the Times.* London: L. Davis and C. Reymers, 1757.

Bunbury, Henry William [Geoffrey Gambado, pseud.]. *An Academy for Grown Horsemen.* . . . London: W. Dickinson, S. Hooper, and Mess. Robinsons, 1787.

———. *The Annals of Horsemanship.* . . . London: W. Dickinson, S. Hooper, J. Archer, and R. White, 1791.

Burdon, William. *Capt. Burdon's Gentleman's Pocket-Farrier.* . . . London: J. Torbuck and J. Rowland, 1742.

Burke, Edmund. *Reflections on the Revolution in France.* 1790. Edited by J. C. D. Clark. Stanford: Stanford University Press, 2001.

Burney, Fanny [Frances]. *Diary and Letters of Madame D'Arblay, Author of "Evelina," "Cecilia," &c.* Edited by her niece [Charlotte Barrett]. Vols. 2–3, *1786–1787.* London: H. Colburn, by Hurst and Blackett, 1854.

———. *The Early Journals and Letters of Fanny Burney.* Vol. 2, *1774–1777.* Edited by Lars E. Troide. Montreal: McGill-Queen's University Press, 1990.

Carter, Mr. *Instructions for Ladies in Riding.* . . . London, 1783.

Cavendish, William, Duke of Newcastle. *A General System of Horsemanship in All Its Branches.* . . . 2 vols. London: J. Brindley, 1743. Facsimile reproduction, with a foreword by William C. Steinkraus, North Pomfret, Vt.: J. A. Allen, 2000. Citations are to the facsimile.

———. *Ideology and Politics on the Eve of Restoration: Newcastle's Advice to Charles II.* Ca. 1658–59. Transcribed with an introduction by Thomas P. Slaughter. Philadelphia: American Philosophical Society, 1984.

———. *A New Method, and Extraordinary Invention, to Dress Horses, and Work Them According to Nature.* . . . London: Tho. Milbourn, 1667.

Clifford, Christopher. *The Schoole of Horsemanship.* . . . London: [By T. East] for Thomas Cadman, 1585.

Cobbold, Richard. *Geoffrey Gambado, or A Simple Remedy for Hypochondriacism and Melencholy Splentic Humours.* London: Dean and Son, 1865.

Cowper, William. *The Entertaining and Facetious History of John Gilpin.* . . . London, 1785.

Cruso, John. *Militarie Instructions for the Cavallrie, or Rules and Directions for the Service of the Horse.* . . . Cambridge: Roger Daniel, printer to the Universitie, 1644.

Dando, John, and Harrie Runt. *Maroccus Extaticus, or Bankes Bay Horse in a Trance.* . . . [London]: [Thomas Scarlet] for Cuthbert Burby, 1595.

Davenant, William. "The Long Vacation in London." In *The Works of the English Poets*, vol. 6, *From Chaucer to Cowper*, edited by Samuel Johnson and Alexander Chalmers, 433–34. London: J. Johnson et al., 1810.

Decastro, Jacob. *The Memoirs of J. Decastro, Comedian.* . . . Edited by R. Humphreys. London: Sherwood, Jones, 1824.

de Grey, Thomas. *The Compleat Horseman and Expert Ferrier.* . . . London: Thomas Harper, 1639.

Descartes, René. *Discourse on Method and the Meditations.* 1637. Translated by F. E. Sutcliffe. London: Penguin Books, 1968.

Dibdin, Charles the Younger. *Memoirs of Charles Dibdin the Younger.* Edited by George Speaight. London: Society for Theatre Research, 1956.

Dickens, Charles. *The Old Curiosity Shop.* Vol. 1 of *The Works of Charles Dickens.* New York: Hurd and Houghton, 1873.

Drinkwater, John. *A History of the Late Siege of Gibraltar: With a Description and Account of That Garrison, from the Earliest Periods.* London: T. Spilsbury, 1786.

Dryden, John. "An Evening's Love, or The Mock-Astrologer." In Dryden, *The Comedies, Tragedies, and Operas.* . . . 2 vols., 1:275–325. London: Jacob Tonson, Thomas Bennet, and Richard Wellington, 1701.

An Elegy in a Riding House: In Imitation of Virgil's First Pastoral. London: J. Robson, 1778.

Freeman, Strickland. *The Art of Horsemanship Altered and Abbreviated, According to the Principles of the Late Sir Sidney Medows.* London: W. Bulmer, 1806.

Gailhard, Jean. *The Compleat Gentleman, or Directions for the Education of Youth as to Their Breeding at Home and Travelling Abroad, in Two Treatises.* London: In the Savoy, Tho. Newcomb for Iohn Starkey, 1678.

Garrick, David. "The Old Painter's Soliloquy upon Seeing Mr. Bunbury's Drawings." In *The Correspondence of Sir Thomas Hanmer, Bart., Speaker of the House of Commons: With a Memoir of his Life,* edited by Sir Henry Bunbury, 377. London: Edward Moxon, 1838.

Griffiths, Ralph, and G. E. Griffiths. *The Monthly Review, Or, Literary Journal: January to April inclusive.* London: Published by s.n., 1793.

Grose, Francis. *A Classical Dictionary of the Vulgar Tongue.* London: S. Hooper, 1785.

———. *Rules for Drawing Caricatures: With an Essay on Comic Painting.* London: A. Grant for S. Hooper, 1788.

Guérinière, François Robichon de La. *School of Horsemanship* [*Ecole de Cavalerie*]. 1729–31. Translated by Tracy Boucher, with an introduction by Jack C. Schuman. London: J. A. Allen, 1994.

Guillet de Saint-Georges, Georges. *The Gentleman's Dictionary.* London: H. Bonwicke, 1705.

H., R. [Howlett, Robert]. *The School of Recreation, or A Guide to the Most Ingenious Exercises of Hunting, Riding, Racing.* . . . London: H. Rhodes, 1701.

Halliwell, James Orchard. *Popular Rhymes and Nursery Tales.* . . . London: John Russell Smith, 1849.

Harrison, Mr. "The Taylor's Soliloquy." In *The Comick Magazine, or Compleat Library,* by William

Hogarth, 26–28. London: Harrison, 1797.

Hawkes, John. *The Meynellian Science, or Fox-Hunting upon System*. . . . 1808. Leicester: Edgar Backus, 1932.

Hayley, William. *Ode to Mr. Wright of Derby*. Chichester: Dennett Jaques, 1783.

Herbert, Henry, Earl of Pembroke. *A Method of Breaking Horses and Teaching Soldiers to Ride, Designed for the Use of the Army*. London: J. Hughs, 1762.

Hobbes, Thomas. *De Cive: Philosophicall Rudiments Concerning Government and Society*. 1642. Oxford: Clarendon Press, 1983.

———. *The Elements of Law: Natural and Politic*. 1650. Edited by Ferdinand Tönnies. 2nd ed., with an introduction by M. M. Goldsmith. London: Cass, 1969.

———. *Leviathan*. 1651. Edited by C. B. Macpherson. Harmondsworth: Penguin Books, 1968.

Hogarth, William. *The Analysis of Beauty*. . . . London: J. Reeves, 1753.

Hope, William. "Supplement of Riding; Collected from the best Authors." In *The Compleat Horseman: Discovering the Surest Marks of the Beauty, Goodness, Faults and Imperfections of Horses*. . . . , by Jacques de Solleysel. London: M. Gillyflower et al., 1696.

An Hue and Cry After M——f Y——h's White-Horse. . . . London: T. Querit, 1747.

Hughes, Charles. *The Compleat Horseman, or The Art of Riding Made Easy*. . . . London: F. Newbery, 1772.

Jackson, J. L. *The Art of Riding, or Horsemanship Made Easy*. . . . London: A. Cooke, 1765.

Landmann, George. *Adventures and Recollections of Colonel Landmann, Late of the Corps of Royal Engineers*. London: Colburn, 1852.

Lavater, Johann Caspar. *Essays on Physiognomy: Designed to Promote the Knowledge and the Love of Mankind*. Translated from the French by Henry Hunter. 3 vols. London: John Murray, H. Hunter, and T. Holloway, 1789–98.

Lawrence, John. *A Philosophical and Practical Treatise on Horses and on the Moral Duties of Man Towards the Brute Creation*. 2nd ed. 2 vols. London: C. Whittingham for H. D. Symonds, 1802.

Lennox, Charlotte. *The Female Quixote, or The Adventures of Arabella*. 1783. Edited by Margaret Dalziel. London: Oxford University Press, 1970.

Leslie, David, 1st Baron Newark. *General Lessley's Direction and Order for the Exercising of Horse and Foot*. . . . London, 1642.

Locke, John. *An Essay Concerning Human Understanding*. 1689. Edited by Peter H. Nidditch. Oxford: Oxford University Press, 1975.

The London Chronicle for the Year 1800. Vol. 87. London: G. Woodfall, 1800.

Markham, Gervase. *Cauelarice, or The English Horseman*. . . . London:

[Edward Allde and W. Jaggard] for Edward White, 1607.

———. *Markhams maister-peece, or What doth a Horse-man Lacke.* . . . London: Nicholas Okes, 1610.

Memoirs of Dick: The Little Poney. London: J. Walker, 1800.

Montagu, Elizabeth. *The Letters of Elizabeth Montagu, with Some of the Letters of Her Correspondents.* . . . Vol. 3. Edited by Matthew Montagu. London: Matthew Montague, 1813.

Montluzin, Emily Lorraine de. "'Oh! He Was All Perfection': The Earl of Orrery's Tribute to His Horse, Posthumously Printed in the *Gentleman's Magazine*." *ANQ* 20, no. 4 (2007): 13–17.

Morgan of Crolane, Nicholas. *The Horse-mans Honour, or The Beautie of Horsemanship.* London: Widdow Helme and J. Marriott, 1620.

———. *The Perfection of Horse-manship, Drawne from Nature; Arte, and Practise.* . . . London: [Edward Allde] for Edward VVhite, 1609.

Mrs. Gilpin's Return, Being the Sequel to Jonny Gilpin of Cheapside. London: T. Davis for Edward Wallis, n.d.

"*Noctes Ambrosianae*, no. 54." *Blackwood's Edinburgh Magazine* 29 (February 1831): 263–64.

Oswald, John. *The Cry of Nature, or An Appeal to Mercy and to Justice, on Behalf of the Persecuted Animals.* London: J. Johnson, 1791.

"Paddy Bull's Expedition." In *Apollo's Lyre; Being a Selection of the Most Approved Songs, Including Those Sung at Vauxhall, Theatres Royal, &c.,* 54–55. London: J. Fowler, [1795?].

Peacham, Henry. *The Compleat Gentleman: Fashioning him absolute in the most necessary & commendable Qualities.* . . . London: Francis Constable, 1622.

Pope, Alexander. "The First Epistle of the Second Book of Horace, Imitated." In *The Poems of Alexander Pope: A One-Volume Edition of the Twickenham Text, with Selected Annotations*, edited by John Everett Butt, 635–58. London: Routledge, 2005.

Reynolds, Joshua. *The Works of Sir Joshua Reynolds.* . . . 2 vols. London: T. Cadell, Jun. and W. Davies, 1797.

S., A. *The Gentleman's Compleat Jockey: With the Perfect Horseman, and Experience'd Farrier.* . . . London: Henry Neime, 1696.

S., F. [Segar, Francis]. *The Schoole of Vertue, and Booke of Good Nourture for Chyldren, and Youth to Learne Theyr Dutie by.* . . . London: Wyllyam Seares, 1557.

Segar, William. *Honor Military, and Ciuill, Contained in Foure Bookes.* . . . London: Robert Barker, 1602.

Sidney, Philip. *The Countess of Pembroke's Arcadia.* Edited by Maurice Evans. London: Penguin Books, 1977.

———. *The Defence of Poesie.* London: VVilliam Ponsonby, 1595.

Smith, Adam. *The Theory of Moral Sentiments.* 1759. Edited by Knud Haakonssen. Cambridge: Cambridge University Press, 2002.

Smollett, Tobias. "An Academy for Grown-Horsemen." In *The Critical Review, or Annals of Literature*, 348–50. London: Published by W. Simpkin and R. Marshall, 1787.

———. *The Adventures of Peregrine Pickle: In Which are Included Memoirs of a Lady of Quality*. 1751. London: Oxford University Press, 1964.

Solleysel, Jacques de. *The Compleat Horseman: Discovering the Surest Marks of the Beauty, Goodness, Faults and Imperfections of Horses*. . . . Translated by William Hope. London: M. Gillyflower et al., 1696.

Somervile, William. *The Chace: A Poem . . . the Third Edition*. London: G. Hawkins, Sold by T. Cooper, 1735.

Stokes, Will. *The Vaulting-Master: Or the Art of Vaulting, Reduced to a Method, comprized under certaine Rules, Illustrated by Examples*. . . . [London?]: Printed for Richard Davis, in Oxon, 1652.

Stringer, Arthur. *The Experienced Huntsman*. . . . Dublin: L. Flin, Castle-Street, 1780.

Surtees, R. S. *Ask Mamma, or The Richest Commoner in England*. 1858. London: Folio Society, 1954.

———. *Jorrocks's Jaunts and Jollities*. . . . 1843. London: Methuen, 1961.

Sympson, Josephus. *Twenty Five Actions of the Manage Horse*. . . . London: Printed for and Sold by J. Sympson and Andrew Johnston, 1729.

Thompson, Charles. *Rules for Bad Horsemen*. . . . London: Printed for J. Robson, 1762.

Thomson, James. "Liberty." In *The Works of Cowper and Thomson: Including Many Letters and Poems Never Before Published in This Country*. . . . , 74–107. Philadelphia: J. Grigg, 1832.

Topham, Edward. *The Life of the Late John Elwes, Esquire*. . . . London: John Jarvis for James Ridgway, 1790.

van Beneden, Ben, and Nora de Poorter, eds. *Royalist Refugees: William and Margaret Cavendish in the Rubens House, 1648–1660*. Antwerp: Rubenshuis & Rubenianum, 2006.

Vernon, John. *The Young Horse-man, or The Honest Plain-dealing Cavalier*. London: Andrew Coe, 1644.

The Vice-Chancellor and the Whole Senate of the University of Cambridge. "Letter to the Most Eminent Prince." In *A Collection of Letters and Poems: Written by several Persons of Honour and Learning, Upon divers Important Subjects, to the Late Duke and Dutchess of New Castle*, edited by Margaret Cavendish, Duchess of Newcastle, 50–52. London: Langly Curtis, 1678.

Weaver, John. *Essay Towards an History of Dancing*. . . . London: Jacob Tonson, 1712.

Westwood, John. "[Carmen Basileuporion sive Regale iter] Royal Journey Ode, or The Royal Journey." Translated by Jackson Bryce. Edited by Timothy Raylor. In "The Cavendish Circle," ed. Richard Maber, special issue, *Seventeenth Century* 9, no. 2 (1994): 179–95.

Wollstonecraft, Mary. *A Vindication of the Rights of Men*. 1790. In Wollstonecraft, *A Vindication of the Rights of Woman/A Vindication of the Rights of Men*, edited by Janet Todd, 1–62. Oxford: Oxford University Press, 1999.

Xenophon. "Xenophon's Treatise on Horsemanship." Translated from the original Greek by Richard Berenger. In Berenger, *The History and Art of Horsemanship*, 2 vols. 1:218–332. London: T. Davies and T. Cadell, 1771.

SECONDARY SOURCES

Andrew, Donna T. "The Code of Honour and Its Critics: The Opposition to Duelling in England, 1700–1850." *Social History* 5, no. 3 (1980): 409–34.

Barad, Karen. *Meeting the Universe Halfway: Quantum Physics and the Entanglement of Matter and Meaning*. Durham: Duke University Press, 2007.

———. "Posthumanist Performativity: Toward an Understanding of How Matter Comes to Matter." *Signs: Journal of Women in Culture and Society* 28, no. 3 (2003): 801–31.

Barker-Benfield, G. J. *The Culture of Sensibility: Sex and Society in Eighteenth-Century Britain*. Chicago: University of Chicago Press, 1992.

Barrell, John. *The Birth of Pandora and the Division of Knowledge*. London: Macmillan, 1992.

———. "'The Dangerous Goddess': Masculinity, Prestige, and the Aesthetic in Early Eighteenth-Century Britain." *Cultural Critique* 12 (Spring 1989): 101–31.

———. *The Political Theory of Painting from Reynolds to Hazlitt: "The Body of the Public."* New Haven: Yale University Press, 1986.

Beghin, Tom, and Sander M. Goldberg, eds. *Haydn and the Performance of Rhetoric*. Chicago: University of Chicago Press, 2007.

Benedict, Barbara M. *Curiosity: A Cultural History of Early Modern Inquiry*. Chicago: University of Chicago Press, 2001.

———. "Reading Faces: Physiognomy and Epistemology in Late Eighteenth-Century Sentimental Novels." *Studies in Philology* 92, no. 3 (1995): 311–28.

———. "The Spirit of Things." In *The Secret Life of Things: Animals, Objects, and It-Narratives in Eighteenth-Century England*, edited by Mark Blackwell, 19–42. Lewisburg: Bucknell University Press, 2007.

Benston, Kimberly W. "Experimenting at the Threshold: Sacrifice, Anthropomorphism, and the Aims of (Critical) Animal Studies." *PMLA* 124, no. 2 (2009): 548–55.

Birke, Lynda, Mette Bryld, and Nina Lykke. "Animal Performances: An Exploration of Intersections Between Feminist Science Studies and Studies of Human/Animal Relationships." *Feminist Theory* 5, no. 2 (2004): 167–83.

Blake, Robin. "A Different Form of Art: Stubbs and Rockingham's

Young Whigs in the 1760s." In *Stubbs and the Horse*, edited by Malcolm Warner and Robin Blake, 42–63. New Haven: Yale University Press, 2004.

Boehrer, Bruce. "Shakespeare and the Devaluation of the Horse." In *The Culture of the Horse: Status, Discipline, and Identity in the Early Modern World*, edited by Karen Raber and Treva J. Tucker, 91–113. New York: Palgrave Macmillan, 2005.

Brandt, Keri. "A Language of Their Own: An Interactionist Approach to Human-Horse Communication." *Society and Animals* 12, no. 4 (2004): 299–316.

Brewer, John. *The Common People and Politics, 1750–1790s*. Vol. 5 of *The English Satirical Print, 1600–1832*, edited by Michael Duffy. Cambridge: Chadwyck-Healey, 1986.

———. *Party Ideology and Popular Politics at the Accession of George III*. Cambridge: Cambridge University Press, 1981.

———. *The Pleasures of the Imagination: English Culture in the Eighteenth Century*. Chicago: University of Chicago Press, 2000.

Bryson, Anna. *From Courtesy to Civility: Changing Codes of Conduct in Early Modern England*. Oxford: Clarendon Press, 1998.

Butler, Judith. *Gender Trouble: Feminism and the Subversion of Identity*. New York: Routledge, 1990.

Canny, Nicholas. "Irish Resistance to Empire? 1641, 1690, and 1789." In *An Imperial State at War: Britain from 1689–1815*, edited by Lawrence Stone, 288–321. New York: Routledge, 2001.

Carré, Jacques. "Introduction." In *The Crisis of Courtesy: Studies in the Conduct-Book in Britain, 1600–1900*, edited by Jacques Carré, 1–11. Leiden: Brill, 1994.

Carter, Philip. *Men and the Emergence of Polite Society, Britain, 1660–1800*. Harlow, UK: Pearson Education, 2001.

Cash, Arthur H. *John Wilkes: The Scandalous Father of Civil Liberty*. New Haven: Yale University Press, 2006.

Clark, Anna. "The Chevalier d'Eon and Wilkes: Masculinity and Politics in the Eighteenth Century." *Eighteenth-Century Studies* 32, no. 1 (1998): 19–48.

Clark, Peter. *British Clubs and Societies, 1580–1800: The Origins of an Associational World*. Oxford: Oxford University Press, 2000.

Cohen, Michèle. *Fashioning Masculinity: National Identity and Language in the Eighteenth Century*. London: Routledge, 1996.

———. "Manliness, Effeminacy, and the French: Gender and the Construction of National Character in Eighteenth-Century England." In *English Masculinities, 1660–1800*, edited by Tim Hitchcock and Michèle Cohen, 44–61. London: Longman, 1999.

———. "'Manners' Make the Man: Politeness, Chivalry, and the Construction of Masculinity, 1750–1830." *Journal of British Studies* 44, no. 2 (2005): 312–29.

Cole, Lucinda. "Introduction: Human-Animal Studies and the Eighteenth Century." In

"Animal, All Too Animal," ed. Lucinda Cole, special issue, *Eighteenth Century* 52, no. 1 (2011): 1–10.

Cole, Lucinda, Donna Landry, Bruce Boehrer, Richard Nash, Erica Fudge, Robert Markley, and Cary Wolfe. "Speciesism, Identity Politics, and Ecocriticism: A Conversation with Humanists and Posthumanists." In "Animal, All Too Animal," ed. Lucinda Cole, special issue, *Eighteenth Century* 52, no. 1 (2011): 87–106.

Colley, Linda. *Britons: Forging the Nation, 1707–1837*. New Haven: Yale University Press, 1992.

Conaway, Charles. "'Thou'rt the Man': David Garrick, William Shakespeare, and the Masculinization of the Eighteenth-Century Stage." *Restoration and Eighteenth-Century Theatre Research* 19, no. 1 (2004): 22–42.

Condren, Conal. "Casuistry to Newcastle: 'The Prince' in the World of the Book." In *Political Discourse in Early Modern Britain*, edited by Nicholas Phillipson and Quentin Skinner, 164–86. Cambridge: Cambridge University Press, 1993.

Conway, Stephen. *The British Isles and the War of American Independence*. Oxford: Oxford University Press, 2002.

Cox, Rosanna. "John Milton's Politics, Republicanism, and Terms of Liberty." *Literature Compass* 4, no. 6 (2007): 1561–76.

Crown, Patricia. "Sporting with Clothes: John Collet's Satirical Prints in the 1770s." *Eighteenth-Century Life* 26, no. 1 (2002): 95–135.

Cust, Richard. "Honour and Politics in Early Stuart England: The Case of Beaumont v. Hastings." *Past and Present* 149, no. 1 (1995): 57–94.

Dabhoiwala, Faramerz. "The Constructions of Honour, Reputation, and Status in Late Seventeenth- and Early Eighteenth-Century England." *Transactions of the Royal Historical Society*, 6th ser., 6 (1996): 201–13.

Dent, Anthony. *Horses in Shakespeare's England*. London: J. A. Allen, 1987.

De Ornellas, Kevin Patrick. "Troping the Horse in Early Modern English Literature and Culture." PhD diss., Queen's University, Belfast, 2002.

Derrida, Jacques. *The Animal That Therefore I Am*. Edited by Marie-Louise Mallet. Translated by David Wills. New York: Fordham University Press, 2008.

———. *The Beast and the Sovereign*. Vol. 1. Edited by Michel Lisse, Marie-Louise Mallet, and Ginette Michaud. Translated by Geoffrey Bennington. Chicago: University of Chicago Press, 2009.

Deuchar, Stephen. *Sporting Art in Eighteenth-Century England: A Social and Political History*. New Haven: Yale University Press for the Paul Mellon Centre for Studies in British Art, 1988.

Dickinson, H. T. *Caricatures and the Constitution, 1760–1832*. Vol. 6 of *The English Satirical Print*,

1600–1832. Edited by Michael Duffy. Cambridge: Chadwyck-Healey, 1986.

Disher, Maurice Willson. *Fairs, Circuses, and Music Halls*. London: William Collins, 1942.

Donald, Diana. *Picturing Animals in Britain, 1750–1850*. New Haven: Yale University Press for the Paul Mellon Centre for Studies in British Art, 2007.

Drayton, Richard. *Nature's Government: Science, Imperial Britain, and the "Improvement" of the World*. New Haven: Yale University Press, 2000.

Edwards, Peter. *Horse and Man in Early Modern England*. London: Continuum Books, 2007.

———. "The Horse Trade in Tudor and Stuart England." In *Horses in European Economic History: A Preliminary Canter*, edited by F. M. L. Thompson, 113–31. Reading: British Agricultural History Society, 1983.

———. *The Horse Trade of Tudor and Stuart England*. Cambridge: Cambridge University Press, 1988.

Edwards, Peter, Karl A. E. Enenkel, and Elspeth Graham, eds. *The Horse as Cultural Icon: The Real and the Symbolic Horse in the Early Modern World*. Leiden: Brill, 2012.

Elias, Norbert. *The Civilizing Process: State Formation and Civilization*. Translated by Edmund Jephcott. 2 vols. Oxford: Basil Blackwell, 1982.

Ellis, Markman. *The Coffee-House: A Cultural History*. London: Weidenfeld and Nicolson, 2004.

Erskine-Hill, Howard. "Pope and the Poetry of Opposition." In *The Cambridge Companion to Alexander Pope*, edited by Pat Rogers, 134–49. Cambridge: Cambridge University Press, 2007.

Fletcher, Anthony. *Gender, Sex, and Subordination in England, 1500–1800*. New Haven: Yale University Press, 1995.

Foyster, Elizabeth A. *Manhood in Early Modern England: Honour, Sex, and Marriage*. New York: Longman, 1999.

Frost, Thomas. *Circus Life and Circus Celebrities*. London: Chatto and Windus, 1881.

Fudge, Erica. *Brutal Reasoning: Animals, Rationality, and Humanity in Early Modern England*. Ithaca: Cornell University Press, 2006.

———. "A Left-Handed Blow: Writing the History of Animals." In *Representing Animals*, edited by Nigel Rothfels, 3–18. Bloomington: Indiana University Press, 2002.

———. *Perceiving Animals: Humans and Beasts in Early Modern English Culture*. Champaign: University of Illinois Press, 2000.

Game, Ann. "Riding: Embodying the Centaur." *Body and Society* 7, no. 4 (2001): 1–12.

Ganev, Robin. "Milkmaids, Ploughmen, and Sex in Eighteenth-Century Britain." *Journal of the History of Sexuality* 16, no. 1 (2007): 40–67.

Garrett, Aaron. "Francis Hutcheson and the Origin of Animal Rights." *Journal of the History of Philosophy* 45, no. 2 (2007): 243–65.

Gatrell, Vic. *City of Laughter: Sex and Satire in Eighteenth-Century London*. London: Atlantic Books, 2006.

George, M. Dorothy. *Catalogue of Political and Personal Satires Preserved in the Department of Prints and Drawings in the British Museum*. Vol. 6, *1784–1792*. London: British Museum, 1938.

——. *Hogarth to Cruikshank: Social Change in Graphic Satire*. London: Penguin Books, 1967.

Gilroy, Amanda. "The Habit and the Horse, or The Suburbanisation of Female Equitation." In *Green and Pleasant Land: English Culture and the Romantic Countryside*, edited by Amanda Gilroy, 45–56. Louvain: Peeters, 2004.

Graham, Elspeth. "The Duke of Newcastle's 'Love [. . .] for Good Horses': An Exploration of Meanings." In *The Horse as Cultural Icon: The Real and the Symbolic Horse in the Early Modern World*, edited by Peter Edwards, Karl A. E. Enenkel, and Elspeth Graham, 37–69. Leiden: Brill, 2012.

——. "Reading, Writing, and Riding Horses in Early Modern England: James Shirley's *Hyde Park* (1632) and Gervase Markham's *Cavelarice* (1607)." In *Renaissance Beasts: Of Animals, Humans, and Other Wonderful Creatures*, edited by Erica Fudge, 116–37. Champaign: University of Illinois Press, 2004.

Gray, W. Forbes. "An Eighteenth-Century Riding School." *Book of the Old Edinburgh Club* 20 (1935): 111–59.

Griffith, Eva. "Inside and Outside: Animal Activity and the Red Bull Playhouse, St. John Street." In *A Cultural History of Animals in the Age of Enlightenment*, edited by Matthew Senior, 101–20. New York: Berg, 2007.

Guichet, Jean-Luc. "Animality and Anthropology in Jean-Jacques Rousseau." Translated by Richard Byrne. In *A Cultural History of Animals in the Age of Enlightenment*, edited by Matthew Senior, 145–56. New York: Berg, 2007.

Hackforth-Jones, Jocelyn. "Mai/Omai in London and the South Pacific: Performativity, Cultural Entanglement, and Indigenous Appropriation." In *Material Identities*, edited by Joanna Sofaer, 13–30. Oxford: Blackwell, 2007.

Haraway, Donna. *The Companion Species Manifesto: Dogs, People, and Significant Otherness*. Chicago: Prickly Paradigm Press, 2003.

——. "Encounters with Companion Species: Entangling Dogs, Baboons, Philosophers, and Biologists." *Configurations* 14, nos. 1–2 (2006): 97–114.

——. *When Species Meet*. Minneapolis: University of Minnesota Press, 2007.

Harris, Bob. *Politics and the Nation: Britain in the Mid-Eighteenth Century*. Oxford: Oxford University Press, 2002.

Harvey, Karen. "The History of Masculinity, Circa 1650–1800."

Journal of British Studies 44, no. 2 (2005): 296–311.

Henricks, Thomas S. "The Democratization of Sport in Eighteenth-Century England." *Journal of Popular Culture* 18, no. 3 (1984): 3–20.

Hilton, Boyd. *A Mad, Bad, and Dangerous People? England, 1783–1846*. Oxford: Oxford University Press, 2006.

Hoppit, Julian. *A Land of Liberty? England, 1689–1727*. Oxford: Oxford University Press, 2000.

Horlacher, Stefan. "Charting the Field of Masculinity Studies, or Toward a Literary History of Masculinities." In *Constructions of Masculinity in British Literature from the Middle Ages to the Present*, edited by Stefan Horlacher, 3–19. New York: Palgrave Macmillan, 2011.

Hudson, Nicholas. "It-Narratives: Fictional Point of View and Constructing the Middle Class." In *The Secret Life of Things: Animals, Objects, and It-Narratives in Eighteenth-Century England*, edited by Mark Blackwell, 292–308. Lewisburg: Bucknell University Press, 2007.

Hulse, Lynn. "'The King's Entertainment' by the Duke of Newcastle." *Viator* 26 (1995): 355–405.

Hunt, Margaret R. *The Middling Sort: Commerce, Gender, and the Family in England, 1680–1780*. Berkeley: University of California Press, 1996.

James, Mervyn. *English Politics and the Concept of Honour, 1485–1642*. Oxford: Past and Present Society, 1978.

Jirousek, Charlotte. "Ottoman Influences in Western Dress." In *Ottoman Costumes: From Textile to Identity*, edited by Suraiya Faroqhi and Christoph K. Neumann, 231–51. Istanbul: Eren, 2004.

Jones, Vivien, ed. *Women in the Eighteenth Century: Construction of Femininity*. London: Routledge, 2006.

Jordan, John Bryce. "'Is He No Man?' Toward an Appreciation of Male Effeminacy in English Dance History." *Studies in Eighteenth-Century Culture* 30 (2001): 201–22.

Kahn, Victoria. *Wayward Contracts: The Crisis of Political Obligation in England, 1640–1674*. Princeton: Princeton University Press, 2004.

Kim, James. "'Good Cursed, Bouncing Losses': Masculinity, Sentimental Irony, and Exuberance in *Tristram Shandy*." *Eighteenth Century* 48, no. 1 (2007): 3–24.

King, Thomas A. *The Gendering of Men, 1600–1750*. Vol. 1, *The English Phallus*. Madison: University of Wisconsin Press, 2004.

Kittredge, Katharine, ed. *Lewd and Notorious: Female Transgression in the Eighteenth Century*. Ann Arbor: University of Michigan Press, 2003.

Klein, Lawrence E. "Coffeehouse Civility, 1660–1714: An Aspect of Post-Courtly Culture in England." *Huntington Library Quarterly* 59, no. 1 (1996): 30–51.

———. "Politeness and the Interpretation of the British Eighteenth Century." *Historical Journal* 45, no. 4 (2002): 869–98.

Kuchta, David. *The Three-Piece Suit and Modern Masculinity: England, 1550–1850.* Berkeley: University of California Press, 2002.

Kwint, Marius. "Astley's Amphitheatre and the Early Circus in England, 1768–1830." PhD diss., Magdalen College, University of Oxford, 1994.

———. "The Legitimization of the Circus in Late Georgian England." *Past and Present* 174, no. 1 (2002): 72–115.

Lamb, Jonathan. *Preserving the Self in the South Seas, 1680–1840.* Chicago: University of Chicago Press, 2001.

Landry, Donna. "The Bloody Shouldered Arabian and Early Modern English Culture." *Criticism* 46, no. 1 (2004): 41–69.

———. *The Invention of the Countryside: Hunting, Walking, and Ecology in English Literature, 1671–1831.* New York: Palgrave, 2001.

———. "Learning to Ride at Mansfield Park." In *The Postcolonial Jane Austen*, edited by You-me Park and Rajeswari Sunder Rajan, 56–73. London: Routledge, 2000.

———. "Learning to Ride in Early Modern Britain, or The Making of the English Hunting Seat." In *The Culture of the Horse: Status, Discipline, and Identity in the Early Modern World*, edited by Karen Raber and Treva J. Tucker, 329–50. New York: Palgrave Macmillan, 2005.

———. *Noble Brutes: How Eastern Horses Transformed English Culture.* Baltimore: Johns Hopkins University Press, 2009.

Langford, Paul. *A Polite and Commercial People: England, 1727–1783.* Oxford: Clarendon Press, 1998.

LeGuin, Elisabeth. "Man and Horse in Harmony." In *The Culture of the Horse: Status, Discipline, and Identity in the Early Modern World*, edited by Karen Raber and Treva J. Tucker, 175–96. New York: Palgrave Macmillan, 2005.

Leonard, Stephen T., and Joan C. Tronto. "The Genders of Citizenship." *American Political Science Review* 101, no. 1 (2007): 33–46.

Lewis, Elizabeth Miller. "Hester Santlow's *Harlequine*: Dance, Dress, Status, and Gender on the London Stage, 1706–1734." In *The Clothes That Wear Us: Essays on Dressing and Transgressing in Eighteenth-Century Culture*, ed. Jessica Munns and Penny Richards, 80–101. Newark: University of Delaware Press, 1999.

Liedtke, Walter A. *The Royal Horse and Rider: Painting, Sculpture, and Horsemanship, 1500–1800.* New York: Abaris Books, 1989.

Lillywhite, Bryant. *London Coffee Houses: A Reference Book of Coffee Houses in the Seventeenth, Eighteenth, and Nineteenth Centuries.* London: George Allen and Unwin, 1963.

MacDonald, Gabrielle Ann. "Horsemanship as a Courtly Art in Elizabethan England: Origins, Theory, and Practice." PhD diss., University of Toronto, 1983.

MacGregor, Arthur. "The Household Out of Doors: The Stuart Court and the Animal Kingdom." In *The Stuart Courts*, edited by Eveline Cruickshanks, 86–117. Phoenix: Sutton, 2000.

Mangan, Michael. *Staging Masculinities: History, Gender, Performance*. London: Palgrave Macmillan, 2003.

Mason, Jennifer. "Animal Bodies: Corporeality, Class, and Subject Formation in *The Wide, Wide World*." *Nineteenth-Century Literature* 54, no. 4 (2000): 503–33.

Mattfeld, Monica. "'I See Them Galloping!': War, Affect, and Performing Horses in Matthew Lewis's *Timour the Tartar*." In *Performing Animals*, edited by Karen Raber and Monica Mattfeld. University Park: Pennsylvania State University Press, 2017.

Maurer, Shawn Lisa. *Proposing Men: Dialectics of Gender and Class in the Eighteenth-Century English Periodical*. Stanford: Stanford University Press, 1998.

Mayer, Andreas. "Man's Animal Nature: Science, Art, and Satire in Thomas Rowlandson's 'Studies in Comparative Anatomy.'" In *Humans and Other Animals in Eighteenth-Century British Culture: Representation, Hybridity, Ethics*, edited by Frank Palmeri, 119–36. Aldershot: Ashgate, 2006.

———. "The Physiological Circus: Knowing, Representing, and Training Horses in Motion in Nineteenth-Century France." *Representations* 111, no. 1 (2010): 88–120.

McGirr, Elaine M. *Eighteenth-Century Characters: A Guide to the Literature of the Age*. New York: Palgrave Macmillan, 2007.

McGuffie, T. H. *The Siege of Gibraltar, 1779–1783*. London: B. T. Batsford, 1965.

McShane, Clay, and Joel A. Tarr. *The Horse in the City: Living Machines in the Nineteenth Century*. Baltimore: Johns Hopkins University Press, 2007.

Moody, Jane. *Illegitimate Theatre in London, 1770–1840*. Cambridge: Cambridge University Press, 2000.

Moore, Helen. "Introduction." In *Amadis de Gaule*, translated by Anthony Munday, edited by Helen Moore, ix–xxviii. Aldershot: Ashgate, 2004.

Moore-Colyer, Richard J. "Horse Supply and the British Cavalry: A Review, 1066–1900." *Journal of the Society for Army Historical Research* 70, nos. 281–84 (1992): 245–59.

Munns, Jessica, and Penny Richards, eds. *The Clothes That Wear Us: Essays on Dressing and Transgressing in Eighteenth-Century Culture*. Newark: University of Delaware Press, 1999.

Myrone, Martin. *Bodybuilding: Reforming Masculinities in British Art, 1750–1810*. New Haven: Yale University Press for the Paul Mellon Centre for Studies in British Art, 2005.

Nash, Richard. "'Honest English Breed': The Thoroughbred as

Cultural Metaphor." In *The Culture of the Horse: Status, Discipline, and Identity in the Early Modern World*, edited by Karen Raber and Treva J. Tucker, 245–72. New York: Palgrave Macmillan, 2005.

———. "Joy and Pity: Reading Animal Bodies in Late Eighteenth-Century Culture." In "Animal, All Too Animal," ed. Lucinda Cole, special issue, *Eighteenth Century* 52, no. 1 (2011): 47–67.

———. "Of Sorrels, Bays, and Dapple Greys." *Swift Studies* 15 (2000): 110–15.

Nelson, Hilda. "Introduction: Antoine de Pluvinel, Classical Horseman and Humanist." In *Le maneige royal*, by Antoine de Pluvinel, translated by Hilda Nelson, vii–xiv. London: J. A. Allen, 1989.

Nussbaum, Felicity. *The Limits of the Human: Fictions of Anomaly, Race, and Gender in the Long Eighteenth Century*. Cambridge: Cambridge University Press, 2003.

———. *Rival Queens: Actresses, Performance, and the Eighteenth-Century British Theater*. Philadelphia: University of Pennsylvania Press, 2010.

O'Brien, John. *Harlequin Britain: Pantomime and Entertainment, 1690–1760*. Baltimore: Johns Hopkins University Press, 2004.

O'Quinn, Daniel. *Entertaining Crisis in the Atlantic Imperium, 1770–1790*. Baltimore: Johns Hopkins University Press, 2011.

Orden, Kate van. "From *Gens d'armes* to *Gentilshommes*: Dressage, Civility, and the *Ballet à Cheval*." In *The Culture of the Horse: Status, Discipline, and Identity in the Early Modern World*, edited by Karen Raber and Treva J. Tucker, 197–222. New York: Palgrave Macmillan, 2005.

Pincus, Steve. "'Coffee Politicians Does Create': Coffeehouses and Restoration Political Culture." *Journal of Modern History* 67, no. 4 (1995): 807–34.

Pocock, J. G. A. *The Machiavellian Moment: Florentine Political Thought and the Atlantic Republican Tradition*. Princeton: Princeton University Press, 1975.

Podhajsky, Alois. *The Complete Training of Horse and Rider in the Principles of Classical Horsemanship*. London: Sportsman's Press, 1991.

Porter, Roy. *The Creation of the Modern World: The Untold Story of the British Enlightenment*. New York: W. W. Norton, 2000.

Porter, Roy, and G. S. Rousseau. *Gout: The Patrician Malady*. New Haven: Yale University Press, 1998.

Poynter, F. N. L. *A Bibliography of Gervase Markham, 1568?–1637*. Oxford: Oxford Bibliographical Society, 1962.

Raber, Karen. "Cavendish's Horsemanship Treatises and Cultural Capital." In *Authority, Authorship, and Aristocratic Identity in Seventeenth-Century England: William Cavendish, 1st Duke of Newcastle, and His Political, Social, and Cultural Connections*, edited by Peter Edwards and

Elspeth Graham. Leiden: Brill, 2017.

———. "From Sheep to Meat, from Pets to People: Animal Domestication, 1600–1800." In *A Cultural History of Animals in the Age of Enlightenment*, edited by Matthew Senior, 73–99. New York: Berg, 2007.

———. "A Horse of a Different Color: Nation and Race in Early Modern Horsemanship Treatises." In *The Culture of the Horse: Status, Discipline, and Identity in the Early Modern World*, edited by Karen Raber and Treva J. Tucker, 225–44. New York: Palgrave Macmillan, 2005.

———. "'Reasonable Creatures': William Cavendish and the Art of Dressage." In *Renaissance Culture and the Everyday*, edited by Patricia Fumerton and Simon Hunt, 42–66. Philadelphia: University of Pennsylvania Press, 1999.

Raber, Karen, and Treva J. Tucker, eds. *The Culture of the Horse: Status, Discipline, and Identity in the Early Modern World*. New York: Palgrave Macmillan, 2005.

Rauser, Amelia Faye. *Caricature Unmasked: Irony, Authenticity, and Individualism in Eighteenth-Century English Prints*. Newark: University of Delaware Press, 2008.

———. "Hair, Authenticity, and the Self-Made Macaroni." *Eighteenth-Century Studies* 38, no. 1 (2004): 101–17.

Raylor, Timothy. "A Manuscript Poem on the Royal Progress of 1634: An Edition and Translation of John Westwood's 'Carmen Basileuporion.'" In "The Cavendish Circle," ed. Richard Maber, special issue, *Seventeenth Century* 9, no. 2 (1994): 173–78.

Read, Alan, ed. "On Animals." Special issue, *Performance Research* 5, no. 2 (2000).

Reese, M. M. *The Royal Office of Master of the Horse*. London: Threshold Books, 1976.

Ridout, Nicholas. *Stage Fright, Animals, and Other Theatrical Problems*. Cambridge: Cambridge University Press, 2006.

Riely, John C. "Horace Walpole and 'the Second Hogarth.'" *Eighteenth-Century Studies* 9, no. 1 (1975): 28–44.

Rizzo, Betty. "Equivocations of Gender and Rank: Eighteenth-Century Sporting Women." *Eighteenth-Century Life* 26, no. 1 (2002): 70–118.

Roach, Joseph. *It*. Ann Arbor: University of Michigan Press, 2007.

———. "Public Intimacy: The Prior History of 'It.'" In *Theatre and Celebrity in Britain, 1660–2000*, edited by Mary Luckhurst and Jane Moody, 15–30. New York: Palgrave Macmillan, 2005.

Roche, Karen Marie. "Picturing an Englishman: The Art of Sir Henry William Bunbury, 1770–1787." PhD diss., University of Exeter, 2008.

Rogow, Arnold A. *Thomas Hobbes: Radical in the Service of Reaction*. New York: W. W. Norton, 1986.

Russell, Jack. *Gibraltar Besieged, 1779–1783*. London: William Heinemann, 1965.

Ruston, Sharon. "Natural Rights and Natural History in Anna

Barbauld and Mary Wollstonecraft." In *Literature and Science*, edited by Sharon Ruston, 53–71. Cambridge: Boydell and Brewer, 2008.

Said, Edward W. *Orientalism*. London: Penguin Books, 2003.

Sarasohn, Lisa T. "Thomas Hobbes and the Duke of Newcastle: A Study in the Mutuality of Patronage Before the Establishment of the Royal Society." *Isis* 90, no. 4 (1999): 715–37.

Saxon, Arthur H. "The Circus as Theatre: Astley's and Its Actors in the Age of Romanticism." *Educational Theatre Journal* 27, no. 3 (1975): 299–312.

———. *Enter Foot and Horse: A History of Hippodrama in England and France*. New Haven: Yale University Press, 1968.

———. *The Life and Art of Andrew Ducrow and the Romantic Age of the English Circus*. Hamden, Conn.: Archon, 1978.

Schiebinger, Londa. *Nature's Body: Gender in the Making of Modern Science*. Boston: Beacon Press, 1993.

Scull, Andrew. *The Most Solitary of Afflictions: Madness and Society in Britain, 1700–1900*. New Haven: Yale University Press, 1993.

Shepard, Alexandra. "From Anxious Patriarchs to Refined Gentlemen? Manhood in Britain, Circa 1500–1700." *Journal of British Studies* 44, no. 2 (2005): 281–95.

———. "Manhood, Credit, and Patriarchy in Early Modern England, c. 1580–1640." *Past and Present* 167, no. 1 (2000): 75–106.

———. *Meanings of Manhood in Early Modern England*. Oxford: Oxford University Press, 2003.

Shoemaker, Robert. "Male Honour and the Decline of Public Violence in Eighteenth-Century London." *Social History* 26, no. 2 (2001): 190–208.

Skinner, Quentin. *Hobbes and Civil Science*. Vol. 3 of *Visions of Politics*. Cambridge: Cambridge University Press, 2002.

———. *Hobbes and Republican Liberty*. Cambridge: Cambridge University Press, 2008.

Smythe, R. H. *Horse Structure and Movement*. 3rd ed. London: J. A. Allen, 1993.

Solinger, Jason D. *Becoming the Gentleman: British Literature and the Invention of Modern Masculinity, 1660–1815*. New York: Palgrave Macmillan, 2012.

Solkin, David H. *Painting for Money: The Visual Arts and the Public Sphere in Eighteenth-Century England*. New Haven: Yale University Press for the Paul Mellon Centre for Studies in British Art, 1993.

Sørensen, Madeleine Pinault. "Portraits of Animals, 1600–1800." Translated by Janice C. Zinser. In *A Cultural History of Animals in the Age of Enlightenment*, edited by Matthew Senior, 157–96. New York: Berg, 2007.

Speaight, George. "Some Comic Circus Entrées." *Theatre Notebook* 32, no. 1 (1978): 24–27.

Spencer, Jane. "'The Link Which Unites Man with Brutes': Enlightenment Feminism, Women, and Animals." Keynote paper presented at the Women's Studies Group Workshop, London, April 24, 2010.

Stoddart, Helen. *Rings of Desire: Circus History and Representation*. Manchester: Manchester University Press, 2000.

Stott, Raymond Toole. *Circus and Allied Arts: A World Bibliography*. 4 vols. Derby: Harpur, 1958–71.

Swart, Sandra. *Riding High: Horses, Humans, and History in South Africa*. Johannesburg: Witwatersrand University Press, 2010.

Tague, Ingrid H. "Dead Pets: Satire and Sentiment in British Elegies and Epitaphs for Animals." *Eighteenth-Century Studies* 41, no. 3 (2008): 289–306.

Thirsk, Joan. *Horses in Early Modern England: For Service, for Pleasure, for Power*. Reading: University of Reading Press, 1978.

Thompson, E. P. *Whigs and Hunters: The Origin of the Black Act*. London: Pantheon Books, 1975.

Thompson, F. M. L., ed. *Horses in European Economic History: A Preliminary Canter*. Reading: British Agricultural History Society, 1983.

Todd, Dennis. *Imagining Monsters: Miscreations of the Self in Eighteenth-Century England*. Chicago: University of Chicago Press, 1995.

Tribe, Keith. *Land, Labour, and Economic Discourse*. London: Routledge and Kegan Paul, 1978.

Tucker, Treva J. "Early Modern French Noble Identity and the Equestrian 'Airs Above the Ground.'" In *The Culture of the Horse: Status, Discipline, and Identity in the Early Modern World*, edited by Karen Raber and Treva J. Tucker, 273–310. New York: Palgrave Macmillan, 2005.

Tuttle, George Palliser. "The History of the Royal Circus, Equestrian and Philharmonic Academy, 1782–1816, St. George's Fields, Surrey, England." PhD diss., Tufts University, 1972.

Voogd, Peter de. *Henry William Bunbury, 1750–1811: "De Raphaël der Carricatuurteekenaars."* Enschede: Rijksmuseum Twenthe, 1996. Exhibition catalogue.

Wahrman, Dror. *The Making of the Modern Self: Identity and Culture in Eighteenth-Century England*. New Haven: Yale University Press, 2004.

Walker, Elaine. *Horse*. London: Reaktion Books, 2008.

———. "'To Amaze the People with Pleasure and Delight': An Analysis of the Horsemanship Manuals of William Cavendish, First Duke of Newcastle (1593–1676)." PhD diss., University of Birmingham, 2004.

West, Shearer. "Wilkes's Squint: Synecdochic Physiognomy and Political Identity in Eighteenth-Century Print Culture." *Eighteenth-Century Studies* 33, no. 1 (1999): 65–84.

Williams, David. "The Right Horse, the Animal Eye—Bartabas and Théâtre Zingaro." In "On Animals," ed. Alan Read, special issue, *Performance Research* 5, no. 2 (2000): 29–40.

Wilson, Kathleen. "Empire of Virtue: The Imperial Project and Hanoverian Culture, c. 1720–1785." In *An Imperial State at War: Britain from 1689 to 1815*, edited by Lawrence Stone, 128–64. New York: Routledge, 2001.

———. *Island Race: Englishness, Empire, and Gender in the Eighteenth Century*. London: Routledge, 2003.

———. *The Sense of the People: Politics, Culture, and Imperialism in England, 1715–1785*. Cambridge: Cambridge University Press, 1995.

Wolfe, Cary. *What Is Posthumanism?* Minneapolis: University of Minnesota Press, 2010.

Wolloch, Nathaniel. "Rousseau and the Love of Animals." *Philosophy and Literature* 32, no. 2 (2008): 293–302.

Woodworth, Megan A. *Eighteenth-Century Women Writers and the Gentleman's Liberation Movement: Independence, War, Masculinity, and the Novel, 1778–1818*. Farnham: Ashgate, 2011.

Worrall, David. *Theatric Revolution: Drama, Censorship, and Romantic Period Subcultures, 1773–1832*. Oxford: Oxford University Press, 2006.

Worsley, Giles. *The British Stable*. New Haven: Yale University Press for the Paul Mellon Centre for Studies in British Art, 2004.

———. "A Courtly Art: The History of 'Haute École' in England." *Court Historian* 6, no. 1 (2001): 29–47.

Worsley, Lucy. *Cavalier: The Story of a Seventeenth-Century Playboy*. London: Faber and Faber, 2007.

Worsley, Lucy, and Tom Addyman. "Riding Houses and Horses: William Cavendish's Architecture for the Art of Horsemanship." *Architectural History* 45 (2002): 194–229.

Youngquist, Paul. *Monstrosities: Bodies and British Romanticism*. Minneapolis: University of Minnesota Press, 2003.

INDEX

agency, 8, 9, 32, 36, 94, 201
ambling, 13, 14, 186, 236 n. 52
American War of Independence, 11, 89, 123, 140–41, 144
Amphithéâtre d'Astley. *See* Astley's Amphitheatre
Amphitheatre of the Arts. *See* Astley's Amphitheatre
Annals of Agriculture, 182–84
Angelo's Academy
    as business, 119
    class, 119, 127
    military connections, 126–27
    social organization of, 113–17
    women within, 117
Angelo, Domenico
    biography, 113
    riding academy (*see* Angelo's Academy)
animal
    acting, 133–36
    cognitive abilities, 137
    language, 32–33, 34, 199
    verbal speech, 30–31, 132, 199
animal studies, 8, 132
appui, 77, 200–201, 204, 215
Aristotle, 15
Astley's Amphitheatre
    accusations of devilry, 138–39
    censorship of, 123
    centaur within (*see* centaur)
    fireworks, 122
    performance program, 124–25, 139
    as a riding house, 161, 163–65
    usefulness, 167–70, 173

Astley's Riding School. *See* Astley's Amphitheatre
Astley, John
    as dancer (*see* dance)
    with the Gibraltar Charger, 149–50 (*see also* centaur)
    masculinity of, 151–52, 154–55, 167, 207
    sexualization of, 153–54, 155
    vaulting (*see* vaulting)
Astley, Philip
    as Angelo's pupil, 120, 126
    biography, 121, 124–25, 127, 128, 138
    horsemanship, 127–28
    manuals, 127
    masculinity of, 142–44, 167, 207
    military service, 141–42
    resistance to, 174, 176, 186–87, 195, 210–11, 217
    royal letters patent, 165–66, 173
    vaulting (*see* vaulting)
Aurispa, Giovanni, 15

Bankes, Joseph, 134–36, 138
Berenger, Richard, 99, 175, 200
bit
    curb, 89–90, 186
    double bridle and bridoon, 90
    snaffle, 89–90, 186
body, wounded, 212–13
Boyle, John, 1–2. *See also* Cork, fifth Earl of; *and* Marston, second Baron of; *and* Orrery, fifth Earl of
Brindley, John, 24
Bunbury, Catherine, 179

Bunbury, Henry Edward, 177
Bunbury, Henry William (Geoffrey Gambado)
  biography, 172, 77
  caricatures by (*see* caricature)
  centaur (*see* centaur)
  fame, 180
  horsemanship manuals, 171–72, 211; reviews of, 171, 180, 223–24; use, 183
  masculinity, 207
  pseudonym, 184–85
  riding house, 217–19
Bute, Earl of, 88–89

caricature, 175–81
cariere, 14. *See also* jousting
Carter, Captain, 98
Carter, Mr. (riding instructor), 97–98, 101–5, 106–9, 113, 125, 170, 174, 217
Cartesian thought, 8, 27, 31, 62, 136, 137
Cavendish, Charles, 23, 25
Cavendish, William. *See* Newcastle, 1st Duke of
centaur
  at Astley's Amphitheatre, 146, 148–49, 158
  for Bunbury, Henry William, 213–14, 219–21
  for Cavendish, William (*see* Newcastle, 1st Duke of)
  centauric Leviathan, 26–37, 65
  definitions of, 35–37, 145–46, 199–200, 201
  image of, 49
  performance of, 52–53
  Platonic or classical, 49–51
  visibility, 54, 59–60
  for women, 101–3
ceremony
  connection to kingship, 62
  horsemanship as, 61–62
  importance of, 60–61, 62
  renunciation of, 72–73, 78
charity, 213

Charles I (king), 16, 17–18, 73, 77, 89–90
Charles II (king), 73, 76
Chevalier d'Eon, 110–11, 116
Chiron, 148
civic humanism
  and art (*see* Royal Academy)
  connection to citizenship, 186, 191–92, 210
  corruption of, 185
  general discussion of, 174–75
  on liberty (*see* liberty)
civilizing process, 5
coffeehouse, 72, 96, 97, 98, 116, 118
Commerson, Philiber, 197
common saddle. *See* riding, sporting
community of honor
  connection to honor, 46–47, 56
  connection to horsemanship (*see under* horsemanship)
  definition of, 46
Cork, fifth Earl of (John Boyle), 1–2
courtesy literature, 6
covenant
  creation with a horse, 31, 34–35, 39–40, 88
  definition of, 26–27
  display of, 40–42, 44, 60, 62, 65
  formation of, 28, 38
Cruikshank, George, 179

dance, 139–40, 150–52, 156, 158, 160, 161, 162, 165, 194, 246n62
Decastro, Jacob, 143–44, 147
Descartes, Réne. *See* Cartesian thought
Diepenbeke, Abraham van, 24
dogs, 103, 104, 105, 108–9, 216
Ducrow, Andrew, 156–57
dueling, 5

effeminacy, 76, 173
Elizabeth I (queen), 17
Elliot, George. *See* Heathfield, Baron
Elliot's dragoons. *See* Fifteenth Regiment of Light Dragoons

Elliot's light horse. *See* Fifteenth Regiment of Light Dragoons

femininity
  connection to horsemanship, 101–5, 109
  ideal, 100–101, 102
  lack of, 105–9
  social spaces, 118
Fifteenth Regiment of Light Dragoons, 126, 137, 141
first nations. *See* Indians
freedom, 26. *See also* liberty
feeling. *See* sentiment or sensibility
fop, 73, 83, 219
fox hunting, 94–97. *See also* riding, sporting

Gambado, Geoffrey. *See* Bunbury, Henry William
Garrick, David, 99, 116, 155, 172
George III (king), 112, 113–14, 116, 122, 123, 149, 158, 159, 182
Gibraltar Charger
  centaur status (*see* centaur)
  and fireworks, 122–23, 148, 149, 167
  and history, 140–41
  ideal horse, 165
  military service, 144, 145–46
  "Ode" on, 147–78
  as a stage (*see under* horse)
Gibraltar, Siege of, 144–45, 158
Gillray, James, 179, 198
gender panic, 140
gout, 93, 184–85
Grose, Francis, 116, 178, 183, 191

haute école
  caricature of, 82
  definition of, 14
  resistance to, 19, 66, 67–68, 110
Haydn, Joseph, 163
Hazlitt, William, 177
Heathfiled, Baron (Elliot, George), 121, 140–41, 144, 145, 146, 148, 163, 165

Henry VIII (king), 16
Herbert, Henry. *See* Pembroke, fourth Earl of
Hobbes, Thomas
  animal intelligence, 30, 33
  animals and body politic, 29
  connection to William Cavendish and Cavendish family, 25–26
  Commonwealth by Acquisition, 38
  Commonwealth by Institution, 38
  covenants (*see* covenant)
  honor, 45
  horsemanship, 62
  human nature, 28–29
  liberty, general (*see* liberty)
  natural liberty, 38
  political theories, 26–29
  power, 44–45, 59, 61
  servant vs. slave, 38–39
  subjectivity, 38
  war, 38
Hogarth, William, 192, 220
Horneck, Catherine, 179
horse
  breeding, 83–84
  conformation, 54, 197
  definitions of, 2, 146–47, 158
  gendering of, 102–4, 147, 196, 206, 207
  memorial, 1–2
  named: Adonis, 149; Formidable Jack, 134, 189; Gibraltar Charger (*see* Gibraltar Charger); King Nobby, 1–2; Le Superbe, 26; Little Military Horse, 134, 137–38, 189; Monarch, 113; Morocco (*see* Bankes, Joseph); Prince, 134
  place in modern scholarship, 3–4
  as a stage, 156–58
  suitable for a woman, 102, 103
  Thoroughbred breed (*see* Thoroughbred)
horse dealer, 197, 203–6

273

INDEX

horseman
    definition, 13–14, 36, 40, 51, 78, 214, 216–17, 219
    visible identification of, 56
horsemanship
    bit use (*see* bit)
    carousel, 161
    ceremony of (*see* ceremony)
    changing practices, 67, 79
    definition, 13, 82, 222–23
    French influences upon, 16, 17
    gendering of, 100, 101, 207
    at jousting tournaments, 59 (*see also* jousting)
    language system, 9, 193–94, 200–201, 202, 204, 219, 222–23 (*see also* appui)
    liberty (*see* liberty)
    minuet, 160–63, 164
    Neopolitan school, 15
    old school, 74, 161, 216
    patriarchy of, 103, 106 (*see also* patriarchy)
    public and private performances of, 54–55, 57–58
    use, 217
horsemanship community
    changing definitions of, 74, 80, 99, 175, 181, 225–26
    general, 46–49, 51–52, 55–56, 195
horsemanship manual
    audience, 7
    authorial connections, 7
    author use, 7–8
    genre changes, 67, 78–79, 80, 219
    genre introduction, 6–7
    sporting, 87
horsemanship, modern school
    critiques of old school, 111
    definition of, 74, 79
    general, 216
    liberty and technology, 90
    methodology, 90–91
horsemanship, old school. *See also* Newcastle, 1st Duke of
    class, 77–78, 112
    definition, 74, 94, 109, 111
    practice of, 110, 113
Hughes, Charles, 152, 172, 186, 198
hunting. *See* riding, sporting
Hyde Park, 69, 108, 117, 180, 214

Illegitimate theatre, 125–26. *See also* Astley's Amphitheatre
Indians, 208, 210, 211
insanity. *See* madmen

James I (king), 185, 187
jockey, 127, 173, 189
Johnson, Samuel, 83, 172, 179, 186, 195
Johnson, the Tartar, 128
jousting
    ceremony of (*see* ceremony)
    general, 58–59, 140
    running at the tilt, 14
    tournament at Welbeck Abbey, 59–60

La Broue, Salomon de, 15, 16, 17, 56, 136
Lapland, 208, 211
liberty
    connection to civic humanism, 88, 192
    definitions, 26–27, 37, 37–38, 88
    in horsemanship, 72, 90–91, 97
    negative liberty, 88
    positive liberty, 88
livery stable, 69
Locke, John, 151, 202
luxury, 73, 75–76, 83, 173, 183, 184, 186–87, 189

macaroni, 83, 116, 140
madmen, 205
manège
    class and use, 74–75, 175
    connection to luxury (*see* luxury)
    connection to tyranny, 87–88
    definition of, 14, 213
    resistance to, 18–19, 66–67, 75, 77, 79
    women, 101-2

Marston, second Baron of (John Boyle), 1–2
masque, 59
masculinity, general, 4, 5, 73, 95
Meadows, Sidney, 118–19, 200
Montagu, Elizabeth, 99–100
Montgomery, first Earl of. *See* Pembroke, fourth Earl of
Moorfields, 206

Newcastle, 1st Duke of (William Cavendish)
  on animal intelligence, 32, 136
  in Antwerp, 56–57
  biography, 23–4
  on ceremony (*see* ceremony)
  on covenant, 39, 41
  covenants with animals, 31, 34, 35
  critiques of, 75–76, 110
  honor, 45–52, 143
  horsemanship: definition of, 34, 66, 206; as politics, 23, 62, 64; manuals, 24–25, 65–67, 74, 175
  liberty (*see* liberty)
  legacy, 114, 221
  on love and fear, 34–35, 39, 41, 62, 65
  masculinity of, 45–46
  on Morocco the horse, 136
  political animality, 23
  republicanism, 42
  sovereignty (*see* sovereignty)
  sporting riding (*see* riding, sporting)
  vaulting (*see* vaulting)
non-horseman, 63, 64

Olympic Pavilion. *See* Astley's Amphitheatre
Omai, 110–11
Orrery, fifth Earl of (John Boyle), 1–2
Oppian, 15

pacing, 14
pantomime, 158
Parrocel, Charles, 24, 221

pathognomy, 53–54
patriarchy, 4, 6
Pembroke, fourth Earl of (Henry Herbert; *and* the first Earl of Montgomery), 126, 163, 175, 200
performativity, 9, 133–34
physiognomy, 53–54, 211, 233 n. 114
Pignatelli, Giovanni Battista, 15, 18, 56
Pitt, Hester, 99
Pliny the Elder, 15
Pluvinel, Antoine de, 15–16, 17, 23, 24
politeness, 5, 72, 98, 112, 117, 118, 151, 193, 199
Price, Thomas, 128

Ratto, Giovanni, 16
racing. *See* riding, sporting
Reynolds, Joshua, 116, 172, 176, 177
riding. *See* horsemanship
riding academy. *See* riding house
riding house
  Astley's (*see* Astley's Academy)
  caricature of (*see* Bunbury, Henry William)
  Cavendish's, 56–57
  changes to, 80, 97, 189
  class, 97, 116
  Domenico Angelo's house (*see* Angelo's Academy)
  early-eighteenth-century houses, 66–67
  Elizabethan, 17
  gendering of, 98–100, 101–2
  illustration of, 57–58
  importance of, 223
  mid-eighteenth-century houses, 112
  sociability, 116
riding school. *See* riding house
riding, sporting. *See also* horsemanship, modern
  breeds (*see* Thoroughbred)
  Cavendish on the practice, 92
  class, 92, 94, 95–97
  common saddle, 87
  connection to the *manège*, 79, 92

275

riding, sporting (continued)
    discourse of warfare, 94–95
    horse-human relationship, 91
    technology and the hunting seat, 87, 90–91
riding the great horse, 74–75, 92, 113, 224
Roberts, Piercy, 195–97
Rousseau, Jean-Jacques, 197
Rowlandson, Thomas, 116, 179, 195, 211–12, 213
Royal Academy, 172, 175–81
Royal Academy for Teaching Exercises (Edinburgh), 111–12, 118, 161, 163
Royal Circus, 152, 160, 198
Royal Grove. See Astley's Amphitheatre
Royal Riding School. See Astley's Amphitheatre

Sagudino, Nicolo, 16
sailors, 195–99
Saint Antoine, Chevalier de, 15, 16, 17, 18, 23
Sampson, Mr. and Mrs. (trick riders), 128, 190
satire. See caricature
seahorse, 208, 209, 211
sensibility, 202–3, 216
sentiment, 201–3
Seven Years' War, 89, 121, 138, 140–41
Shoreditch, 206
Simon of Athens, 14
Smith, Adam, 185
Smithfield, 206
Soubise, Julius, 119, 126–27
sovereignty
    animal, 29
    defined by Thomas Hobbes, 26, 27, 59, 63
    display of (see ceremony)
    indivisibility of, 63
    overthrow of, 64–65
    understood by William Cavendish, 34, 37, 39, 41–44, 59, 63
sportsmen, 92. See also riding, sporting
Stuart, Henry (prince), 16, 18, 23

Stuart, John, 88–89

Thames River, 122, 148, 149
tailor, 184, 184–91, 192, 208–10
theatre acts, miscellaneous
    "The Blunt Tar, or True Love Rewarded," 197
    General Jackoo, monkey, 168
    Jack Junk, 197
    Learned Pig, 168
    Monstrous Craws, 125, 197–98
    "The Taylor Riding to Brentford" or "The Hunted Tailor" or "The Tailor's Disaster" (see tailor)
    Vincent Lunardi, 168
Thompson, James, 190
Thoroughbred, 85, 87
Tremamondo, Angiolo Domenico Maria. See Domenico Angelo
Tremamondo, Anthony Angelo Malevolti, 161

Valenciennes, Siege of, 143–44, 147
Varo, 14
vaulting, 128, 129–32, 153, 155, 161
Virgil, 14

Walpole, Horace, 172
Welbeck Abbey, 23, 55, 59
West, Benjamin, 116, 118
Wilkes, John, 89, 116, 189, 191–93
Wolfe, James, 159
Wouverman, Philips, 221

www.ingramcontent.com/pod-product-compliance
Lightning Source LLC
Chambersburg PA
CBHW021938290426
44108CB00012B/879